STEVE HOUGHTON

THE BRITISH SNIPER
A CENTURY OF EVOLUTION

FOREWORD BY **MARTIN PEGLER**

Printed and bound in Great Britain by TJ International, Padstow, Cornwall
First Printing, 2018

Cover Design & Image Editing: Martin Latham
Interior Design & Typesetting: SWATT Books Ltd.

ISBN 978-1-3999-3783-2

Swift and Bold Publishing
Victoria Hill,
Eye, Suffolk
IP23 7HJ

www.swiftandboldpublishing.com

Eternally Grateful, and
Always in My Thoughts,

for
Harry and Marjorie

Acknowledgements

I would like to thank the below named individuals and organisations who have helped me in a multitude of ways with the writing of this book.

Frank Fletcher
John Tilstone
Roger Payne
Nigel Greenaway
Hugh Keir
John Coffey
Chris Harrison
Nathan Davies
Georg Oberaigner
Martin Pegler
Colin Shorthouse
Richard Stork
Tony Watts
Chris Pappas
Ministry of Defence
Accuracy International
4th Battalion The Rifles
Imperial War Museum
Royal Armouries Museum
Royal Green Jackets Museum, Winchester
Durham Light Infantry (DLI) regimental collection
Riflecraft Ltd
G.E. Fulton & Son
MJ Services (GB) Ltd
United Scientific Instruments Ltd
Rotec Ltd

I also extend my thanks to all those who along the way have shared their memories and knowledge of this fascinating subject which has been invaluable to me as I have strived to complete this book.

I would also like to thank my wife, Pam, for her patience and understanding which has not been limited to my all-consuming writing of this book but extends to all the years I have been collecting the paraphernalia associated with this subject. She has at times shown great restraint and self-control when I have uttered the universally recognised words, "I have to have it, it's rare" which she has learnt to be a precursor for my parting with a chunk of our money, therefore Pamela I give special thanks to you.

The British Sniper:
A Century of Evolution

A Modern Study of

British Sniper Equipment

1915 – 2018

Steve Houghton

The Great War Sniper's Song

Now, all you young snipers that snipe at the Hun, You'll get lots of Boches and lots of fun, If you'll only remember these few simple rules they are some that are taught in the best sniping schools.

The first thing is patience; don't worry or fret if a shot every day you don't happen to get. But if you can knock out the Hun that you seek, it is well worth your while if you've waited a week.

Conceal your emplacement with scrupulous care for the Boches are watching the line everywhere. And, once you are spotted, they won't be polite, but they'll crump and they'll crump and they'll crumple you quite.

The back of your loophole must always be dark. For a light shining through it will make a good mark. Put your head in the light, as you're likely to do. And a bullet will soon let the light into you.

When you open the loophole, just mind how you go. Don't be in a hurry, be careful and slow. And wait a few minutes before you look out. In case you've been spotted by Herr Sauerkraut.

Don't let your scope or your rifle stick through. And don't rest the muzzle whatever you do, for you must remember your shots will go high. And the Boches you're shooting aren't up in the sky.

Beware the wild woodbine's insidious charm. Though when you're off duty a whiff does no harm. But your loophole's a chimney, and it is no joke if your post is betrayed by a trickle of smoke.

A sniperscope's good to shoot over the top. You can worry the Hun from all over the shop. But look out for your flanks, and don't put up your head, or one of these days you will find you are dead.

Report everything that you see through the day, and send it along without any delay. So that ere it's too late they can ring up the guns, who are always delighted to stir up the Huns.

Quick movement avoid for it catches the eye, keep out of the sun when it shines in the sky. Remember your shadow may give you away if out in the open you're sniping by day.

To all of our snipers here's luck and success. May your bullets all go to the proper address. Just stick to the precepts in this little rhyme, and you'll get lots of Huns at three-halfpence a time!

Courtesy of Nigel Greenaway

"The sniper moves close to the enemy, kills quickly and cheaply, and is rarely supported by other arms. Yet despite this comparatively efficient way of fighting, the sniper has become the object of odium. Yet the odium is irrational. While mines mangle and shells mutilate – producing lingering death or permanent injury, at little risk to the sapper or gunner – the sniper gives a quick kill and takes the risk of detection and destruction."

Royal Marines Headquarters, Lympstone

Contents

Foreword

Since the Great War, when it was belatedly recognised that sniping had become an indispensable element of modern warfare, the sniper has both literally and figuratively lived in the shadows. What he did, how he did it and the tools used were shrouded in secrecy and a certain amount of myth. To a great extent, this was due to the attitude of the snipers themselves, who were mostly quiet, introspective individuals, not given to drawing attention to themselves. The snipers of 1915–1918 were equipped with ordinary MkIII Short Magazine Lee-Enfields onto which were grafted a somewhat bewildering array of mounts and scopes. These did the job, more or less, but they were designed by people with little concept of the requirements of sniping. That the British and their Commonwealth allies were able, by 1918, to claim superiority in the sniping war possibly says more about the men than their equipment. The first chapter of this extraordinarily detailed book gives the reader some idea of what a slow and difficult process this was to achieve and how much time, effort and energy was applied to try and produce rifles to do a job that had hitherto never been considered, particularly in an environment where mass production was the wartime priority. Over the last two decades much new information has come to light, much of which has never before been published, and Steve Houghton has gone to great lengths to provide illustrations of some exceedingly rare examples of surviving rifles. His use of anecdotal accounts adds greatly to their story and puts flesh onto the bones of what is an extremely technical subject.

Post 1918, there still lingered in the British Army a Victorian attitude to sniping, which was regarded as unseemly, somewhat cowardly and rather ungentlemanly. This rather ignored the facts of modern warfare, which had seen the introduction of poison gas, flamethrowers, and the deliberate targeting of civilian populations. Nevertheless, if left to their own devices, most senior British Army officers in the inter-war years would have been perfectly happy to have seen the whole embarrassing concept of sniping eliminated. Not all armies shared this opinion, however, and the widespread use of snipers by the Germans in the Blitzkrieg forced the British into a rapid re-evaluation of the situation. As a result, a new rifle was introduced, albeit still based on the service Enfield. This time,

however, it was properly built, with an excellent scope/mount combination and the Enfield No. 4 (T) was to be arguably the best of its type used in any theatre of war. Almost inevitably post-1945, sniping fell into the doldrums once again. Whilst an improved variant, the L42A1, was introduced, it was merely a stopgap weapon that ignored the fact that modified service rifles were simply no longer adequate. The development and production of the now famous Enfield and its No. 32 telescopic sight have been covered in earlier books, but Steve has included much additional information on their construction and service life, accessories and the varied and often eclectic equipment used by snipers. It is the most complete history of the development of the No. 4 (T) and its successor, the much overlooked L42A1, to date.

I think the culmination of this remarkable book is the chapter dealing with the development and eventual introduction of the radical Accuracy International L96A1 rifle. For the first time, a purpose-designed sniping rifle was issued to the British sniper, providing him with the cutting edge tool that he so desperately needed. Until now, little has been published on this important weapon and much of what exists is misinformation, speculation and sometimes complete fabrication! The L96 chapter provides the reader with a complete history of its design, manufacture, teething troubles, service issue and some remarkable accounts of its combat use, as well as detailed illustrations. If for no other reason, this chapter alone makes this book an important addition to sniping literature.

I can state with some authority that to cover such a broad subject as a century of British sniping is nothing less than a labour of love. I congratulate Steve Houghton on a publication that has covered a difficult subject in an informative and interesting manner. Having written one or two books on the subject, I know this is far from easy to achieve. If you have any interest whatsoever in the subject of sniping, then this book must be considered an absolute necessity.

Martin Pegler, Limoges, France, 2018

The British Sniper: A Century of Evolution

Introduction

95TH RIFLES.
TALAVERA 1809.

Ever since the advent of rifling, thought to be in the fifteenth century, every advanced nation in the world has strived to better the concept. Stabilising a projectile in flight by making it spin was no great discovery, as it was already understood in the days of the slingshot.

For centuries a rifle was expensive to produce and to purchase, as, much like today, a precision long range rifle is often an expensive bespoke product produced as a one-off and out of reach of the masses. This made such a firearm almost elitist, owned only by the wealthy and privileged. For any armed power it was a cost-prohibitive way forward. Nevertheless, nations strived and the technology of the tools and machinery behind the production of rifling was explored until rifled barrels could be mass produced economically. You could say this was the birth of sniping; it was when man's obsession with placing a small projectile precisely on a target area began, although the term "sniping" universally recognised today did not appear until the late eighteenth century and is thought to have arisen in British colonial India. The title was thought to have been awarded to an individual who displayed the skilled marksmanship required to successfully hunt the snipe game bird, which is an exceptionally agile bird in flight.

The advantage of a capability to direct accurate fire on an enemy from a distance at which the enemy had no means of striking back was not lost on military commanders in Europe during the eighteenth century, however it would not be until 1800 that the British Army would adopt its first standard issue rifle: the Baker rifle designed by Ezekiel Baker, a master gunsmith of Whitechapel, London. Trials were held in order to select the new rifle to arm the new Rifle regiments who would play a major part in the defeat of France during the Napoleonic Wars. During the trial the Baker rifle placed eleven of the twelve shots it fired on a six foot diameter target at a distance of 300 yards. After this display of supreme accuracy it was hastily adopted and designated Pattern 1800 Infantry Rifle and served in the British ranks well into the 1830s, notching up many great triumphs through the thirty-odd years it served in the British Army. One such feat of marksmanship with a Baker rifle in 1808 can be compared with another feat of marksmanship with an Accuracy International Arctic Warfare rifle in 2009. The first occurred when Thomas Plunkett of the 95th Rifles, armed with a Baker rifle, shot the French General Colbert from his horse as he led a charge against the 95th during their retreat to the Spanish port of Corunna and then dispatched the bugler who ran to his general's aid. Design, trial and development would continue with an emphasis on pushing the boundaries of the distance at which lethal marksmanship could be achieved. Fast forward 200 years to Afghanistan, 2009, and Corporal of Horse of the Blues and Royals, Craig Harrison, armed with a .338 calibre Arctic Warfare rifle, also delivered two deadly shots on a Taliban machine gun team at a staggering 2,474 metres.

Although the two rifles and the distances concerned could not be any further apart, the two events bear many synergies. The distances were for their day both incredibly far and beyond the intended capabilities of the weapons in question. The initial shot in both instances was confirmed with a second lethal shot and both events have been questioned and drenched in disbelief ever since. The compelling thing in both events is that the basic principles are the same and both men were doing the same job; both were exceptional marksmen and both were pushing their equipment to perform beyond the expectations of those who designed and built it.

As we entered the twentieth century and with the arrival of the Great War it would not be Great Britain who would introduce military sniping to the conflict, or to modern warfare for that matter. The Germans were far more advanced in the use of a telescoped rifle and utilised the deer and boar hunters from the vast German forests with whom they formed Jäger battalions. In the opening months of the Great War they would prove to be devastatingly deadly, and the situation forced the British to respond, at which point military sniping became indelible within the British Army.

Since 1915 the British Army has fallen in and out of the sniping fold but has still managed to field several of the world's finest sniper rifles and has since set the bar very high in what it takes to produce a skilled and proficient sniper. The principles first established 100 years ago in the trenches of the Western Front have barely changed and have since been adopted by others, becoming doctrine within the sniper ranks of foreign armies. *The British Sniper: A Century of Evolution*, is a study of the sniper's weapons and equipment chronologically and tells the story of how British sniping rifles, equipment and observation instruments have developed from the early fledgling days of 1915 to the present. The development of British sniper rifles over the last century has sometimes been ad hoc but always innovative, and the engineering involved has at times been breathtakingly detailed.

Chapter 1
Baptism of Sniper Fire

4th August 1914 saw Great Britain cross the start line of the Great War, a four year long conflict which would prove to be one of the deadliest episodes in human history resulting in 38 million casualties. The conflict also proved to be the gateway to the British Army's sniping journey, a journey we are still on today.

In 1914 British forces possessed no real sniping capability and were very much a volunteer army which did however lay large emphasis on individual marksmanship as a result of the painful lessons inflicted by the Boers during the Boer War from 1899–1902, finishing just twelve years earlier. The changes to musketry training that immediately followed the conflict raised the marksmanship standards within the army to an exceptionally high standard which would be demonstrated in the opening engagements of the Great War, particularly that of the Battle of Mons where the relatively small BEF (British Expeditionary Force) held off a significantly larger German force at the Mons–Condé Canal until the French Fifth Army unexpectedly retreated, exposing the British right flank. The military feat pulled off by the small BEF that halted the German Army was largely credited

to the individual mastery of the bolt action rifle: the British rifleman could deliver accurate rapid bolt action fire which was reported by the Germans as being like machine gun fire.

The absence of scoped rifles in the British armoury was not an oversight or an indication the British Army was poorly equipped, but quite deliberately excluded as a result of a common objection to sniping in a military capacity which ran much deeper than the ranks within the army and was indeed viewed in many corners of society as abhorrent, inhumane and an unsporting action that was given no real consideration by the then War Office. As the British and German opposing forces dug in across Europe, months of stalemate set in which led to the development of all manner of ways

to industrially slaughter men and destroy equipment.

At this time the Germans, in complete contrast to the British, had no political or social reservations where sniping was concerned and set about deploying snipers to the trenches straight away. In addition, with the outbreak of war the aristocratic Duke of Ratibor sent out across Germany a call for arms, or to be more accurate telescopic sights and rifles, which was well received by the German people. In support of the war effort they donated a staggering 20,000 civilian hunting rifles and scopes, the scopes mainly being Fuess, Voigtlander, Goerz and Kahles commercial telescopes. It is not recorded as to how many of these rifles/scopes were actually put into service, but fortunately for

RIGHT: This extract from the discerning gentleman's newspaper The Field is dated July 1915, almost a year to the day the Great War began. Mr H.A. Bryden's appeal for telescopic sights is an illuminating glimpse into desperate times and appears in the newspaper just two months after the War Office appointed the Ministry of Munitions to oversee an official sniper rifle conversion. *(Courtesy Nigel Greenaway)*

PREVIOUS PAGE: A sniper of the 18th Battalion, London Regiment (London Irish Rifles) on a daylight patrol in Albert firing his rifle to silence a German sniper, 6th August 1918. Note his rifle is fitted with a PPCo telescope. The image also demonstrates why large sniper knee pads were eventually produced.

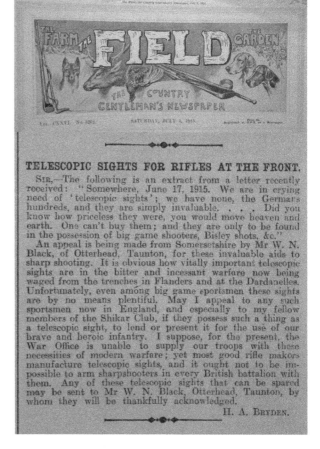

German logistics the popular 7.92mm hunting round was the same calibre as their military service round which aided them perfectly and I would assume rifles donated of this calibre would have certainly been pressed into service particularly in the early stages of hostilities. In addition to the rifles collected from the populace, the German Army was issuing a service sniper rifle and was by this time enjoying huge success sniping at the British as daily routine meant moving through the trenches, some stretches of which had to be built up.

We look back and assume all the trenches were over six feet deep with fire steps and ladders to go over the top, and in large part they were, but the trench lines snaked across the landscape for considerable distances which inevitably meant in places the topography of the land made for some short distances of quite shallow trench, exposing heads and shoulders. The German forest boar and deer hunters were plying their trade effectively, disrupting British movements, morale and exerting total control of "no-man's land", a problem the British had no answer to in the opening months of the conflict.

British inventiveness came to the rescue; necessity being the mother of invention, the men in the trenches sought to tackle the problem long before the War Office stepped in.

Officers and men were writing home asking for the family hunting rifle, many of which were scoped to be sent to the trenches for sniper duty. There were also a good number of large calibre big game hunting rifles sent which were used to good effect on German steel loophole plates and so successful that the War Office placed contracts for ammunition for these weapons to keep them in service. Former shooting clubs were being asked to send club target sights which included the Galilean optical sight, or open sights which consisted of a front and rear lens arrangement which attached to the rifle and were open, as the two lenses were not contained within a tube that would otherwise form the telescopic sight.

RIGHT: This feature taken from a 1915 September issue of The Field newspaper indicates the War Office were at this stage purchasing these sights in the thousands and all manufacturers were vying for contracts to supply. The War Office are on record as officially adopting only three types of this sight but in reality many versions by alternative manufacturers made it to the Front through a variety of avenues. Continued on next page. *(Courtesy Nigel Greenaway)*

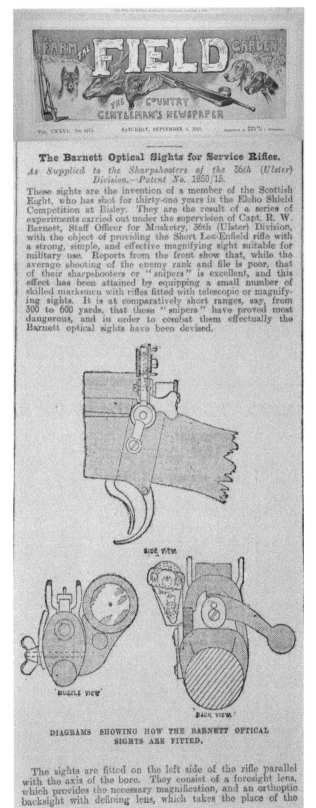

THE FARM · THE FIELD · THE GARDEN

THE COUNTRY GENTLEMAN'S NEWSPAPER

Vol. CXXVI. No. 3271. SATURDAY, SEPTEMBER 4, 1915.

The Barnett Optical Sights for Service Rifles.

As Supplied to the Sharpshooters of the 36th (Ulster) Division.—Patent No. 1850/15.

These sights are the invention of a member of the Scottish Eight, who has shot for thirty-one years in the Elcho Shield Competition at Bisley. They are the result of a series of experiments carried out under the supervision of Capt. R. W. Barnett, Staff Officer for Musketry, 36th (Ulster) Division, with the object of providing the Short Lee-Enfield rifle with a strong, simple, and effective magnifying sight suitable for military use. Reports from the front show that, while the average shooting of the enemy rank and file is poor, that of their sharpshooters or "snipers" is excellent, and this effect has been attained by equipping a small number of skilled marksmen with rifles fitted with telescopic or magnifying sights. It is at comparatively short ranges, say, from 300 to 600 yards, that these "snipers" have proved most dangerous, and in order to combat them effectually the Barnett optical sights have been devised.

SIDE VIEW.

MUZZLE VIEW.

BACK VIEW.

DIAGRAMS SHOWING HOW THE BARNETT OPTICAL SIGHTS ARE FITTED.

The sights are fitted on the left side of the rifle parallel with the axis of the bore. They consist of a foresight lens, which provides the necessary magnification, and an orthoptic backsight with defining lens, which takes the place of the

OPTICAL SIGHTS.

SIR,—My attention has been drawn to a letter from Mr Ernest H. Robinson under the heading "Telescope Sights" which appeared in your issue of Aug. 21, and in view of the public importance attaching at this juncture to the choice of a strong, simple, and effective optical sight, I am permitted by the General Officer Commanding the 36th (Ulster) Division to write a few lines in reference to the optical sights with which our sharpshooters are already equipped.

I have no wish to damp Mr Robinson's enthusiasm for the Lattey sight. It certainly has the merit of cheapness, and if anyone is enamoured of "the regulation aim" he may now enjoy a measure of magnification while continuing to "align the sights on the centre of the lowest part of the mark, the top of the foresight being in the centre of, and in line with, the shoulders of the U or V of the backsight," in accordance with *Musketry Regulations*, Part I., par. 202. It is scarcely necessary, however, for Mr Robinson, in the supposed interest of the Lattey sight, to disparage other optical sights which have already done good work at the front and elsewhere. He writes: "Unfortunately the several adaptations of this idea (the simple two-lens system) which have been put on the market, such as the Ulster sight, invented by Mr Caldwell, or the well-known B.S.A.-Martin combination, introduce complications which render some special instructions and practice necessary before they can be used by a soldier who is an ordinary good shot with the Service sights."

I need not defend Armourer-Sergt. Martin's adaptation of the B.S.A. sight to optical users, though I am sure that anything turned out by his firm will be efficient and workmanlike. As for "the Ulster sight invented by Mr Caldwell," there is certainly no "complication" about it comparable with that of "the regulation aim" described in official language above. To look through a peepsight and make the spot in centre of foresight coincide with what you want to hit, this surely is the *ne plus ultra* of simplicity! It is claimed for the Ulster Division optical sights that "any marksman of average ability can be taught to use them in half an hour." In the case of a marksman of Mr Robinson's ability the period of instruction might safely be reduced to five minutes.

As in the case of the Lattey sight, the bayonet can be fixed while the Ulster sights are in position. Attached, as they are, to the left side of the rifle, these sights do not interfere with the rapid manipulation of the bolt, and they have what we consider the unique advantage of leaving the regulation sights available either as a "finder" or for use in case a target suddenly presents itself at a longer range than those for which the optical sights are designed.

I am glad to observe from your note to "Canadian Mounted Rifleman's" letter that you favour fixed sights for "sporting and other rifles which are used away from ranges." The Ulster Division optical sights are for all practical purposes fixed sights, for there is only one adjustment to provide for the rise from point blank range to distances of 500 and 600 yards.

As my own name has recently been associated with these sights, may I say that my claim to fame is a very limited one. In January last I laid down to the best of my ability the conditions of the problem to be solved, and I had subsequently the honour of "inventing the inventor."

R. W. BARNETT (Captain attached General Staff).

Seaford. Aug. 29.

[We append extracts from the printed matter inclosed with Mr Barnett's letter. Applications relating to the same should be addressed to Sharman D. Neil Ltd., Opticians, 22, Donegall-place, Belfast.—ED.]

regulation aperture sight so little employed. Strength and simplicity are the distinguishing features of the optical sights. It is claimed that any marksman of average ability can be taught to use them in half an hour.

Aim is taken through the orthoptic or peephole by placing the round black spot in the centre of the foresight on the object to be fired at. For all practical purposes the rifleman shoots from point blank range up to 600 yards with fixed sights. The backsight has one movement only, which provides for the difference of elevation between 200 and 500 yards. Taking the first-class figure target, with its figure 1ft. 6in. in height, as a convenient illustration, the firer, with the 200 yards sight, aims at the bottom of the figure at 100 and 200 yards, at the centre of the figure at 300 yards, and 1ft. above the figure at 400 yards. With the 500 yards sight he aims at the bottom of the figure at 500 yards, and 1ft. above the figure at 600 yards.

Special Features.

1. The optical sights, being fitted on the left side of the rifle, do not interfere in any way with the rapid manipulation of the bolt. Neither do they prevent the use of the regulation sights if a target suddenly presents itself at a longer range than those for which the optical sights are designed.

2. The regulation sights, when adjusted to the estimated distance, form an excellent "finder," enabling the marksman to pick up his target quickly in a bad or difficult light.

3. The bayonet may be fixed when the optical sights are on the rifle, though this is undesirable, as it involves (with Mark VII. ammunition) aiming down from 3ft. to 1½ft., *vide Musketry Regulations*, Part I., par. 159.

4. The construction of the optical sights is so strong that they are not likely to be injured or put out of adjustment even by the rough usage of the field. In the event, however, of a lens being broken, the rifle is not out of action, for the regulation sights can be used instead without a moment's delay.

5. When not in use the optical sights are carried separately in a strong and compact leather case suitable for the belt or pocket.

ABOVE: In this 1915 newspaper extract it would appear the gentleman who has submitted the piece does clearly have an interest in the Barnett Optical Sight and writes heavily in favour of it against the Lattey Optical Sight which was one of the War Office purchased sights. The Barnett sight was known better as the Ulster Sight due to its popularity with the Ulster Division. *(Courtesy Nigel Greenaway)*

Three of the most common open sights found during WW1 with British troops are illustrated. *TOP*: the Lattey open sight, *BOTTOM LEFT*: the Ulster/Barnett sight and *BOTTOM RIGHT*: the Gibbs sight.

The Galilean optical sight, of which several patterns existed, offered a very low power of magnification as well as a fine crosshair or dot in the forward lens for aiming. They were utilised on the Western Front where they served as a crude tool in the counter sniper effort on the Short Magazine Lee Enfield rifle, but were somewhat fragile and prone to damage. From the assortment of Galilean sights available at the time only three models were officially adopted by the War Office and are noted in the List of Changes as being the Lattey, Neill and Martin sights, which were all formally approved between May and September 1915. Easy to manufacture and considerably cheaper to buy, by the end of the war in 1918 the government had procured 79,900 Sights, Optical for Rifles; significantly less in comparison were the estimated 13,000 Sights, Telescopic for Rifles.

Hunting rifles were arriving and were immediately rendered useless as they used non-standard ammunition of which there was none, or a rifle sent from home had a very short service life as it became useless when the small quantity of nonstandard ammunition that arrived with it ran out, or if it failed mechanically as there were no spare parts for these custom firearms, many of which were very fancy for the day and were more suited to the Scottish hillside with a formal hunting party than the tough life many went on to serve in the trenches. However telescopes were not discarded, particularly if they could be fitted to the MkIII and MkIII* SMLE service rifle.

A disorganised counter sniper effort picked up pace on the part of the British as the German sniping campaign was having its desired effect. The German snipers of the Jäger battalions were skilled and ruthless in equal measure and built a hefty tally killing and wounding exclusively with head shots. A large proportion of the casualties were officers and NCOs; the rank structure was being damaged but more importantly the morale of the men was suffering terribly. The problem needed combating and therefore cunning and inventiveness would play a huge part.

LEFT: Pictured is 2nd Lieutenant Oliver Lenn MC of the 2nd Battalion, the Durham Light Infantry, in the spring of 1915. The photograph depicts him attempting some sniping along the British front line at a place called Hobb's Farm, northeast of Houplines, Armentiéres. His field service cap has been turned around back to front, avoiding the shine from the two small brass chinstrap buttons which could give his position away. This young officer of around 20 years of age is posing in the spring sunshine, whilst holding a .303 in. Mauser sporting rifle. The Marquis of Londonderry loaned this rifle made by John Rigby of London to the 2nd Bn. DLI in 1914 as a sniper rifle and later in 1919 presented it to the Officers Mess. The rifle is also pictured below as it can be found today at the Regimental Museum, Durham.

ABOVE: A sniper's post of the 2nd Durham Light Infantry. This large sniper's post in the roof of Hobb's Farm (in front of Houplines) shows on the left of the image the Mauser sporting rifle presented for sniping to the Battalion by the Marquis of Londonderry. Note the three draw telescope and iron loophole plates. Also note the sandbags filled with bricks and rubble. January–April 1915.

A number of ways to defeat the enemy sniper evolved; hunting instincts came to the surface and when it came to eliminating German snipers, the German who made the fatal mistake of setting a routine ran the risk of facing a number of British rifleman secreted along the trench who were tasked with opening up with a volley of fire the minute the German revealed his position, or those more skilled at the black art would need to be lured out with such things as the dummy head, or a chink of light from a false loophole. In fact a whole industry evolved off the back of trapping and luring German snipers. The Royal Engineers set up a large factory at Wimereux in France dedicated to camouflage, and this is where the incredibly lifelike dummy heads were made of papier mâché moulded from plaster casts taken from employees at the

ABOVE: The engraved plaque which is fixed to the rifle's butt stock reads, "This rifle, which, in the hands of The 2nd Battalion The Durham Light Infantry accounted for a number of Germans during the Great War, was lent to the regiment by the Marquis of Londonderry and was subsequently presented by him to the Officers Mess. 1919".

ABOVE: A group of the women's workforce pictured in their workshop making papier mâché dummy heads.

ABOVE: Curiously real, these dummy heads are made to look like Officers and NCOs. They are presented here over the parapet of a sandbag wall as they would appear to the enemy.

works. The heads were then painted by accomplished artists to look lifelike and to appear like an NCO or officer, the latter the prize of every German sniper and by whom many met their fate.

The dummy heads were sent to the intelligence sections of every battalion with a pamphlet specially written after a great deal of effort by the engineers at Wimereux who had explored the best and most precise way to expose the head in a realistic manner which would ultimately fool the German sniper and draw his fire. The frustrations of the sniping and scouting sections are, though, recorded as the heads arrived and found their way to the intended recipients but the specially prepared pamphlets rarely ever accompanied them. Therefore initially the use of the heads was ad hoc with limited success which brought about the specific training in the use of the device at all the sniping and scouting schools on the Western Front. The schools taught the use of the dummy head as a two-man operation; the technique to raising the head above the trench parapet in a realistic manner was crucial by one man whilst the second man observed with a periscope several feet away looking for the muzzle flash of the enemy sniper. After the schools took over the training in the use of the dummy head every intelligence section eventually had at least one officer or NCO trained in its use, and the success rate improved enormously with a high percentage of shots pinpointed out to 250 yards. The Germans' most popular quarry would often in the end be a lure that would get many into trouble.

Having spied his prize deliberately exposed through the loophole in an observation post, or in a fleeting glimpse above the trench line, the prize would be too much to ignore and on releasing his shot he would compromise his own position to the British periscope spotter working with the dummy head – and on doing so a British sniper would return the compliment with deadly effect.

LEFT: In the absence of a dummy head troops would commonly expose some form of headdress above the parapet. In this case a Royal Irish Fusilier uses a pith helmet on the muzzle of his rifle to draw the fire of a troublesome Turkish sniper in an effort to make him compromise himself, Gallipoli, 1915.

LEFT: Although this image of British soldiers searching a German during a trench raid is almost certainly staged for propaganda the German sniper rifle was on the raider's list of priority items to be returned to British lines. Many German sniper rifles were captured this way and then used with deadly effect by British snipers.

Many German sniper rifles were captured this way as well as through raids on the German trenches and once in British hands they were turned effectively back on the Germans which demonstrated what the British could achieve with a purpose built and well set up sniping rifle. Now the Germans were being effectively sniped back at, the balance of power shifted slightly which led to the development of the trench loophole and sniper plates, which were large steel armour plates first used by the Germans.

Several examples were captured through trench raids and brought behind the British lines where they were developed further with the help of Major Hesketh-Prichard.

He first equipped the plates with a swing plate which when pushed to one side revealed a hole just big enough to shoot a sniper rifle through; when closed it prevented chinks of light being revealed behind the plate which when observed would indicate that someone was sitting behind it. The effectiveness of the British counter sniper campaign

led to the Germans producing steel body armour which, although impossible for their own snipers to use, was used to protect vulnerable key personnel from British sniper fire. When sniping from a trench the German sniper did, however, use a steel brow plate which hooked onto the front of the helmet via the two Frankenstein-like studs the German Great War helmet was famous for. The brow plate was simply a thick steel plate which defeated the bullet with brute strength and could only be worn by the sniper when

RIGHT: Loophole plates were a German creation; produced by Krupp Works, Essen they appeared in a variety of shapes and sizes, and were hastily adopted by the British in a more static role, being used widely in the construction of observation posts and sniper positions. This image is staged propaganda but features a plate which was almost mobile and could be hastily positioned.

ABOVE: The Germans employed body armour extensively along with helmet plates in an attempt to defeat the British sniper's bullet. Although the German loophole plate became commonplace in the British trench, albeit with some modifications, body armour did not.

standing vertical using the parapet of a fire trench.

In 1915 the War Office deployed the Ministry of Munitions to oversee the designs of a British sniper rifle. In May of that year their seal of approval for the commercial fitting of telescopic sights to the Short Magazine Lee Enfield MkIII service rifle was passed and the involvement of firearm and optics manufacturers was encouraged. The Periscopic Prism Company, Holland & Holland as well as J. Purdey & Sons immediately registered their interest, amongst others. The Periscopic Prism Company were the first to arrive at a conversion design that met with War Office approval and from that point the practice of accuracy testing newly manufactured SMLE rifles in house began and those showing above average grouping accuracy were set aside for sniper conversion.

ABOVE: A rare WW1 image capturing the moment a German sniper's bullet passes through a member of a British artillery gun team. Note, the rest of the gun crew are not yet aware their team mate has been hit. The puff of dust from his clothing can be clearly seen as the bullet impacted. German snipers often used the report of the artillery gun to mask their own shot which helped to conceal their position. Note the sniper selected the lanyard man who fired the gun which aided him in getting his timing right.

SMLE MkIII & MkIII*
Periscopic Prism Co (PPCo) Conversion/PPCo Telescope

Technical Specification	
Calibre	303in
Magazine Capacity	10 Rounds
Overall Rifle Length	44.5in
Barrel Length	25.2in
Twist Rate	5 Groove, LH 1 in 10 Twist
Combat Weight	10lb
Iron Sights	Graduated to 2000 Yds
Conversion Approval Date	4th May 1915
Converted By	Periscopic Prism Company
Scope Mounted	Offset, Left Side
Quantity Converted	4800

LEFT: The wrist markings show a 1915 BSA MkIII. Enfield were the predominant manufacturer, however BSA also supplied rifles of a suitable accuracy.

The Periscopic Prism conversion was the most common of the four principal Great War sniper conversions and it was the first sniper rifle to be officially adopted by the British Army. Note the very low position of the telescope affording the sniper a low profile. Also note the lack of volley sights: the swell of the fore-end here is allowing for the range dial of the volley sight but the fitting has clearly been omitted, common amongst the later converted rifles.

RIGHT: Snipers of the 9th Battalion the Black Watch pose for a picture at Arras Cathedral in 1917. Note the lack of volley sights on their PPCo converted rifles, the leather 1914 pattern slings and the signaller spotting telescopes on the ground.

The first official conversion, which of all the Great War sniper rifle conversions would be the most prolifically produced by far, involved the mounting of what was essentially a copy of the Fuess Helios 3 scope modified by PPCo to incorporate a primitive deflection, or windage adjustment capability. The scope tube was steel with the internal components being mainly brass. The scope had two power magnification and focus capability operated by a small knob fitted to a square plate that contoured the scope tube and was designed to be close fitting to prevent dirt and water entering the slot, in which the focus knob travelled left and right. Just

forward of the focus adjustment the elevation drum also sat on top of the scope tube and was a brass dial. Graduated to 600 yards, it carried a scribed line indicating each dead zero which, to be selected, required the slackening of a clamping screw, turning the dial to the desired range and then tightening the clamping screw again. This of course was calibrated to the external ballistics of the standard .303 inch MkVII ball ammunition.

The deflection adjustment provided cannot really be described as windage adjustment as there is no datum to adjust for wind and it certainly would not have been used for such a purpose. The adjustment

is performed with the use of two capstan screws which can be found on each side of the scope tube level with the elevation drum. The adjustment is done by turning the screw head that sits proud of the scope tube. Screwing the left screw in adjusts the bullet's path right, and screwing the right screw in adjusts the bullet's path left. The screw heads both have a small hole drilled straight through so a small bar or wire could be used as leverage when adjustment is required. The Periscopic Prism Company scope can be commonly found with two styles of ocular housing, the Long Cone and the Short Cone, the latter having a much steeper taper and

LEFT: Looking directly down on the Periscopic Prism Co telescope, the range drum arrangement can be seen. Note the scribed lines graduating the telescope's range to 600 yards. The left and right capstan screws for lateral adjustment and the focus adjustment are also clear to see.

LEFT: The rings illustrated here show how there are two retaining screws on the underside fixing directly into the scope tube.

LEFT: The uppermost part of the scope tube has been engraved with the PPCo markings which conveniently fall between the two rings which commonly bear the rifle serial number on the left and patent details on the right.

being stepped in its profile. A further design feature added by PPCo was a sturdy brass ring that screwed on to the objective lens end of the scope tube to protect the lens and tube rim from heavy knocks.

The telescope had a detachable mount which was a single fitting meaning the scope was held in two rings but was a single piece, retained with two screws and in some cases sweated, or soft soldered, in place.

The single piece rings unit had a male dovetail profiled slider which slid into a single piece mount with a female dovetail to receive it. The mount was fixed to the left side wall of the receiver via five 5BA cheese head screws and was equipped with a steel leaf spring and release catch so the scope could be easily attached/detached. Although original mounts are rare, enough still exist for two slightly differing designs to have been noted. One design has a deep release catch that extends below the dovetail, furthermore this deep thumb catch design also tends to have the bottom left and right corners of mount rounded off. The alternative

design has a much shallower release catch that sits shallow of the dovetail; this design of mount tends to have the bottom left corner left square. It is common to find the issued rifle serial number stamped between the mounting screw holes. The scope when detached was housed in a cylindrical leather carry case lined commonly with a red felt material. The leather case was embossed with the serial number of the rifle and it is not uncommon to find examples today bearing more than one rifle number.

ABOVE: The PPCo mount is fixed to the receiver wall with five cheesehead screws between which the rifle serial number is commonly stamped; more often the digits are placed individually between fixings. The mount featured has a shallow release catch with square bottom left and right corners as opposed to an alternative mount which has a deep release catch and rounded corners. (Please note this is a faithful recreation mount. Manufactured by Roger Payne and fitted by Richard Stork.)

Telescope, Periscopic Prism Company

Technical Specification	
Manufacturer	Periscopic Prism Company
Length	12.25in
Weight	18oz
Objective Lens DIA	19mm
Field of View	9.5 degrees
Magnification	2 X
Reticle	Post and Wire
Range Graduations	100–600 Yds
Focus Capability	Yes
Lateral Adjustment	Yes. Capstan Screws L&R
Mount Type	Single

ABOVE: The PPCo reticle of post and wire design. This reticle would be set to feature in British sniper scopes for almost the next 100 years.

The Periscopic Prism Co Ltd telescope illustrated here in profile as well as four quartered angles. Note the stepped profile eyepiece as opposed to the rarer coned profile. The ring's male dovetail slider is visible as is the sturdy brass ring which protects the objective lens against heavy knocks.

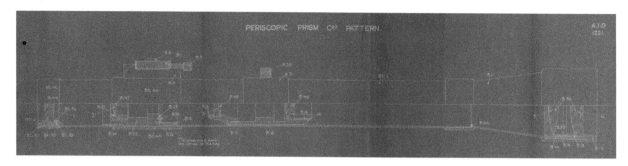

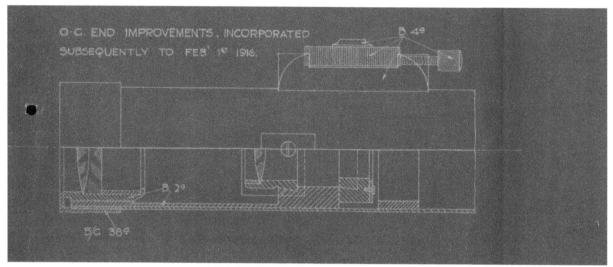

ABOVE: These original PPCo blueprints illustrate the external appearance of the telescope as well as the detail concerning internal components and lenses. Note the enlarged drawing detailing internal improvements made in 1916.

ABOVE: The PPCo telescope's leather carry case is cylindrical and commonly lined with red felt material. These cases carry the matching rifle's serial number embossed into the leather; it is also common to find several rifle numbers on these cases.

Whilst the 4,000 PPCo conversions were being produced the demand for sniper rifles was clear. The Periscopic Prism Company was running at full capacity with their conversion which left something of a void in supply if the army's appetite for these weapons was to be satisfied. Therefore the War Office looked to other companies to get involved with the supply of sniper rifles. The numbers of converted SMLE rifles were boosted by the sporting gun companies of Holland & Holland and J. Purdey & Sons Ltd using an Aldis scope mounted in detachable double fitting rings and mounts designed by the two respective companies. When looking closely at the design of the rings of both Purdey and Holland & Holland, it could be argued their designs may have originally started as an overbore system changed under the instruction of the army who heavily favoured the offset design as it allowed the rifle to be reloaded via the charger bridge of the rifle. Instead, the new conversions still followed the PPCo design of side mounting the scope, and the opportunity to improve the design by introducing an overbore mounted scope was lost, much to the disappointment of Major Hesketh-Prichard (referenced fully on page 35).

SMLE MkIII & MkIII*
J. Purdey & Sons Conversion/Aldis Bros Telescope

Technical Specification	
Calibre	303in
Magazine Capacity	10 Rounds
Overall Rifle Length	44.5in
Barrel Length	25.2in
Twist Rate	5 Groove, LH 1 in 10 Twist
Combat Weight	10lb
Iron Sights	Graduated to 2000 Yds
Conversion Approval Date	4th May 1915
Converted By	J. Purdey & Sons
Scope Mounted	Offset, Left Side
Quantity Converted	1400 approx

LEFT: Although in the image the year date looks to be 1916, it is in fact 1915. A common anomaly created during an era when machinery in comparison to that of today was primitive and many processes were done by hand. Such oddities can be found on a great many Enfield rifles all the way to the L42A1 rifle which was not obsolete until the 1990s.

A very fine example of an SMLE MkIII converted to sniper specification by J. Purdey & Sons, and fitted with an Aldis No. 1, or 2 telescope. Note this example still has the volley sights present.

LEFT: A British sniper pair operating in Gallipoli, 1915. Note the spotter with the three draw telescope observing over the shoulder of the sniper; although weapons and spotting scopes have moved on considerably the practice is still routinely seen today.

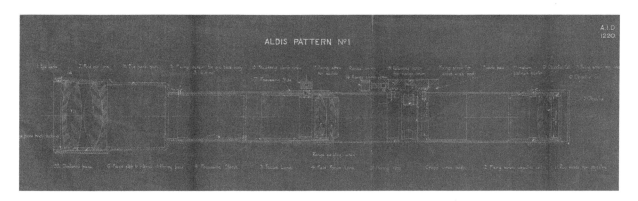

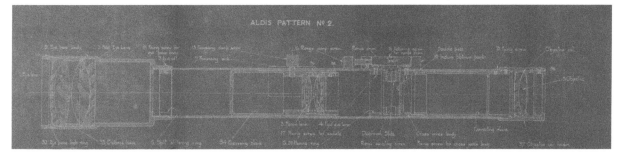

ABOVE: Original blueprints of the Aldis No. 1 and 2 telescopes detailing the internal components and lenses. Externally both of these telescopes looked identical with the differences between them being wholly internal, mainly relating to the range drum and objective lens and prisms.

The Aldis telescope was manufactured at the Aldis Brothers factory in Hall Green, Birmingham. Aldis telescopes encountered today commonly bear a 1915 or 1916 date and evolved to four models in total, simply designated No. 1, 2, 3 and 4. Aldis would almost overtake the PPCo's telescope with an estimated 3,000 being produced for military use also being preferred by the troops who used them as well as historically being viewed as the best of those which the British fielded during WW1. The four models all varied slightly from each other with only the No. 4 being noticeably different in its features. The models 1, 2 and 3 all looked the same with the differences between them being mainly inside the instrument and being related to the lenses and internal operation of the range drum. Externally models 1 and 2 share the range drum clamping screw position rear of the drum pointing to the ocular end of the scope whereas models 3 and 4 share the same drum clamping screw design, placing it forward of the drum, and also incorporated a stop screw in the scope tube in line with the clamping screw, so it could not be unscrewed and lost.

Model No. 3 had a significant redesign of its range elevating mechanism which it shared with model No. 4. The fourth model looked very different as it incorporated larger lenses, the larger objective lens offering significantly better light gathering capability. The steel tube at the eyepiece was also a coned design rather than a separately manufactured eyepiece

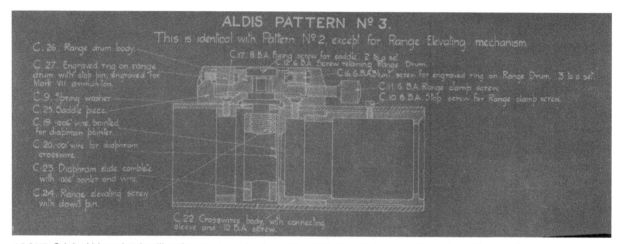

ABOVE: Original blueprint detailing the range mechanism of the Aldis No. 3 telescope. The note on the drawing makes reference to the design being identical to the No. 2 pattern with the exception of the range elevating mechanism which is illustrated here in large detail.

BELOW: The original Aldis No. 4 drawing detailing the inner workings of the telescope. The model No. 4 is instantaneously recognised by its coned eye piece and forward facing range drum retaining screw, the coned eye piece being the one feature that separates it from the three models that preceded it.

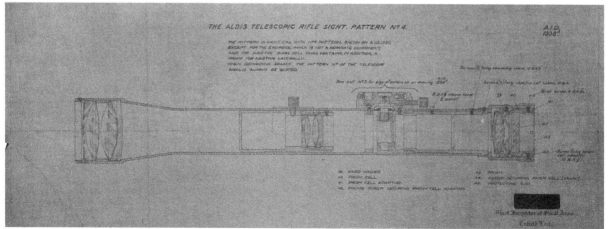

ABOVE: A close-up view of both the front and rear mounts of the Purdey system.

ABOVE: A closer view of the sturdy rear mounting lug which protrudes away from the rifle. The lug's job is to simply locate the rear scope ring and hold it securely in position.

with a stepped profile which attached and secured by screws and this is the single most obvious distinctive feature when looking at an Aldis No. 4 model. The third and fourth models also came with an enlarged objective lens housing so an adjustable prism could be fitted in order to give lateral adjustment, however it should be noted that several examples of the third model suggest not all of these models received the modified objective lens prism. Designs one and two did not have this feature as the mounts they were destined to be set up in had lateral adjustment built in.

The Purdey mount system is today the most commonly found conversion type with an Aldis scope of which 1,400 were fitted in 1915 and 1916. It is a double mount system in that it has a separate front and rear mount. The scope is mounted offset to the left of the receiver and is fitted with separate front and rear rings. The rear mount which fixed to the receiver wall and is situated just behind the receiver ring is hard up against the scooped recess which accommodates the thumb when charging the magazine. This rear mount has a lug which protrudes ninety degrees to the rifle and accommodates the rear swan-necked scope ring, which simply

hooks into place in a rearward fashion.

The front mount slips onto the barrel, sitting just forward of the chamber which places it centrally in the wood of the rear hand guard which of course has to be modified. The mount in its entirety is essentially in three pieces; the first two pieces clamp around the barrel and are hand finished to suit the radius of the barrel they are being fitted to. This part of the mount carries a female dovetail which allows the fitting of the third and final piece of the mount which is male dovetailed so they slot together. The third piece which is the section exposed of the woodwork carries a round hole

centrally to its top face that accepts a lug fitted to the underside of a flat arm protruding at ninety degrees to the scope.

This flat arm and front scope ring is one single piece. When the rear swan-necked hook is sited and the front lug is pushed home the scope is locked into place by a small roll-over catch on the front mount which when engaged locks the front lug in the recess. Lateral adjustment was made possible in the Purdey mounts through the front mount. Screws situated on both sides allowed the dovetail to be moved left and right by slackening one and tightening the other.

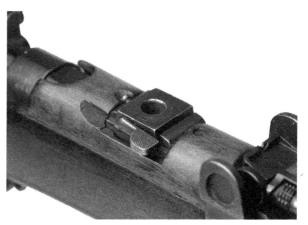

ABOVE: A closer view of the front mount exposed by a heavily modified hand guard. The roll-over lever is in the open position.

Telescope, Aldis Bros No. 3

Technical Specification	
Manufacturer	Aldis Brothers, Birmingham
Length	10.8in
Weight	17.75oz
Objective Lens DIA	19mm
Field of View	9 degrees
Magnification	3 X
Reticle	Post and Wire
Range Graduations	100–600 Yds (some 1–8)
Focus Capability	Yes
Lateral Adjustment	None (late variants had prism adjustment)
Mount Type	Double

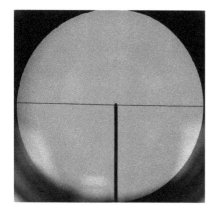

On first appearances this Aldis telescope could actually be a No. 1, 2 or 3 model as aesthetically they are the same, however the detail in the range drum and its forward facing locking screw gives away that it is in fact a No. 3. This model carries a 1916 date and typically has the post and wire reticle. The sequence of images illustrate the elegant swan's neck rear ring as well as the flat arm of the front ring which carries the male lug on its underside.

A great example of the leather carry case for the Aldis telescope, slightly oval to accommodate the rings. This example came complete with instructions for the adjustment of the telescope in the lid and is numbered to rifle 8053.

The side mounted PPCo and Aldis scopes laid bare the British lack of sniping knowledge and experience as the set-up appeared to enable the firer to quickly get a clip of rounds into the rifle, as standard for the infantry rifleman in the fight. The lack of understanding was not necessarily on the part of the design team but more on the part of the army not realising the sniper fed his ammunition singly. The side mounted scope also proved to be cumbersome in that the user often didn't know whether to shoot with his dominant right eye or, as the scope lay most definitely parallel to the left side of the rifle's body, whether he should attempt to shoot with the left eye. Furthermore the offset scope made shooting through the steel loophole plates extremely difficult which led to the snipers altering the apertures in the loophole plate themselves.

Brian Sharp, who served with 2/5th South Staffordshire Regiment in 1917, wrote:

"I was a corporal of the Scout and Sniper section of 2/5th Bn South Staffordshire Regt in France 1917. At one time we relieved the Canadian army in the Lens sector and I saw and talked to them about their equipment superior to ours, usually the Ross Rifle.

"We were handicapped because some genius on high decided that the Aldis sight must be offset to the left so as to clear the breech for rapid fire! So we needed to cut a large loophole or slits one for the rifle and one for the sight. This was rectified in W.W.2."

Courtesy of Nigel Greenaway

The arrival of the rifle seemed to create more problems than it solved, which were exacerbated by the complete lack of training of the men who were selected to carry them. It appeared the sniper rifle was met with huge scepticism by those who weren't involved directly with the activity; a staggering level of ignorance was displayed at certain levels of command even after the German sniper had illustrated so well what the effects of a well fought sniper campaign could have on the enemy.

The complacency was such that the quartermaster, having received brand new sniper rifles, would not bother to issue them out and when they did finally find their way into the trench they were often given to the best shot in a section or platoon, despite the individual not necessarily displaying any enthusiasm for the subject. To make matters worse, the rifles were seldom zeroed and set up for the user.

Arthur Barraclough, who served with 1/4th Duke of Wellingtons from 1916–1917, wrote:

"After a battalion sniper had got himself sniped, they gave me the job, being a bloody fair shot. You dug your own trench, just big enough to fit in and raise your rifle, then you just lay down quietly waiting for someone to strike a light or fire a shot. Sometimes I used to throw a brick just to attract someone to have a shot, but I never caught anyone as far as I know.

"It was a lousy job lying there in the cold and wet. The Huns were crack shots. New chaps would have a quick peep over the top, just for

a moment, but only if they didn't know anything. If you put your arm up to scratch your head, you'd have a bullet through the palm of your hand."

Courtesy of Nigel Greenaway

There were problems; a lack of coherent training and education was rendering the British sniper programme useless and was compounded by the lack of knowledge of the commanders who gave no real thought to the character of those they selected for the callous job of sniping. We must remind ourselves that the men of this war came from much simpler backgrounds than those of our modern age who are fed a daily diet of death and violence through a host of modern media and are to some degree desensitised; in comparison the WW1 British soldier was God-fearing and led his life in accordance to the strict religious upbringing a great many experienced in the day. Taking a life had to be justified to many, who, in turn, hesitated and wrestled with their own conscience before pulling the trigger.

R.A. Chell wrote in September 1915:

"After about fifteen minutes quiet watching with my rifle in a ready position I saw a capless bald head come up behind the plate. The day was bright and clear and I hadn't the slightest difficulty in taking a most deliberate aim at the very centre of that bright and shiny plate, but somehow I could not press the trigger. To shoot such a 'sitter' *so deliberately in cold blood required more real courage than I possessed. After a good look round he went down and I argued with myself about my duty. My bald-headed opponent had been given a very sporting chance and if he were fool enough to come up again I must shoot him unflinchingly. I considered it my duty to be absolutely ready for that contingency. After about two minutes he came up again with added boldness and I did my duty. I had been a marksman before the war and so had no doubt about the instantaneousness of that man's death. I felt funny for days and the shooting of another German at 'stand to' the next morning did nothing to remove those horrid feelings I had."*

'*Courtesy of Nigel Greenaway*

However, there was a British officer, Major Hesketh-Prichard DSO, MC (1876–1922), who prior to the war was an explorer, big game hunter and keen marksman who also possessed incredible foresight and was well aware of the failings that had beset the British sniping campaign. He would often visit the trenches and spend time with the men carrying the now issued sniper rifle. He would experience first-hand the lack of knowledge displayed by individuals who were tasked with carrying the equipment and how best to use it.

He championed the cause and knocked on every door in order to get the High Command to wake up to the failings but also to understand the success that could be won if they got their act together and delivered an effective sniping campaign to

ABOVE RIGHT: Major Hesketh Vernon Prichard, later Hesketh-Prichard, was aged 37 on the outbreak of war and was rejected twice by the army due to his age. He was eventually successful in being accepted as a Press Officer which took him to the front lines in 1915. He was appalled at the daily losses of soldiers to German snipers which were anything from five to twenty men a day. He began a campaign to improve individual marksmanship and counter the German sniper threat. In August 1915 he was given permission to formalise sniper training within the army after which his reputation travelled far and wide. *(Courtesy Nigel Greenaway)*

LEFT: The artist of this caricature of Major Hesketh-Prichard is unknown but it was reportedly drawn whilst its creator was at the Linghem School of Sniping.

ABOVE RIGHT: A very rare copy of the course content from the First Army School of Scouting, Observation and Sniping. Note the cover is marked "Do Not Take Away. Course Use Only". *(Courtesy Nigel Greenaway)*

the enemy. Major Hesketh-Prichard argued hard and after quite an uphill struggle the High Command relented and the authority to set up a sniper school at the rear of the trench lines was granted. The Second Army sniper school was the first of its kind and was established in December 1915, and Major Hesketh-Prichard's First Army school was opened in the summer of 1916 in the village of Linghem, Pas-de-Calais and would become pre-eminent under his command. The success of the fledgling sniper training schools led to each of the British five armies on the Western Front having one. It was at these schools that men were properly selected by the traits in their character deemed preferable for such work as sniping and scouting and indeed the characteristics required would later be published in training literature to aid instructors to identify men with such qualities.

Men selected and put forward for such duties attended one of the sniping and scouting schools where they were introduced to the rifle and its particular need for cleanliness, especially the bore, the scope and its operation and care. The men were taught the importance of the preservation of the barrel and how its accuracy would start to fall away after just a few hundred rounds, so it was never used for any other duty than that of sniping. In fact the sniper would carry a duty rifle as well as the sniper rifle. They were also taught the effects of certain types of ammunition on the life of the sniper rifle's barrel such as tracer. First used by the British in 1915, its invention was spurred on in an effort to defeat the Zeppelin airships which, filled with hydrogen gas, were incredibly flammable. They were also introduced to and taught the importance of the use of armour piercing ammunition used by snipers to defeat German loophole plates. A small quantity of this ammunition was carried but was used sparingly. Its introduction largely made the big game rifles used initially for the task of "loophole busting" redundant. Because of the heavy wear inflicted on the bore by armour piercing ammunition it was mainly reserved for only the most lethal and effective of German snipers operating from behind a loophole plate.

LEFT: Men of the American 77th Division receiving instruction in camouflage and sniping from a British instructor at Moulle. A camouflaged sniper is lying concealed between the officer and the men.

Observation and Spotting Equipment

Once the sniper students were taught how to correctly zero the rifle and were proficient in keeping it accurately zeroed the craft could now be taught in detail. The British, unlike their German counterparts, paired up and operated as a sniper pair; camouflage, concealment and the art of observation were taught and again, unlike the Germans who seemed only to favour the binocular, the British sniper pair were taught to observe predominantly with the three draw x20 magnification signaller telescope which could see into shadow and had the power to show a great deal of detail.

The men were taught to swap and share observation duties to avoid tiredness and eye strain and both men could use the sniper rifle as effectively as each other. The British soldier seemed to be naturally suited to sniping structured in units usually of one sergeant, one corporal and sixteen snipers equipped with eight signaller telescopes and eight sniper rifles. He operated all day, every day, but favoured dawn and dusk best and enjoyed good hunting over the winter months when the sky was leaden and no-man's land was full of mist and gloom. The signaller telescope came into its own in these conditions, revealing tell-tale details the trained observer would be looking for.

Prismatic binoculars were, although on the whole scarce, made available to snipers and were an effective accompaniment to the three draw telescope carried in the main by the sniper whilst the spotter used the primary tool, the spotting scope.

The prismatic binocular issued was a fixed six power magnification of No. 2 and No. 3 specification produced prolifically from Ross and Zeiss designs by a plethora of manufacturers who were awarded contracts to produce anything from a few hundred units to a couple of thousand. The principal manufacturer was A. Kershaw and Sons Ltd of Leeds, who incidentally recruited three key personnel from Carl Zeiss (London) Ltd. 15th June 1916 saw the company take receipt of a colossal order from the War Office for 25,000 No. 3 Mk1 binoculars. They were constructed from lenses and prisms supplied by Barr and Stroud, Thomas Cooke and Sons and Taylor Hobson but after some time Kershaw's took over the manufacture of such parts themselves, producing lenses and prisms of a higher quality. By 29th December 1917 5,678 sets had been delivered, and by February 1918 the specification had moved to Mk2.

ABOVE & RIGHT: The signaller telescope was first identified as the ideal spotting instrument by Major Hesketh-Prichard and Major Crum. The MkII telescope was manufactured by several companies through War Department contracts and varied in quality from one manufacturer to another, the variance mainly being in the quality of the lenses.

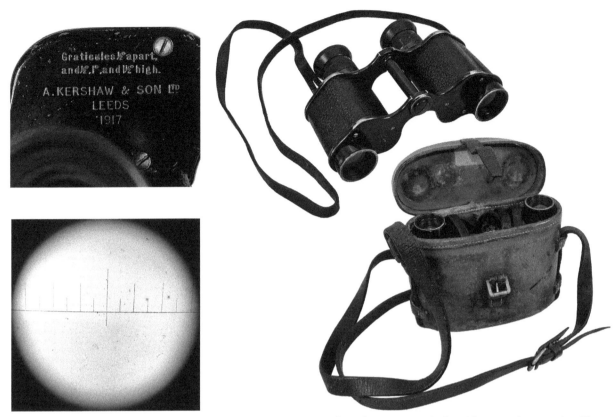

ABOVE: The prismatic binocular of the Great War was like the signaller telescope manufactured by several companies. Those early examples were issued with graticules for ranging in the right hand lens, a feature which has been present in the same right hand lens of every issued binocular to this day.

Captain Thomas Arthur Tatton MC

The following caricatures sketched in ink on lined notepaper are a fascinating glimpse into the ordinary daily life of one officer who served with the Rifle Brigade during the Great War. Research was carried out to try and identify the artist of the caricatures which were found with a letter addressed to R.C. Hargreaves Esq and dated April 1915. The only reference to the artist is Tom. T. The letter begins: *Dear Old Poteus (?) I'm most awfully glad to hear about your MC: its grand and everyone here is awfully pleased about it. I am sending you the little illustrations you know so well, with a few new ones.*

It seemed to me that the familiar reference to an officer who had just been awarded a Military Cross strongly suggested that the letter

An observer on the Salonika Front in 1916. He is using the MkII signaller telescope mounted in a MkV tripod with the legs splayed. This cumbersome use of the tripod led to the tripod legs being shortened by signallers and observers in WW1, however the shortened variant is more synonymous with the WW2 sniper.

writer and artist of the caricatures was also an officer. Making that assumption it ought to be possible to identify an officer serving in 4RB with the first name Tom and a surname beginning with T. Checking the war records of 4RB in the 1915 regimental chronicle, only one candidate emerges: Thomas Arthur Tatton who was serving in D Company.

Tatton was educated at Eton and Oxford and was commissioned into

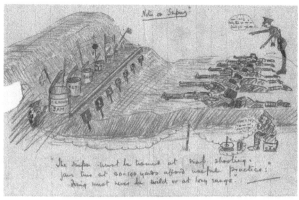

the Rifle Brigade in 1912. He served with the 1st Battalion at home during 1913 but joined the 4th Battalion before they embarked for France on 20th December 1914. Shortly after writing this letter he was wounded on 7th May 1915. He served with this battalion until 1916 when he was posted to the 3rd Bn Rifle Brigade with whom he was serving when he was awarded a Military Cross. The citation for this award, which was published in the *London Gazette* of 26th September 1917, reads: *For conspicuous gallantry and devotion to duty. During an advance he led his*

company with the utmost gallantry against the obstinate resistance of the enemy, and it was due to his personal example that his company advanced as far as it did. During the next forty-eight hours he kept up the spirits of his men by his splendid cheerfulness and coolness under exceptionally trying circumstances.

He was badly wounded while serving with 3rd Battalion. He subsequently returned to the 4th Bn and went to Salonika with them and then on to India. Tatton died on 19th July 1968 at his home in Churston Ferrers aged 75. In his

obituary published in the *Royal Green Jackets Chronicle 1968* the author wrote:

Tom came out with 4th Battalion to Quetta in 1919, in command of D Company. As a brother officer rifleman, he was the best of company and the kindest of men and had not an enemy anywhere. His "D" troop was a very happy one. He made the most of what Quetta offered, and was an exceptionally keen horseman and a keen polo player. In his later years he was far from well but bore it with great courage.

As British success grew the number of sniper schools increased in France as well as being established in the UK under the new brand of scouting and sniper training. Major F.M. Crum (1872–1955) was an officer of the Kings Royal Rifle Corps who like Major Hesketh-Prichard could see the future of sniping was to be crucial as part of the wider campaign. Major Crum was a highly experienced sniper and had set up and run many scouting and sniper training schools, personally developing and writing the course content. He wrote initially to aid the training of snipers and went as far as personally funding one such document which he had published in December 1917, distributing it as training pamphlet *SS.195.* Titled Scouting and Patrolling, the booklet would be the first to be dedicated to scouting, patrolling and sniping in a formal written document as a training aid. He was largely recognised as the leading authority on the subject, and was requested by High Command to lecture commanding officers and sniper school commandants on the subject, as being an active sniper himself he could report the most current information to his audience.

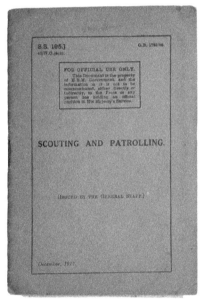 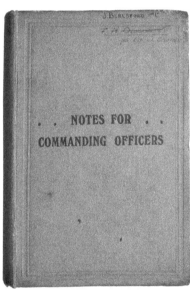

ABOVE: Two notable publications of the Great War written by Major Crum. Pamphlet SS195 was the first formalised written teaching aid for snipers. Later to aid officers with trained scout snipers under their command he wrote further to assist them when deploying these highly trained men. (*Courtesy Nigel Greenaway*)

His credentials did later ensure his position as being responsible for the structured cohesion between the schools in the UK and France, and his writing developed further with handbooks prepared and aimed at the officers in the trench who had scouts and snipers under

their command. The pocket sized handbook gave these commanders the best guidance as to how to use these highly trained men, and how best to utilise their specialist equipment. After the war when the Major left the Army he continued to lecture on the subject and wrote further about his experiences as a sniper during the war years and produced further written works on the subject.

Major F.M. Crum's dedication to the development and training of British snipers during WW1 is unsurpassed by anyone else of the time and his steadfastness to his commitment undoubtedly stunted his career. His efforts were recognised by future snipers, one being none other than the most successful and highest scoring British sniper of WW2, Harry Furness, who felt compelled to compile a biographical document of Major Crum's sniping and scouting career, a gesture from one revered sniper to another.

Research Notes on Major F.M. Crum. Sniper-Officer, World War One

By Harry M. Furness

Frederick Maurice Crum, born, 12th October 1872.

He served as an Officer during the Boer War with the Mounted Infantry.

He was wounded in one arm during the Boer War, and suffered problems evermore.

In October 1915 he joined the 8th battalion Kings Royal Rifle Corps, serving as battalion 2i/c.

His batman with the 8th battalion was Rifleman Mathews, a trained sniper.

As a career infantry officer, he often praised the professional efficiency of the enemy he was facing. In fact of the German Army soldiers he told everyone he respected them as being patriotic to their Fatherland and admired their many qualities. He was also known to admit that he disliked having to snipe and shoot down such brave enemies.

Major Crum led patrols into No Man's Land to attack forward enemy trenches so that he could secure some examples of their Krupp's of Essen made iron loopholes from which the enemy marksman fired in reasonable safety. At that time the British had no such iron loopholes, but from those Major Crum captured we had our own well designed loopholes made, in fact with the additional designs of Major H. Hesketh-Prichard the designs included sliding double loopholes which enabled our snipers to shoot at an angle as well.

A recorded incident concerning Major Crum was of an occasion on the 30th July 1915 when from a forward position in No Man's Land the Major was spotting with his Scout Regiment Telescope a party of German soldiers at a distance of 700-yards, and the specialist trained sniper with him was Corporal Evans. The sniper Corporal killed three of the enemy at that long distance using his SMLE sniping rifle fitted with an Aldis telescopic sight.

In October of 1915 Major Crum had assembled a team of 10 trained snipers in his battalion to deal with German snipers who were using thick iron shields as cover. Major Crum on a leave from the trenches went to a London gunsmith and purchased a heavy calibre Elephant rifle and ammunition out of his own pocket to deal properly with these snipers. He was not alone in buying such heavy calibre weapons, for other Sniper-Officers were known to have possessed such private weapons which they used in trench warfare.

Major Crum taught at the Senior Officers School at Aldershot Command at two periods, early 1917, and again in 1918. He lectured battalion Commanding Officers on sniper deployment. In 1917 Aldershot Command Sniper's School issued training pamphlets which were written mostly by Major F.M. Crum. An official army booklet reference SS195 was the first available in May 1917, the title was "Scouting, Sniping and Observation" compiled by Major F.M. Crum, who at that period was based at General Headquarters in France, as their Scouting & Sniping Expert.

Most of his brother Officers had the opinion he would have been a Lt. Colonel in rank had he not been such a rebel against old-fashioned ideas of the elderly General Officers who didn't understand his forthright enthusiasm for sniping. At one stage he was offered a senior status position to wander the various frontal areas wearing the blue & red armband to signify special duties. He refused as he knew he would be taken away from the tasks he had chosen to be with the snipers.

Major Crum toured many Army Formations in his role as Sniper-Officer. He often took with him a large wooden box in which he had lantern slides, and cine film which he could project onto a white cloth from the projector he carried. He had these slides and film specially made for him by the Official War Photographers who were in France to provide propaganda photos and several newsreel films for the U.K. His slides and film demonstrated the techniques he had taught at the

Sniper Schools. It is thought the remainder of these slides and films may still be in the archives of The Imperial War Museum (?).

Major Crum was demobilised from the army in August 1918, as his old wounds from the Boer War were proving troublesome. Throughout W.W.1 the Major could have left the Army at time of his choosing due to the problems of ill health he suffered, mostly from old war wounds. But he insisted on carrying on his work training snipers, he was a thoroughly dedicated sniper enthusiast, and had more than earned higher promotion and decorations for his frontline bravery, but he was overlooked by higher command.

In April 1917, Major Crum had arranged with a film laboratory in Wardour Street, London, to cut and edit the films he sent of Scout-Sniper training. The films were made under the direction of several Sniper-Officers each commanding a different Army School for snipers. These important and most valuable films cannot now be traced, they would be priceless now.

In June 1917, the Canadian Army set up their own Sniper's School. For initial advice they requested visits from the two best known Sniper-Officers. Major H. Hesketh-Prichard and his close friend Major F.M. Crum.

Sniping Instruction assumed such importance, that from the 21st to 24th July 1917, a special conference was called for all S.O.S. School Commanders to attend at Boulogne. Each School Commandant was called upon to lecture in great detail their training methods, and to pass on the latest incoming field intelligence concerning German Army sniper methods and deployment. The newest equipment was shown and demonstrated by official contractors and requests for specific equipment was noted to be passed on to suppliers. It was perhaps the most important Sniper's Conference held in France during W.W.1.

1st. S.O.S. was at that time based in a farmhouse in Linghem, from June 1917.

2nd. S.O.S. was under the command of Sniper-Officer Major Sclater.

3rd S.O.S. was based in Albert.

In May 1916, Major Crum initiated a Sniper School to be held at Brigade H.Q. at A.C.Q. General Skinner, a sniper enthusiast himself, was in command of that Sector. The firing range for training snipers was built in a nearby chalk quarry. The course lasted for four weeks with day and night training sessions. In July 1916 Major Crum travelled again to train Snipers and Observers, based at Arras Brigade H.Q. with their intelligence.

Throughout W.W.1 Major Crum carried a lucky charm, it was in fact a Swastika emblem badge the ages old Greek symbol which was later adopted by Hitler for his N.S.D.A.P. In the U.K. Major Crum's home was with his elderly mother at her home in Longworth, Stirling, Scotland. He lived there until around 1921. Details of his earlier, and most post W.W.1 Scouting Association career as a senior scoutmaster can be found in the archives of The Scout Association, London, SW7 5BR. Around the year 1950 November, it is known that Major Crum was still at his home known as "Kenmuir" in Rosneath, Scotland.

It was assumed that his wartime diaries were handed over for preservation to the local Histories Archive Library in Stirling, no recent trace found however.

Major Crum had some of his work printed for him at the offices of "The Journal" 9, King St, Stirling, Scotland. This newspaper is no longer listed as such in that area, the archives were taken over by another newspaper group. Still to be checked. His last book was printed by The Journal in 1950.

His Christian names have to be checked, as well as his Army number, and any decorations???

Courtesy of Nigel Greenaway

"The Gentleman Sniper"

By Harry M. Furness

How can you be a gentleman, and at the same time a Sniper? Surely a travesty of terms? Yet that is how even in present times we view the unique service given to the art of the military sniper by the British Officer in the trenches of World War One. He was of course Major F.M. Crum, who served with The King's Royal Rifle Corps.

But how many soldiers past and present, even know of him? Few I reckon, for he was without doubt a very much under-stated pioneer of the modern age Army Sniper. He came into his own in the trench warfare of France in early 1915 onwards for prior to that he had been bombarding the War Office in London from the entire start of the war to be allowed to get to the frontlines and to put his ideas of sharpshooting into practice. Surely the War Office was then lax not to jump at this offer? But the facts are somewhat different, for London H.Q. were well aware that Major Crum was already advanced in age and still suffering from war wounds he received during his service in the Boer War. So no matter how eager he was to fight again, there were genuine reasons to hold him back so younger, fitter Officers were sent to the frontline.

But perseverance pays off, and by 1915 Major F.M. Crum got his wish, he moved over with a new battalion of the K.R.R.C., he was in fact offered the promotion to command the battalion, but he declined the offer as he felt his still troublesome wounds would prevent him giving the last ounce of energy a battalion C.O. must give every hour of the day and night. Instead he took up the 2nd in command position, as that too had certain advantages in that he could spend more time on his determination to set up a special corps of highly trained marksmen who would be trained to shoot with selected rifles on which were mounted telescopic sights.

German snipers had already made the British infantry pay a bloody price in dead and wounded right from the start of the war in 1914. For we know that The Freiherr Der Herzog von Ratibor, an aristocratic titled German shooting fanatic and hunter of real merit, had right from the first hint of war looming liaised with the High Command of the German Army in Berlin that specially selected marksmen mainly recruited from the large number of forest hunters employed by the State and private landlords who controlled the huge German forest lands. Soon he had assembled a large number of Jägers and found that there were not enough suitable service rifles in the war stores to give each soldier his own sniping weapon. But he considered that to be a minor setback, for he then advertised widely throughout Germany requesting to buy or loan for the national cause as many telescopic sights as possible. The German population are on the

whole military-minded, and take a pride in their soldiers, so it took very little time before the Duke (Herzog translates to Duke in English) had over 20,000 useable telescopic sights ready for mounting onto Mausers and Mannlichers. The Jägers knew their business so little training was needed, it made little difference to them between shooting at fast moving game animals in the forests, to drilling holes into British Tommies unused to such surgical precision shooting which often came from long range.

So that was the position facing the likes of Officers and their men just sent over from the British Isles to go into a new kind of deadly warfare in the trenches where even to glance quickly over the parapet could mean a bullet through the head. The Germans lined their trenches with trained snipers from before first light until the last shreds of light in the sky to pick off anyone careless enough to give him a sight picture.

So finally, you want to know why we think of him as The Gentleman Sniper? Well that's easily answered, for we have to stand back and admire a little the sort of man who was known to dislike having to kill the enemy, no Rambo hatred with this man, ready and willing to wipe off the entire earth anyone who seemed likely to be his enemy. No, for the Major he was constantly telling anyone who would listen that he had such a deep respect for the decent honourable German soldiers opposed to him that he was upset every time he shot yet another soldier he caught fair and square in his crosshairs, and believe me the Major built up a very handsome tally by the end of the war, a gentleman right to the end.

Postscript: Why if he was so good did he remain as a Major you are asking? Fair enough question, and a possible reason was he was

in his own way a rebel, he just didn't conform to what was expected of the Officer Class of those days. He mixed easily and readily with the lower ranks, saw their point of view, and was indeed A SNIPER, one considered by the military hierarchy as an evil-necessity of war, a man who doesn't play "cricket" in the associated senses, instead his game was deadly indeed, a very different kind of "sport". He demonstrated beyond all doubt his ideas on the Art of Sniping had proved successful beyond all expectations, and to cap it all had wanted to share his experiences by writing a new type of Sniper's field manual, but he did so without official permission. He just went ahead and wrote his treatise, had it published privately at his own expense of no more than a 1000 copies print run, then he gave them away to interested Officers to train their men. He was ordered by an armchair General back in his safe Chateau to stop immediately sending out his manuals, and to send what was left to H.Q. He replied politely with an apology for not first seeking permission to write on a subject he knew better than most, and added he couldn't send them the remainder of his stock of manuals as all had been sent off to requests received.

So it cost him the promotion he so richly deserved, but his old wounds were proving so troublesome to him by then that he returned to the U.K. to serve the remainder of his service at least lecturing on the specialization he had so very greatly improved.

He was a close friend of Major Hesketh-Prichard, another very talented Sniper-Officer of the W.W.1 period.

Courtesy of Nigel Greenaway

ABOVE: A sniper school demonstration shows a rifleman in a conventional prone fire position next to a camouflaged sniper in a low Hawkins-style position.

The British application of snipers was now structured, with every sector on the Western Front having a scout sniper section developing tactics which were carried back to the sniper schools with the NCOs selected as training staff. The course content continued to evolve and expand with a technical element starting to be established. The disciplined routine of compiling detailed observation logs, the demanding skills of judging wind strength, estimating distance as well as the effects of the wind over distance, were now being taught in depth alongside the traditional skills of camouflage and concealment.

The range of skills being taught were now encapsulated in the new course Scouting and Sniping which was producing a highly proficient sniper, in fact even by late 1916 more trained snipers were being produced than converted rifles. As the requirements of the British sniper became more apparent the telescope, particularly the Aldis telescope, began to receive modifications which in the period 1915–1916 saw four models of Aldis scope enter the conversion programme. The models one to four appeared chronologically as the modifications changed the model number; the third model received the adjustable objective lens prism and the fourth model received the adjustable prism as standard being fitted to the J. Purdey & Sons rifle as the mounts lacked sufficient lateral adjustment.

ABOVE: The basic equipment of the Great War sniper. The principal items illustrated here were indeed simple but were set to evolve, with some items being omitted such as the bayonet whilst others such as the carry case would become a constant over the 100 years, seeing development which would transform it into a highly specialised item in support of the sniper's role.

ABOVE: Sniper and observer from the 1/4th Battalion, Royal Berkshire Regiment in the roof of a barn at Anton's Farm near Ploegsteert Wood during the spring of 1915. Note the spotter on this occasion is using the prismatic binocular.

SMLE MkIII & MkIII*
Holland & Holland Conversion/Aldis Bros Telescope

Technical Specification	
Calibre	303in
Magazine Capacity	10 Rounds
Overall Rifle Length	44.5in
Barrel Length	25.2in
Twist Rate	5 Groove, LH 1 in 10 Twist
Combat Weight	10lb
Iron Sights	Graduated to 2000 Yds
Conversion Approval Date	4th May 1915
Converted By	Holland & Holland
Scope Mounted	Offset, Left Side
Quantity Converted	1000 approx

LEFT: The wrist markings show this rifle to be Enfield built in 1916 to MkIII* specification.

The Holland & Holland converted MkIII* SMLE rifle illustrated here shows a modification to the rear sight protector which appears necessary for the front mount to fit. Also, note the rear hand guard is missing. A common issue with this conversion as the hand guard itself was perhaps over modified in order for the mount to fit which led to an unreliable fit. Hand guards were lost and dare I say it thrown away as a result. Note the exposed section of barrel: its appearance looks almost polished and the black finish which would otherwise be present, having been hidden beneath the wood has long been rubbed away by the many hands that have handled it.

ABOVE: The British snipers in this image are armed with Holland & Holland converted rifles and pose with a captured Gewehr 98 German issue service rifle with its saw back bayonet fixed, also note the Pickelhaube helmets, often a source of much amusement to those who posed with them.

The Holland & Holland mount system is rarer and far less encountered today than the Purdey system and is again a double mount with the scope rings also in a separate forward and rear arrangement. The front mount was similar to the Purdey system in that it clamped around the barrel forward of the chamber sitting central to the rear hand guard, which required a modification to fit around the mount assembly. Original surviving examples have been noted to have had the rear hand guard missing as a result of it being deliberately left off the rifle, presumably due to its modification being unsatisfactory, or simply unreliable in some way, maybe by removing itself too often to the point that it was lost, discarded or broken. The example here also has the missing section of rear hand guard and the wear to the finish on the barrel would suggest the rifle was used in this fashion. The front mount was a robust steel block which slightly overhangs the left side of the receiver; the overhang carries in it a slot cut which a steel pin passes through. The steel pin accommodates the hook of the forward projecting arm of the front scope ring.

Any similarity that may exist between the H&H and the Purdey mounts ends there as the roll-over lever and means of lateral adjustment has been transferred to the rear. The rear mount which is

ABOVE: The front mount from above. Note how it has been slightly set into the ear of the rear sight protector. The seam of the two sections that come together around the barrel is also visible as is the pin of which the claw foot of the front ring locates.

fixed to the left side of the receiver and hard up against the receiver ring has an oblong square cornered recess which accepts a male insert of the same dimensions attached to the rear scope ring. This insert has a semi-circular cut-out positioned half way in its forward edge. When the forward scope ring hook is located and the rear scope rings attachment is inserted a roll-over lever is operated and locks the rear ring in the recess, utilising the semi-circular cut-out in the scope's insert.

The lateral adjustment is uniquely situated in the rear scope ring which is actually in two pieces. The scope ring carries a female dovetail and the attachment that slots into the mount has a male dovetail which enables the two to slot together forming on first appearances a single piece rear ring. Screws on both sides of the rear ring assembly can be slackened and tightened to enable the upper section attached to the scope to move left and right on the dovetail joint.

ABOVE: The fixings that attach the rear mount to the receiver wall are visible here, however the third fixing is concealed behind the roll-over lever.

BELOW: A view of both the front and rear mounts from above. The roll-over lever is currently in the open position and deploys the locking pin by pushing the lever down and through 180 degrees where it rests, mirrored to its position in this image. Note the polished section of barrel which indicates this example has been without its rear hand guard for some years.

Telescope, Aldis Bros No. 1

Technical Specification	
Manufacturer	Aldis Brothers, Birmingham
Length	10.8in
Weight	17.5oz
Objective Lens DIA	19mm
Field of View	9 degrees
Magnification	3 X
Reticle	Post and Wire
Range Graduations	100–600 Yds (some 1-8)
Focus Capability	Yes
Lateral Adjustment	None
Mount Type	Double

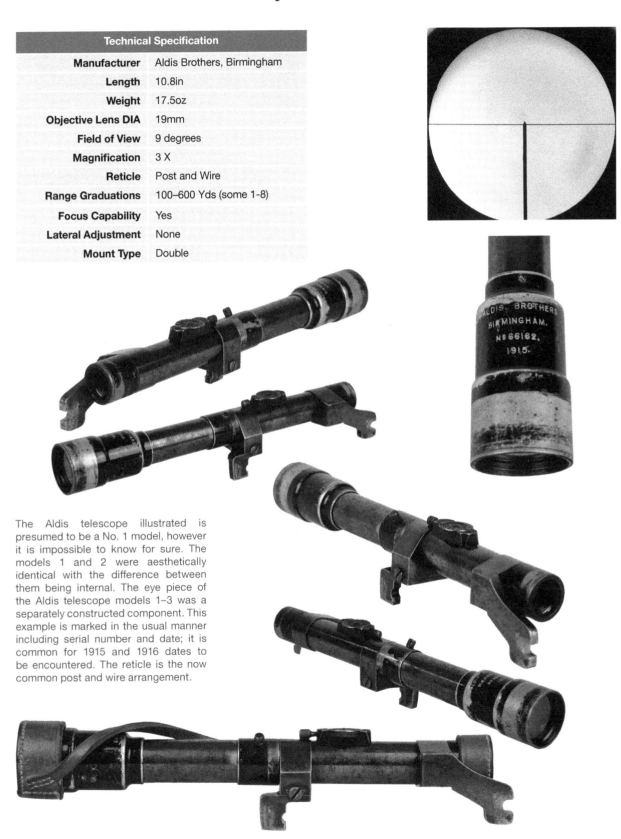

The Aldis telescope illustrated is presumed to be a No. 1 model, however it is impossible to know for sure. The models 1 and 2 were aesthetically identical with the difference between them being internal. The eye piece of the Aldis telescope models 1–3 was a separately constructed component. This example is marked in the usual manner including serial number and date; it is common for 1915 and 1916 dates to be encountered. The reticle is the now common post and wire arrangement.

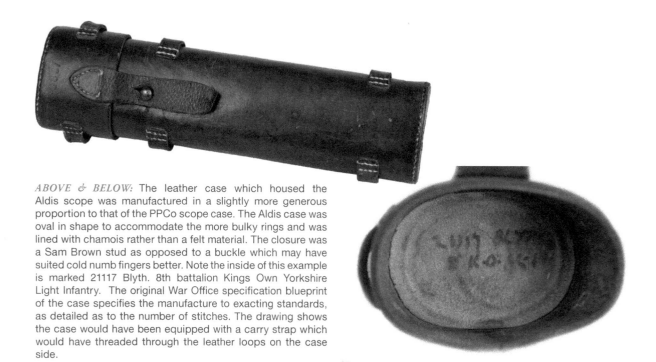

ABOVE & BELOW: The leather case which housed the Aldis scope was manufactured in a slightly more generous proportion to that of the PPCo scope case. The Aldis case was oval in shape to accommodate the more bulky rings and was lined with chamois rather than a felt material. The closure was a Sam Brown stud as opposed to a buckle which may have suited cold numb fingers better. Note the inside of this example is marked 21117 Blyth. 8th battalion Kings Own Yorkshire Light Infantry. The original War Office specification blueprint of the case specifies the manufacture to exacting standards, as detailed as to the number of stitches. The drawing shows the case would have been equipped with a carry strap which would have threaded through the leather loops on the case side.

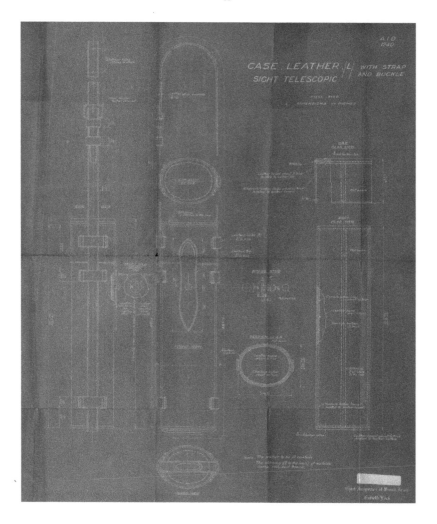

With the Periscopic Prism Company, Holland & Holland and J. Purdey & Sons Ltd all supporting the war effort with their respective sniper conversions, they were restricted by the speed at which the telescopes could be manufactured and therefore the requirement for sniper rifles still presented itself as unquenchable which led a fourth SMLE sniper conversion to enter the fray. The British lacked the industrial ability to manufacture optical instruments on a truly industrial scale and were forced to look further afield; this led to the adoption of the American Winchester B4 and A5 models of telescope. These telescopes were delivered with two styles of reticle: either a delicate crosswire or a single post with no wire. Winchester produced the single post reticle by using a standard sewing needle to create the post, a wonderful act of initiative from a bygone age.

The Winchester telescope conversions were carried out by Whitehead Brothers with 907 sniper rifles supplied. The four variants of conversion spanned the SMLE MkIII and MkIII* rifle and collectively by 1918 they numbered approximately 13,000, all converted mainly on Enfield built rifles with a good number of BSA rifles in the mix.

The four Great War sniper rifles featured here are the most commonly encountered and are those that were converted in any real significant numbers, however there were other conversions produced in much smaller batch sizes using telescopes manufactured by Watts, Evans, Fidjland and Jeffrey. The WW2 sniper Harry M. Furness, who after his own exploits became a keen historian on the subject in the post-war years, unearthed an MoD file many years ago during his own study work which contained the following detailed list of contracts for sniper rifle conversions awarded by the War Office between September 1915 and October 1916. The document also lists contracted purchases of Galilean open sights between October 1915 and June 1916.

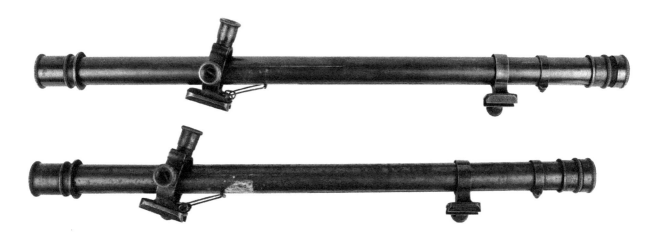

ABOVE: The Winchester telescope models A5 and B4 are illustrated side by side. The B4 model is featured below the A5 and is marginally shorter, but with the exception of this it is the same telescope.

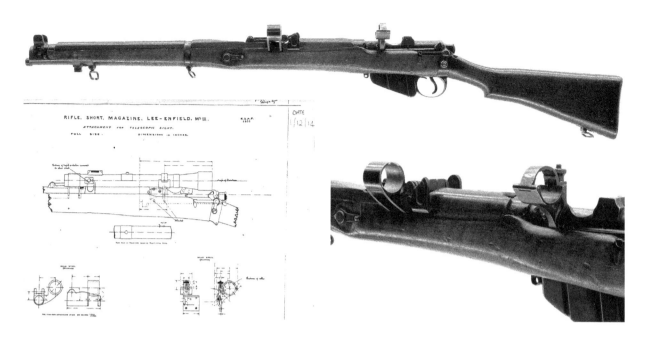

ABOVE: A very rare survivor of one of the alternative small batch conversions. John Rigby & Co. Enfield No. 1 MkIII sniper rifle, manufactured 1914, serial number L 780. A former Pattern Room rifle most possibly converted as per drawing dated 01.12.1914 for a contract to supply and fit telescopes to twenty-one rifles by John Rigby & Co., the contract dating 13.01.1915. Front base/ring attached to barrel, rear base/ring attached to receiver. Unique in combining rings and bases to a single piece by having the scope itself removable with a bayonet-type locking mechanism. The scope which would in all likelihood have been a Fuess type scope transitional to PPCo locked in place by rubber shims on top of a split rear scope ring (not present on rifle shown) and additional positioning/locking stud added to the scope tube. The original drawing indicates usage of 25mm tube (rifle shown 1" tubes). Note removal of left side rear sight protector to clear lateral adjustment capstans of scope.

Telescopic Sights

Date	Manufacturer	Equipment	Quantity
14/9/1915	J. Purdey & Sons	Fitting Telescopic Sights	90
7/10/1915	Holland & Holland	Fitting Telescopic Sights	100
7/10/1915	Whitehead Bros.	Fitting Telescopic Sights	200
19/10/1915	J. Bartle & Co.	Fitting Telescopic Sights	2000
28/10/1915	Periscopic Prism Co.	Supply & Fit Telescopic Sights	4000
8/11/1915	Whitehead Bros.	Fitting Telescopic Sights	6
12/11/1915	J. Purdey & Sons	Fitting Telescopic Sights	200
13/11/1915	D. Frazer & Co.	Fitting Telescopic Sights	36
3/12/1915	Holland & Holland	Fitting Telescopic Sights	100
14/12/1915	Whitehead Bros.	Fitting Telescopic Sights	200
5/1/1916	J. Purdey & Sons	Fitting Telescopic Sights	100
19/1/1916	W. Jeffrey & Co.	Supply Sights Telescopic	50
24/1/1916	Holland & Holland	Fit Telescopic Sights & Supply Leather Cases	100
25/1/1916	J. Purdey & Sons	Fit Telescopic Sights & Supply Leather Cases	200
2/2/1916	W. Evans	Supply & Fit Telescopic Sights	50

Date	Manufacturer	Equipment	Quantity
14/2/1916	Whitehead Bros.	Fitting Winchester Telescopes	500
24/2/1916	Holland & Holland	Fit Telescopic Sights & Supply Leather Cases	200
24/3/1916	J. Purdey & Sons	Fitting Telescopic Sights	200
31/5/1916	J. Purdey & Sons	Fitting Telescopic Sights	200
1/6/1916	Holland & Holland	Fitting Telescopic Sights	200
3/8/1916	E.R. Watts & Sons	Spare Parts for Telescopic Sights: 5 Items; No. of Parts	132
19/9/1916	Periscopic Prism Co.	Prism Mounts, Complete: 3 Items; No. of Parts	72
30/9/1916	Aldis Bros.	Fit Telescopic Sights with Bartle Fittings	700
20/10/1916	Aldis Bros.	Supply Sights Telescopic	2254
18/10/1916	Aldis Bros.	Fit Telescopic Sights with Bartle Fittings	700

Galilean Open Lens Sights

Date	Manufacturer	Equipment	Quantity
29/10/1915	S.D. Neill Ltd.	Rifle Sights, sets of	4000
8/12/1915	J. & R. Fleming Ltd.	Lattey Lens Sights	3000
8/12/1915	Precision Eng. Co.	Mountings for Lattey Lens Sights	3000
22/12/1915	Alexander Martin	Martin Lens Sights	575
22/12/1915	Alexander Martin	BSA Optical Sights	80
19/2/1916	J. & R. Fleming Ltd.	Lattey Lens Sights	2600
19/2/1916	Knights & Cattrell	Lattey Lens Mountings	2000
25/2/1916	Precision Eng. Co.	Lattey Lens Mountings	2000
7/3/1916	J. & R. Fleming Ltd.	Lattey Lens Sights	2000
14/6/1916	F.H. Glew	Radium Composition Glass Tubes: Optical Sights for Rifles	180,000

The company W. Jeffrey & Co listed as supplying fifty telescopes in January 1916 was in fact more of a specialist when it came to big game hunting rifles. The company enjoyed more success supplying these large calibre rifles than they did their telescopes and it is on record that the W. Jeffrey big game rifle was procured for the purposes of "loop hole busting". In the early months of the war when Britain was at a disadvantage and very much playing catch up the War Office bought up many civilian supplies of telescope, in fact anything that could be mounted on an SMLE rifle was purchased in the period before things were standardised with the introduction of the Periscopic Prism Company conversion.

The list of civilian sporting telescopes that have been recorded as entering service in that early period are Gibbs, Baker, Westley Richards, Rigby as well as some German and Austrian scopes such as Goerz, Kahles and Fuess, presumably stocks purchased before the outbreak of hostilities. The listed figures which account for such War Office pre-contract purchases of telescopic sights from these various makers are recorded as 2,914. Pre-contract purchases of Galilean open sights are also listed as a quantity of 1,400 Lattey manufactured sights procured early in 1915.

SMLE MkIII & MkIII*
Whitehead Brothers Conversion/Winchester Telescope

Technical Specification	
Calibre	303in
Magazine Capacity	10 Rounds
Overall Rifle Length	44.5in
Barrel Length	25.2in
Twist Rate	5 Groove, LH 1 in 10 Twist
Combat Weight	9lb
Iron Sights	Graduated to 2000 Yds
Conversion Approval Date	4th May 1915
Converted By	Holland & Holland
Scope Mounted	Offset, Left Side
Quantity Converted	907

ABOVE: These wrist markings show this example as being Enfield manufactured in 1916 to MkIII* specification.

This exceptional example of a Whitehead Bros converted SMLE carries a Winchester A5 telescope. Note the palm swell of the fore-end allowing for a volley sight dial which has been omitted from the specification due to its MkIII* build specification, however even if the rifle had been MkIII, being a sniper it may well have still been built without the volley sights. I would suggest this rifle is wearing one of the last MkIII specification wood sets before the proportions of the fore-end were altered, consigning the volley sight to history.

ABOVE: The front mount of the Whitehead Bros conversion is essentially a steel angle shaped to that of the rear sight protector ear. Although the mount appears to be fixed solidly to the metalwork of the rifle it is in fact fixed to the wood of the fore-end as the rear sight protector itself fixes to the fore-end with a single screw visible from the underside of the rifle.

The third most commonly encountered scope to be employed by British snipers during the Great War was the Winchester A5 procured by the government from the U.S. Winchester Repeating Arms Company. The instruments were purchased and it is believed some of these were also the similar, but smaller B4 models. The A5 model however was to make up the lion's share of the order and is certainly the model most encountered today. The scopes were mounted to the SMLE rifle by the Whitehead Brothers company using their own mounting system which consisted of a double mount arrangement.

The front and rear mounts were essentially angle iron and the front was shaped and fitted to the side of the left rear sight protector ear. The obvious downside to this was that the rear sight protector was actually fitted to the wooden fore-end which moved as the wood contracted and expanded. The bracket was mechanically fixed with three screws. The rear mount was also shaped and fitted to the left receiver wall just in front of the scooped recess that accommodated the thumb when charging the magazine.

This mount was also mechanically fixed with three screws, and both the front and the rear mounts were fitted with male dovetail mounting blocks, each mechanically fixed with two screws. The scope was fitted with a front and a rear ring which carried the female dovetail blocks to complete mounting to the rifle. The front was a simple arrangement, but the rear dovetail block was mounted to the underside of the scope's adjustment apparatus.

The telescope had no internal means of adjustment, enabling the manufacturer to produce a very slimline instrument, very different to the scopes the troops had become accustomed to. The A5, B5 and B4 models shared the same design and means of adjustment which was installed over the rear mount. The scope tube was held under a spring-loaded tension against the elevation and windage adjustment knobs. The scope unusually moved forward on recoil and had to be physically pulled back by the sniper before the next shot, hence the grippy rings at the eyepiece.

Genuine Great War Winchester scopes are generally found today bearing British military ownership marks in the form of an Enfield

BELOW: Again the rear mount is essentially a simple steel angle shaped to contour the receiver wall. Both the front and rear mounts act as a platform to carry the male dovetail blocks.

inspection mark and broad arrow ownership mark on the scope's female dovetail mounting block, although several telescopes that have the SMLE serial number engraved on the tube and backfilled with red paint do not appear to bear the War Department acceptance marks as described above. It is presumed these telescopes were the first to be received and were fitted straight away whilst the telescopes that followed went into stores where they were properly received and marked with the correct government ownership marks. It should also be noted that these properly marked telescopes did not receive a rifle serial number engraving to the tube when fitted at conversion.

ABOVE: The Enfield inspection and broad arrow ownership marks are visible either side of the patent. This telescope does not bear a rifle serial number which is in keeping with these telescopes that generally have one such mark or the other.

Telescope, Winchester A5

Technical Specification	
Manufacturer	Winchester Repeating Arms Company
Length	16in
Weight	6oz
Objective Lens DIA	18mm
Field of View	3.2 degrees
Magnification	5 X
Reticle	Crosshairs/Post
Range Graduations	None
Focus Capability	Yes
Lateral Adjustment	Yes
Mount Type	Double

ABOVE: The Winchester telescopes were supplied with two reticle patterns. A fine cross hair or a single post with no wire is found today in surviving examples; it also offered a much greater power of magnification to its contemporaries.

The Winchester A5 telescope illustrated still bears the serial number of the SMLE rifle it was paired to. The serial number G2838 is coarsely engraved on the scope tube and backfilled in red paint and as is common with the Winchester telescopes marked in this way it does not carry any military ownership marks.

ABOVE & LEFT: The leather carry case for the A5 telescope was bucket shaped. The example illustrated still bears the SMLE serial number W8118 and is unit marked to the 6th Battalion Royal Fusiliers.

It is also a documented fact that Britain's hunger, or lack of industrial capability, to manufacture optical products such as telescopic sights, camera lenses and range finders as well as binoculars and trench periscopes resulted in the extraordinary circumstances whereby exploration of a deal with Germany was sought, Germany whose industrial proficiency in the manufacture of such products was such that it was in a position to supply thousands of units of each product each month. Government officials from both sides held discussions in neutral Switzerland. In return for the supply of optical units Germany requested that Britain supply it with rubber of which we had good colonial supplies; however the actual result, or agreement, seems to have evaporated in the mists of time.

I would suggest no deal was struck; the number of units being discussed at the time ran into the tens of thousands across a broad array of products and I would imagine there would be plenty of German examples still around today wearing the broad arrow if such an agreement had existed.

No. 17114 Pte. Thomas Barratt, late S. Staffs. R. (Tipton).

For most conspicuous bravery when as Scout to a patrol he worked his way towards the enemy line with the greatest gallantry and determination, in spite of continuous fire from hostile snipers at close range.

These snipers he stalked and killed. Later his patrol was similarly held up, and again he disposed of the snipers.

When during the subsequent withdrawal of the patrol it was observed that a party of the enemy were endeavouring to outflank them, Pte. Barratt at once volunteered to cover the retirement, and this he succeeded in accomplishing.

His accurate shooting caused many casualties to the enemy, and prevented their advance.

Throughout the enterprise he was under heavy machine gun and rifle fire, and his splendid example of coolness and daring was beyond all praise.

After safely regaining our lines, this very gallant soldier was killed by a shell.

ABOVE: This London Gazette clipping brings to life the exploits of one Great War sniper, Private Thomas Barratt, who was clearly made of stern stuff and a capable sniper. However, as so typical of the Great War, luck would often play a huge part in determining who would live and who would die. *(Courtesy Nigel Greenaway)*

By late 1917 Major Crum was made responsible for the total co-ordination of scout and sniper training across the British Army. A well organised scout sniper training infrastructure now existed and constantly morphed with the introduction of new equipment, and with the training staff coming directly from a sniping background in the trenches they brought with them the most current experiences of the British sniper on the ground.

Aided by advances in technology, the sniping campaign on the Western Front was now being firmly won by the British; the tide had most certainly been turned from entering the war with no real sniper presence to dominating "no-man's land" and constantly harassing the German lines and inflicting constant pressure on the morale of the German troops. This success was the result of a highly proficient sniper being routinely turned out by the scouting

and sniper training schools. The men recruited into the profession were handpicked because they suited the criteria of intelligence, tirelessness and physical strength as well as demonstrating the making of a good shot. The desired qualities were very much evident in Pte Thomas Barratt of the South Staffordshire Regiment who was posthumously awarded the Victoria Cross, the announcement of which was printed in the *London Gazette*.

The Sniper's Garment

The German snipers from the Jäger battalions, made up of men who had a hunting background in the vast German forests, opened the sniping campaign and remained hugely successful in the initial months of the war, however they found themselves pitted against the Scottish ghillies who largely formed the Lovat Scouts Regiment which in turn had a significant influence on the training of British snipers. It was the Lovat Scouts who brought the ghillie suit to the battlefield.

The suit was a form of camouflage initially used to help the Scottish ghillie, or deer hunter, on the hillside blend in when in pursuit of the red deer. The ghillie suit was predominantly made from hessian sacking which enabled the wearer to melt away in a natural landscape. The base colour of the hessian matches the natural colour scheme which is further enhanced by adding some natural foliage from the immediate environment. The end result is a superb form of camouflage which blends and breaks up the outline of the human form. So effective was it that the suit was adopted immediately and as the landscape descended from grassy fields and woodland to a brown moonscape the suit was simply

ABOVE: Two original examples of the British sniper gown from the Great War. Very simple garments, often a trench coat customised and hand painted. The practice of adding strips of hessian sacking to break up the human outline is also illustrated.

ABOVE: These surviving examples of mitt and headdress are perfectly camouflaged with russet colours for the muddy bare wasteland of the Western Front. Note the headdress completely shrouds the sniper's head and has a small gauze mesh panel to see through.

ABOVE: This sniper demonstrates the use of a hessian sandbag as a head shroud. The sacking has been painted with the addition of tree bark attached to the top, showing effective camouflage could be made from commonly found items that littered the battlefield.

ABOVE: A Lovat Scout in prone firing position, dressed in a full sniper gown. His demonstration is on the heathland of Bisley camp.

ABOVE: Fake shell-shattered looking trees often stood anonymously in and around no-man's land concealing scout observers and at times snipers.

altered to match the environment. No longer was there a need to add foliage, mainly as there was none; the suit simply evolved and became a gown with hood and mitts.

Sniper gowns were made mainly by the men in the trench and from whatever materials they could lay their hands on. Anything and everything was put to use, whether hessian sacking or an old trench

coat. As the landscape changed and became a featureless, muddy, cratered wasteland the sniper gown was painted in rustic colours and spattered in multiples of browns, greens, reds and even white. It has to be said some of the original examples closely resemble the British Army's current MTP (Multi Terrain Pattern) camouflage of today that was adopted in 2011.

Efforts to deceive the enemy didn't end with a highly effective camouflage suit. The British developed imitation trees which were modelled on an actual tree selected in no-man's land, or what was left of the tree after the shelling turned woodlands into broken stumps. The fake model tree would be installed by work parties in the dead of night. Noise from their activities would be muffled by a diversionary shelling or machine gun fire so by daylight all looked as it did the previous day, however what looked perfectly normal from the German lines now concealed an observer or sniper who had the reach they needed on a section of the German trench to carry out their respective duty whether it be recording German movements, or daily routine by the observer, or the sniper delivering deadly sniper fire to disrupt the enemy's activities, or to break morale of troops who otherwise felt they were out of reach of such a threat.

Another well used method for the British sniper to access areas of the German trench which would otherwise be difficult would again

BELOW: The dummy carcass of a horse laid out here at one of the sniper schools. The internal area looks to have been created with the use of a barrel.

ABOVE: The author's artistic impression depicts a British sniper who is about to crawl into the belly of a fake horse made of hessian and padded out with straw. The tactic helped conceal British snipers in the most unlikely of places, enabling them to access areas of the German lines that were otherwise unreachable, and went a long way to breaking German morale.

involve some fakery. It is a sad and lasting indictment on mankind that not only were we addicted to the blood lust of killing each other, we dragged the horse into the carnage as well, with approximately half a million horses and mules being acquisitioned after a national census. Of these seventy-five percent would perish, if not by direct enemy fire, then through disease and starvation which would also take their toll during the war. Many war horses lay dead, their carcasses littering no-man's land in varying states of decomposition. The British, seeing this as an opportunity, made oversized imitation carcasses from hessian fixed to a light frame and stuffed with straw to look like the bloated remains of a horse. The sniper would crawl into the fake carcass through the belly where he would wait for an opportunity to

offer itself. His patience would, more often than not, pay off, the reward being an opportunity to deliver deadly sniper fire on a confused enemy.

In the years 1915 and 1916 the British struggled to produce sufficient numbers of the SMLE rifle. Even with thousands of rifles being reclaimed from the dead and wounded in no-man's land and returned to England for refurbishment, sufficient supply was still a struggle. The MkIII became a MkIII* after the design saw the withdrawal of the magazine cutoff which technically authorised the MkIII* designation but further amendments to the specification of the rifle were made. By late 1916 a great many of the men who were highly trained in musketry were dead, killed in offensives such as the Battle of the Somme. The training

infrastructure at home in England was now turning out a basically trained infantryman; there was no time to teach a recruit how to use the volley sights of an SMLE rifle, or how to adjust his sight laterally for wind, so these features were also dropped from the rifle's specification. This, coupled with the simplification of parts for manufacture, saved raw material in an attempt to aid the war effort but also made the manufacture of the rifle quicker and easier. Furthermore, the War Office turned to the United States and requested a number of .303 inch calibre rifles manufactured by the Winchester Arms Co, Remington and Eddystone. Eddystone were a subsidiary company of Remington who were based in Ilion, NY. Designated Pattern 1914, they didn't materialise in the UK in any real numbers until 1917 when the changes made to the design of the SMLE had taken effect and supply of the MkIII* rifle was now back on track and the shortages were overcome. The vast majority of the Patt 14 rifles were put in Cosmoline type grease and packed away, not to see the light of day again until WW2.

A number of rifles were set aside and sent to the sniper schools in England for trial and appraisal. The Remington and Eddystonè rifles were found to be manufactured to a looser tolerance and not as accurate as the Winchester manufactured rifles which were reported as being a joy to shoot and demonstrating superior accuracy at all distances over the SMLE; in fact the iron sighted Patt 14 rifle was preferred over a telescoped SMLE.

It is no secret that the SMLE could not be all things to all men and was indeed a superlative infantryman's rifle capable of reliability in the most difficult field conditions, however, it was not the ideal weapon for sniper conversion and its service was dogged with complaints by snipers regarding its suitability as a sniper rifle. The side mounted scope on a flexible receiver, its relatively light barrel, rear locking bolt and lack of accuracy, particularly beyond 300 yards using the .303 inch MkVII ball ammunition, made it a difficult weapon to master.

In late 1917 it is reported that a captured German sniper rifle became the inspiration for a new British sniper rifle to replace all the SMLE variants. The captured weapon carried a light Hensoldt telescope mounted with detachable claw foot mounts. The rifle was returned to England where it was assessed and found to be far superior to the SMLE family of sniper rifles.

In the second half of 1917 the Small Arms Committee met a number of times to discuss the creation of a new sniper rifle which would better that of the captured German design. A committee meeting dated 12th September 1917 and titled "Mounting of Telescopic Sights on .303 Rifles" has its minutes recorded. Minute 21 tells of the German example and how a 1914 rifle had already been set up with an Aldis telescope in similar overhead mounts for testing and approval by the sniper schools in France. The meeting further discussed a modification of the mounts to include two "give and take" screws for lateral adjustment as opposed to the one screw the German model had and how there were 750 Aldis telescopes ready for fitting after approval by the schools in France.

The Pattern 1914 rifle selected with its Aldis telescope fitted with new claw foot mounts was sent to France for field trials where it outperformed the SMLE models, but it was still falling short of the standard demonstrated by the captured German example. It was let down by the scope; it was felt the telescope was inferior to the Hensoldt Wetzler fitted to the captured example. Work began to

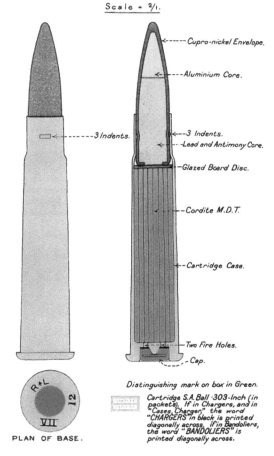

ABOVE: An early Ministry of Munitions specification drawing of the S.A. Ball, .303 inch round. MkVII. Note the propellant is Cordite MDT and the drawing gives detailed notes to the markings applied to packaging.

design a lighter superior scope to replace the Aldis which had served so well on the SMLE, with the assistance of Lord Cottesloe and Lt. Col. L.H. Robinson, the latter being the Chief Inspector of Small Arms at Enfield Lock. Their design delivered a new lightweight telescope which also influenced the design of the claw foot mounts. The objective lens had within it an adjustable prism for lateral adjustment which eliminated the need for any "give and take" screws in the mounts. The new telescope arrived in early 1918, and was designated Sight Telescopic Model 1918.

Now mounted overbore via claw foot mounts, the new rifle was designated in April 1918 .303-inch Pattern 1914, Mk1* W (T), the letter "W" denoting that it was built on a Winchester manufactured rifle. The Periscopic Prism Company carried out the conversion of 2,000 units overseen by the Ministry of Munitions, but they were unfortunately sent to France too late to be tested in the same way as the SMLE was as hostilities ended in November 1918. So history largely looks back at the Pattern 1914 Mk1* W (T) as the inter-war rifle which never had the opportunity to earn a reputation or develop its own pedigree on the battlefield.

Chapter 2
The Quiet Years

Post 1918 saw the Patt 1914, Mk1* W (T) largely retired to stores. Although on issue to over 100 battalions at roughly eight per battalion, sniping stayed low as a priority due to the War Office not recognising it as a skill worth investing in after the defence cuts that followed the Armistice. It was scaled back as though obsolete, with very little military training provided and no advancement on what had been learnt in France during the war years. 1921 saw the Small Arms Committee meet to discuss the future use, if any, for the SMLE sniper rifle and after much deliberation as to whether they should have been issued to the territorial battalions the decision was instead taken to break them up.

The array of rifle, mount and scope combinations that sat in the armouries was obviously a result of the work in progress that was the British Army entering the sniping fracas and such a large "tool chest" complicated matters. It was largely felt the costs surrounding their issue would have been excessive due to the logistical problems thrown up by the different scopes and mounts that would have required ongoing maintenance and repair as well as the ongoing training infrastructure required to use them.

Therefore the SMLE sniper rifle entered its decommission at Weedon Royal Ordnance Depot where the mounts were in many cases scrapped and a number of Aldis No. 1, 2, 3 and 4 scopes were kept back and packaged for long-term storage. The remaining scopes

PREVIOUS PAGE: A WW2 sniper inspecting the barrel of his 3 T rifle. Note the canvas covered scope case for his Model 1918 telescope.

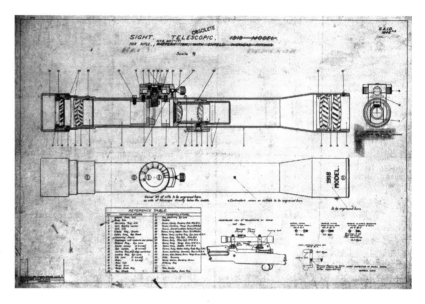

ABOVE: This original specification drawing of the Model 1918 telescope provides a plan as well as two section views of the telescope numbering all of its parts. The accompanying table lists the corresponding parts 1–39. The Model 1918 telescope was manufactured by the Periscopic Prism Company with the exception of seventy-nine examples produced by BSA as part of an Irish Constabulary Contract.

BELOW: An original specification drawing titled Rifle, No. 3, Mk 1 (T). The drawing details the objective lens and prism, focus adjustment arrangement, the range drum graduated to 1,000 yards as well as the fitting arrangement to the rifle. The position of the engraving of both the rifle's serial number and manufacturer's name are specifically denoted.

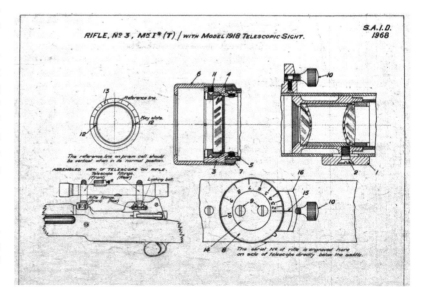

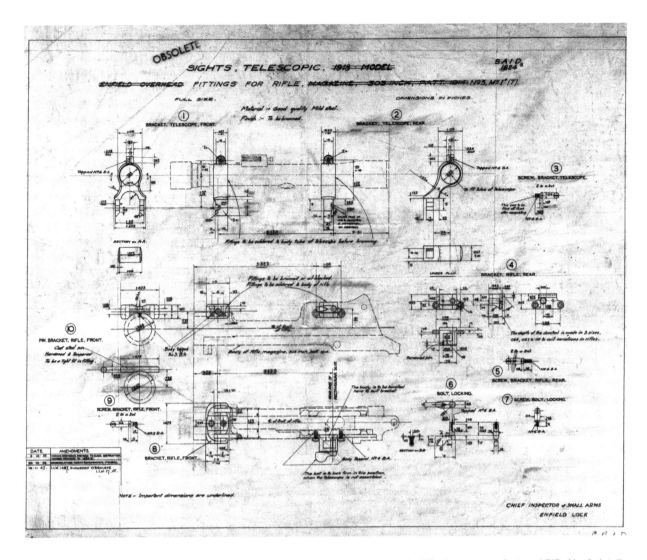

ABOVE: This original drawing detailing the fitting of the Model 1918 telescope to the Winchester manufactured Rifle No. 3 details with absolute precision the mounts and their fitment to the receiver. The drawing also carries amendments dated 1937, 1939 and 1947.

were all sold off back to companies such as Holland & Holland who carried out the original wartime conversions, where they were commercially refurbished and sold into the post-war sporting market, this being the main reason why complete original WW1 sniper rifles are so scarce today, and original mounts almost impossible to find.

The inter-war period saw the slow redistribution of the Pattern 1914 Mk1* W (T) rifle to Commonwealth countries, Australia seemingly receiving the lion's share. I say this as today many of the surviving original examples appear to have Australian military acceptance marks. It would appear the British Army now only had a skeleton involvement in sniping, however the sniper rifle was still in the armoury and the wheels of updating and replacing obsolete equipment did turn, although very slowly.

Pattern 1914 Mk1* W (T)
Periscopic Prism Company Conversion/PPCo Model 1918 Telescope

The Rifle No. 3 Mk 1 (T), formerly .303-inch Pattern 1914, Mk1* W (T), was originally conceived in the latter stages of WW1 to replace all of the SMLE variants that went before it, but went on to serve predominantly in WW2. The example illustrated has a sling swivel fitted forward of the internal magazine compartment. Clearly a WW2 modification, it was also common in WW2 to see the 3T fitted with a birchwood cheek rest like that of the 4T.

Technical Specification	
Calibre	303in
Magazine Capacity	5 Rounds
Overall Rifle Length	46.4in
Barrel Length	26in
Twist Rate	5 Groove, LH 1 in 10 Twist
Combat Weight	10 lb
Iron Sights	Graduated to 1600 Yds
Conversion Approval Date	11th April 1918
Converted By	Periscopic Prism Company
Scope Mounted	Overbore
Quantity Converted	2000 approx (Qty of 79 also produced by BSA Co)

ABOVE: A British sniper student is using a No 3 T rifle on the range at a sniper training school in France, 27th July 1944.

The Pattern 1914 rifle ordered by the British government at a time when the SMLE rifle could not be produced quickly enough arrived after some economical belt tightening delivered the desired effect, putting the SMLE rifle's production numbers back on track. The iron sighted Patt 14 rifle eventually started to arrive in the UK in late 1916 and was sent to the sniping schools in France for evaluation. It was immediately found to demonstrate superior accuracy to the SMLE; in fact many students shot more accurately with an iron sighted Pattern 1914 rifle than they did with a scoped SMLE. The sniping schools' only criticism was of the rear sight, which at their request and for sniping use was made adjustable in much finer increments which in turn led to the "F" Rifle which was issued on a scale of three per battalion late in the war.

The Patt 14 rifle was also selected as the platform for the new sniper system that would replace all of the SMLE rifles converted through the war. The new sniper system was radically different from any of the SMLE conversions as finally – and to the relief of many – the scope was to be mounted overbore in a double claw mount arrangement.

The front mount sat on top of the forward portion of the receiver immediately behind the hand guard retaining ring and was mechanically fixed with two screws. The mount was symmetrical: both left and right of the mount carried an identical square recess through which a pin travelled. The position of this front mount obscured the serial number of the weapon so it became standard practice to reposition on the right ear of the rear "F" sight protector.

The rear mount was set into the wall of the left protector ear of the rear sight and was mechanically fixed with two screws and was flat topped with a square recess and roll-over lever. The scope was equipped with separate rings, the front formed by two "legs" that carried forward facing hooks that engaged with the pins in the front mount recesses. The rear ring presented to the rear mount a single rearward facing hook which travelled from the centre line to its offset position via an elegant sloped angle. When inserted into the mount's square recess the single hook was locked in place when the roll-over lever was operated. The Model 1918 scope was mounted in mounts that had no lateral adjustment; instead the scope itself was equipped with an internal prism that was adjusted after the final fitting to its chosen rifle.

ABOVE: The front mount is situated on top of the most forward section of the receiver. The mount acts to simply locate the double claw feet of the front scope ring against a steel pin in each of the slots.

ABOVE: The rear mount operates in a similar manner to that of the rear mount found on the Holland & Holland converted SMLE. The foot of the rear scope ring drops into the square recess and is locked when the roll-over lever is pushed 180 degrees, deploying the locking pin inside the mount. Note the rear mount is set into the left sight protector ear wall.

Telescope, PPCo Model 1918

Technical Specification	
Manufacturer	Periscopic Prism Company
Length	9.6in
Weight	12 oz
Objective Lens DIA	19mm
Field of View	7.5 degrees
Magnification	3 X
Reticle	Post & Wire
Range Graduations	100–1000 Yds
Focus Capability	Yes
Lateral Adjustment	Yes (internal Prism)
Mount Type	Double

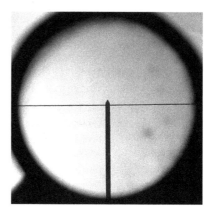

ABOVE: The eye piece was coned in shape and marked Model 1918, commonly with a broad arrow acceptance mark. The reticle was the British post and wire pattern found in all but the U.S. manufactured Winchester telescopes.

The Model 1918 telescope, with its rings and mounts, completed a unique British sniper rifle in its day as it delivered what many had been calling for: a sniper rifle with an overbore mounted telescope. The scope was, in comparison to the telescopes that preceded it, quite petite.

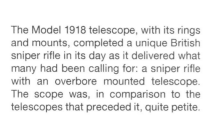

ABOVE & RIGHT: The Model 1918 telescope was provided with a rigid carry case covered with canvas material and finished with a leather buckle strap and long leather carry strap. The canvas case was not as durable as the leather cases that preceded it, which makes this particular case quite rare today.

ABOVE: A British sniper student takes aim through the Model 1918 sight of his No. 3, Mk1* T rifle on the range at a sniper training school in France, 27th July 1944. The No. 3 T had by this period become a training rifle which had to be mastered before the student could be introduced to the No. 4 T.

It was recognised in the 1920s that the SMLE rifle had seen better days and going forward an updated infantryman's rifle was required. The slow wheels of change turned and after some development a further SMLE design was pondered over, the SMLE MkV, but the design didn't travel that far from the original rifle. Later in 1931 a further improved model, MkVI, was produced by RSAF Enfield for troop trials. Further simplification was required as well as a heavier barrel to overcome the SMLE's lack of accuracy over 300 yards. Therefore in 1931 and 1933 an estimated total of 3,000 new .303 inch calibre trials rifles were produced by RSAF Enfield and designated Rifle No. 4 Mk1.

Considerable emphasis was put on the speed with which the new rifle could be produced which involved simplifying production techniques as well as reducing and simplifying complicated parts that took time to manufacture; the lessons learned in the Great War, when production of the SMLE was slow and labour intensive, were being addressed. The new trials rifle shared many of the SMLE's features but a heavier barrel, stiffer action and aperture rear sights significantly improved the shooting ability of the new rifle and stood the new design in good stead in the following years through troop trials and endurance field testing. It endured these well and was re-designated .303-inch Rifle No. 4, Mk1 as part of the army's new numbering nomenclature, which changed to a number and mark system, so the Pattern 1914 Mk1* W (T) rifle became .303-inch Rifle No. 3 Mk1* T and the old SMLE was re-designated Rifle No. 1.

The following post trial years saw the trials No. 4 Mk1 rifle put into stores where it remained until the outbreak of WW2 in 1939. Once again Britain was woefully unprepared for a sniping campaign, and entered the conflict with a dated rifle of Great War vintage which was supported by training literature that was quite weak, written off the back of lessons learnt in the previous conflict waged from static heavily defended trench systems. The opening engagements of WW2 saw the British suffer one defeat after another, being pushed back towards the coast on a daily basis, culminating with Operation Dynamo, the evacuation of Dunkirk in May/June 1940. The lack of inter-war investment in the military was laid bare and consequently led to a rushed effort to field a capable sniper rifle with trained snipers to use it.

Chapter 3
Birth of an Icon

A Patrol Goes Out on the
Anzio Bridgehead

 On entering WW2 Great Britain was not only experiencing an acute shortage of snipers, but also sniper rifles, having redistributed huge numbers of the No. 3 Mk1* T to the Commonwealth during the inter-war years. It was estimated the British Army required some 4,000 units to be of full strength whilst on a war footing, and in 1939 the real figure was trailing this massively. With the exception of the 3,000 shelved trials No. 4 Mk1 rifles, the No. 4 rifle was not available and it would not be until mid-1941 that a facility was set up to start production. The opening months of the war saw Great War dated No. 1 rifles and 1907 pattern bayonets still serving as the British Army's main infantryman's rifle and edged weapon.

The exceptional work done for sniping by the Great War officers and men had set the standard and had manicured the style by which British snipers would operate. However, the British sniper entering the Second World War would fight a very different campaign to his forebears; theirs had been a more static fight which predominantly involved fighting over the same ground which they came to know intimately and they often sniped at relatively short distances. The WW2 sniper, although in the early stages armed with WW1 vintage equipment, would take receipt of a very well-engineered sniper rifle built on a standard infantry rifle equipped with a scope that would allow his shot to be controlled against the effects of wind and gravity, and routinely over considerably longer distances. He would fight a very mobile and largely rural European campaign as the British Army advanced to Germany and to some degree like his forebears had to learn on the job as new scenarios presented themselves; sniping was after all just like all other forms of war fighting and morphed and evolved as one side tried to outwit the other.

The British sniper was, I would suggest, most comfortable fighting in the rural environment where his training in camouflage, concealment and stalking could be applied, and this is what he was most proficient at, but as the advance met towns and villages it was inevitable that urban sniping had to be adopted. This was a particularly deadly environment which brought with it a whole host of lethal hazards such as booby traps left to meet and greet and murder holes in walls and rooftops, an environment that forced sniper pairs to operate in static positions which, if occupied for too long, or too frequently, were easily identified, the consequences of which were very often murderous artillery and/or mortar fire from which there was little escape. Just a few of the hazards the sniper would have to quickly acquaint himself with if he was to survive.

The six years of WW2 moulded the British sniper into what we largely recognise today: a skilled individual who, in plain sight of his enemy, can camouflage himself and stalk to within a range at which he can deliver a single deadly shot on his selected target.

PREVIOUS PAGE: A sniper pair patrolling on the Anzio Bridgehead in 1944. Note the No. 32 telescope is stowed away and the rifle is cocked. Also note the rifle looks to be early production, or possibly a trials example with the round cocking piece and waisted foresight protector. Interestingly note the cut of the woodwork around the extraction port which looks to have been cut to suit a trials rifle magazine cut off. *(Courtesy Nigel Greenaway)*

Rifle No. 3 Mk1* (T) A
Alexander Martin Conversion/Aldis Bros Telescope

Technical Specification	
Calibre	303in
Magazine Capacity	5 Rounds
Overall Rifle Length	46.4in
Barrel Length	26in
Twist Rate	5 Groove, LH 1 in 10 Twist
Combat Weight	11 lb
Iron Sights	Graduated to 1600 Yds
Introduced	1940
Converted By	Alexander Martin
Scope Mounted	Offset Left Side
Quantity Converted	421 approx

The Alexander Martin conversion received designation Rifle No. 3, Mk1* (T) A. The conversion with its offset WW1 vintage telescope which was not detachable from the rifle was in some ways inferior to the Pattern 1914 Mk1* W (T) conversion, suggesting it was in 1939 a conversion hastily readied for war.

The only option on the table in 1939 which would address the severe shortfall at that time with any urgency was a revised conversion of the No. 3 Mk1* T. At the end of the Great War many thousands of Pattern 1914 rifles were put into storage with roughly 10,000 Winchester manufactured models packed and earmarked for potential future sniper conversion and it would be a small number of these rifles that would enter a new conversion programme with Alexander Martin of Glasgow. The contract appeared to have run from 1939–1941 with a total of 421 units produced and on its issue to snipers it was designated Rifle No. 3 Mk1* (T) A, the "A" denoting an Aldis scope, although it should be noted there were examples fitted with a Great War Periscopic Prism Co scope, and there is one example which currently resides with the

Birmingham Proof House which was fitted with one of the smaller produced Evans telescopes.

Unfortunately any information that may have once been available as to the breakdown of conversions that were fitted with an alternative telescope to an Aldis model appears to have long disappeared. The delivery of the rifle began with an initial batch of 400 units after which the production of a second batch of 400 rifles commenced, but after just twenty-one rifles were converted the order from the War Department for the 3T (A) was cancelled.

The training literature available to the sniper referencing this equipment was *Military Training Pamphlet No. 44. Notes on the Training of Snipers,* first printed in October 1940, and received the first of its revisions in July 1941. The most obvious change was a detailed fold-out section providing fully illustrated

instructions on the construction of a ghillie suit. Further revisions would be issued through the war along with a more in-depth supplement in 1944 but the next sniper training pamphlet would not appear until after the war in 1946.

Although there are examples recorded as being fitted with an alternative telescope to an Aldis scope the conversion did largely involve the mounting of one of the Great War reserved Aldis models, many of which carried the barred out serial number of the SMLE it was originally fitted to in WW1. The early conversions used No. 1 and 2 scopes but later the No. 4 model was the standard. The design and setting up of the rifle seemed to be a step backwards in that the telescope was once again mounted offset to the left and was not detachable from the rifle. It was this that maybe contributed to its very short service

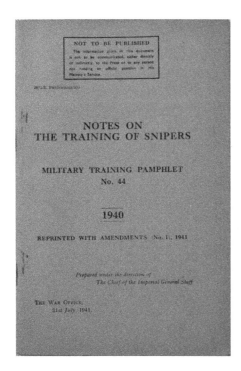

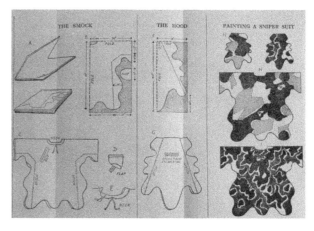

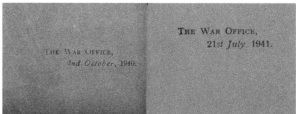

ABOVE: The early 1940 dated training literature was the only written guidance for sniper instructors for some time. Pamphlet No. 44 received several amendments before redistribution in 1941, the most obvious being the inclusion of a fold-out section detailing the field construction and camouflaging of a sniper smock. Further amendments would be issued later in the war.

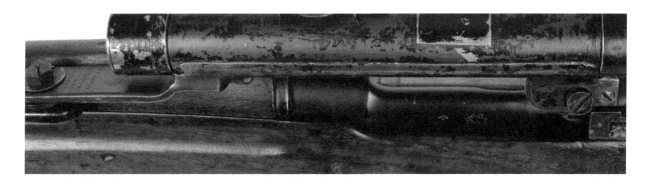

ABOVE: The mount illustrated here in its entirety. Note the scope is soldered into the cradle which in turn bolts onto the rifle.

life and to why such a small number of rifles saw conversion. However it is interesting that the Alexander Martin gun company should have opted for such a conversion after the hugely successful overbore mounting of the Model 1918 telescope on the same rifle.

Given the situation in 1939, I would suggest the conversion arrangement which was arrived at was to satisfy the criteria the War Department issued: in all likelihood to make it cheaply, and more importantly quickly. It was for all intents and purposes a stopgap whilst RSAF Enfield worked on a more thorough solution.

The mounting system is a double mount arrangement with the forward mount being clamped around the barrel in front of the chamber section from which a flat web protrudes ninety degrees to the rifle through a cut-out in the hand guard. The flat metal bracket carries a hole centrally to receive the flat arm that sits on top of it and which comes off the continuous semi-circular cradle that carries the scope; the flat arm and front mount web are joined and mechanically fixed with a single bolt.

The cradle that supports the scope travels the full length of the scope's tube body and although on first appearances looks to mechanically fix to a rear mount, it is in fact one single piece. The ears of the rear sight protector are cut down and the rear sight has been removed, and a simple peep sight now bridges the two former rear sight protector ears. Just forward of the peep sight and within the housing that formerly held the rear sight is a threaded web that serves as one of the two fixings points of the rear mount arrangement. The rear fixing is achieved by the cradle being soldered to an angle that uses its ninety degrees to fix to the left rear sight protector wall and to the threaded web on top of the rifle in the old rear sight housing. There would appear to be some lateral adjustment in this rear fixing arrangement, however I suspect the scope that is soldered into the cradle provided the lateral adjustment via an internal prism.

RIGHT: A view from the opposite side shows the rear fixing arrangement of the bracket. Note the battle sight has been removed, the sight protector ears have been reduced and have been converted to an anchorage point for the bracket, and a peep sight has been installed also.

Telescope, Aldis Bros No. 2

Technical Specification	
Manufacturer	Aldis Brothers, Birmingham
Length	10.7in
Weight in the mount	20 oz
Objective Lens DIA	19mm
Field of View	8 degrees
Magnification	3 X
Reticle	Post & Wire
Range Graduations	100–600 Yds
Focus Capability	Yes
Lateral Adjustment	Some Models
Mount Type	Double (None Detachable)

A rare image of a Rifle No. 3 Mk1* (T) A fitted with a Great War Periscopic Prism Company telescope more commonly found on a 1915 SMLE.

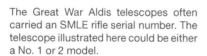

The Great War Aldis telescopes often carried an SMLE rifle serial number. The telescope illustrated here could be either a No. 1 or 2 model.

Rifle No. 4 Mk1 (T)

Ex Trials Rifle RSAF Enfield Conversion/No. 32 Mk1 Telescope

Whilst the Alexander Martin converted rifle was slowly filling the gap in 1940 it would appear the shortcomings of Rifle No. 3 Mk1* (T) A were not lost on the army and RSAF Enfield explored a number of avenues to improve the weapon. The 10,000 Winchester No. 3 rifles put into stores at the end of the Great War had continued consideration for conversion and it would also seem the No. 32 telescope would now be the next generation of sniper optics regardless of the platform. A bracket very similar to the bracket we now recognise as the standard No. 32 bracket was designed in 1940 and in fact only two were ever manufactured and do not survive today. However the drawings dated 25th May 1940 do, and show how the No. 32 telescope was provided with a mounting system for Rifle No. 3. But of course history now tells us Rifle No. 3 never went beyond Rifle No. 3 Mk1* (T) A in any sniper capacity, the demise of the new bracket and its intended conversion being in the same period as conversion Mk1* (T) A also fell to the wayside. Instead the latest technology that lay in Rifle No. 4 led the way and with Rifle No. 4 being not very far away from mass production at this point it would appear time and resources were directed towards a full and final sniper conversion in this rifle.

RIGHT & ABOVE: The search for a capable sniper rifle took RSAF Enfield in a number of directions. The Winchester built Rifle No. 3 was initially a contender for a completely revised conversion. The bracket illustrated is a reproduction as no original examples exist, however the original fabrication drawing does and is what was used to recreate this bracket that served as a creative stepping stone to what we recognise today as the No. 32 scope bracket.

Three thousand trials No. 4 Mk1 rifles were removed from stores and prepared for service. It is widely accepted that 1,403 rifles were sent to RSAF Enfield for sniper conversion and it is possible this number was not entirely made up of trials rifles. In addition there may have been a number of early 1941 production rifles; unfortunately it is now impossible to say with any certainty but a good historical picture of what more than likely happened has been aided by the arrival of the World Wide Web. The arrival of the internet age has enabled collectors from all over the world to cross reference what they know and importantly what they own, throwing into the mix some surprises along the way and changing the information we had and what we thought to be accurate to something entirely new. For example it was widely agreed that Fazakerley No. 4 rifles were never converted, however several early examples have surfaced and are now on record, a small snippet of history helping piece back together the bigger historical picture.

The production rifle differed slightly from the trials example. The trials rifle carried the SMLE in its appearance in some ways. The butt stock was SMLE-like, carrying a brass butt disc and the component parts such as trigger guard and stock bands were finished to a very high standard.

The production rifle was simplified; for speed and ease of manufacture the fore-end proportions were slimmed down; the butt disc, magazine cutoff and retained cocking piece were all dropped from the specification, and the hinged front band was changed to a non-hinged design. The front sight protector which on the trials rifle was an attractive "waisted" shaped component did go into production as an Mk1 foresight sight protector, however its fancy shape was soon simplified to a straight walled component part of which we readily recognise today on a standard production 4T as well as the L42.

The wood sets that were used through the 4T development were limited to just three. The trials rifle which was produced to a high standard in peacetime conditions was fitted with an attractive pale English walnut, however, the early 1941 and 1942 converted production rifles were fitted with beech wood sets – a hard wood which at a time when the war effort was consuming huge quantities of timber was available in good quantities in the UK, though only a few still survive today. The final and most common wood set is that of North American black walnut which was imported and used from 1943 to 1945 and is by far the most common wood set encountered. If you own a 4T today it is more than likely wearing a black walnut wood set.

Furthermore the production rifle carried many marks of selection,

ABOVE: This trials rifle butt stock is a beautiful pale English walnut and bears a brass butt disc like the SMLE. Note the cheek rest which is birch wood and typical of what was also fitted to the No. 3 T rifle.

ABOVE: The trials waisted foresight protector became Mk1 but was subsequently simplified for manufacture as was the front band which on the trials rifle carried a swivel and was hinged. Like the SMLE the trials rifle was fitted with a magazine cut off, of which the wood was cut deeply to accommodate. Note the lack of an "S" mark on the boss where the magazine cut off attaches, entirely in keeping with a trials example. The trials cocking piece was also SMLE-like and was retained. The retaining screw seen here was dropped from the production rifle, however the round style cocking piece remained.

inspection and completion the trials rifle did not. The trials rifle on the other hand carries the EFD inspection mark on almost every component part and with such a small number converted by RSAF Enfield in the first place surviving examples that are complete and original are rare and highly collectable today.

It would be interesting to know how the accuracy of the trials rifle converted to 4T compared with the production converted rifle. I feel the trials No. 4 T rifles were supplied as a quick fix at a time when there were shortages of everything post Dunkirk when the British Army was being overhauled. Roughly half of the available trials rifles were sent for conversion and,

given the relatively high number in comparison to the total available, I doubt they were set aside through an accuracy selection test as was the case with the production rifle, although it has to be said the trials rifles were manufactured to very high standards in peacetime. But the twenty plus thousand production No. 4 T rifles converted were selected by an accuracy test and the ratio of rifles built to find one that passed the accuracy test for sniper conversion is staggering and translates as roughly fifty rifles manufactured to find one that shoots an above average group. Scale this sort of ratio down to a pool of 3,000 rifles to choose from and add into the equation an accuracy test, and

I would suggest the number of trials rifles that would have met the criteria for conversion would have been in single figures. Unfortunately today the trials No. 4 T is a rare beast and those original examples that are still around number a handful, all in various conditions of wear and tear. The opportunity to conduct any kind of comparison test shoot is sadly long gone.

View of a Figure 12 target through a No. 32 Mk 3 telescope at 100 yards. Note the rear sight under the scope; interestingly it is a trials rear sight with its ball bearing just visible as are the two nodules it rests between when deployed.

Rifle No. 4 Mk1 (T) ex Trials Rifle RSAF Enfield Conversion/No. 32 Mk1 Telescope

Technical Specification	
Calibre	303in
Magazine Capacity	10 Rounds
Overall Rifle Length	44.5in
Barrel Length	25.2in
Twist Rate	5 Groove, LH 1 in 10 Twist
Combat Weight	11 lb
Iron Sights	Graduated to 1300 Yds
Introduction	1941
Converted By	RSAF Enfield
Scope Mounted	Overbore
Quantity Converted	1405 approx

LEFT: The wrist markings show this rifle was manufactured as part of the 1931 batch. Note the "A" serial number prefix which denotes the rifle as a trials rifle. The "A" tells an inspector that this rifle consists of some incompatible parts.

This trials No. 4 Mk1 (T) rifle wears an attractive English walnut wood set. The quality of all its parts is exceptional and are all marked with an Enfield inspection stamp. A level of quality and detail which could only be afforded to a peacetime project. With the exception of the magazine this example is complete and fully matching as a trials rifle converted to sniper configuration and bears none of the inspection, acceptance and completion marks you would expect to find on a production 4T.

LEFT: Lance Corporal A.P. Proctor, a sniper with the 56th Division in Italy, cleaning his rifle, 24th November 1943. Note the rifle is a trials rifle still in complete trials trim prior to any FTR alterations which it would have undoubtedly been subject to later, possibly 1945, which seems to be the year many of the trials rifles received their new barrels and wood furniture.

Telescope, No. 32 Mk1 and Backup Sights

A prototype telescope designated No. 32 had at that time been trialled with a view to mounting it on the Bren gun, a scrapped idea, however it was suitable, and it was sitting on the shelf.

RSAF Enfield, who was responsible for the entire conversion programme of the trials rifle to sniper configuration, designed a bracket for mounting the No. 32 Mk1 telescope overbore which involved the scope being held permanently in a bracket that would be removable from the rifle. It is now clearly understood that two brackets which closely resembled each other existed but it is unclear if the bracket designed to mount the telescope on the No. 4 rifle evolved from that of the bracket designed to mount the scope on the No. 3 rifle, or if both projects were running simultaneously alongside each other. Weighing in at around two pounds in its bracket and with a three power magnification, the No. 32 Mk1 telescope came equipped with elevation and windage drums for correction of the bullet's path.

The drums were only effective after the telescope had been zeroed to the rifle on the firing range. Once the desired zero was achieved the elevation and windage drums needed to be returned to the zero graticule line on the drum which

ABOVE: The underside of Tool No. 32 Sighting Telescope Mk1. OS 3901 is illustrated here. The two outer lugs that locate into the recesses of the locking ring on the scope's drum can be seen. The recess in the centre of the tool's drum locates onto the lug of the drum's central lead screw. The tool mounted on the scope's drum appears quite sound but the cumbersome cross bar handles made its operation difficult and it was often likened to a three handed operation.

ABOVE: The Mk1 tool close up, clearly marked with designation and Optical Stores number.

RIGHT: The Mk1 tool replaced with two tools commonly known as key and tongues. The key can be seen here located in the recesses of the drum's locking ring whilst the tongues grip the drum scale and locate onto the drum's central lead screw.

involved an operation which has been commonly described as a three handed operation. The task of adjusting the elevation and windage drums was carried out with the use of a tool which was housed in the lid of the No. 8 carry case and retained by two sprung steel clips. The Tool, No 32 Sighting Telescope Mk1. OS 3901, was reportedly borderline incapable of the job it was designed to do. Both the elevation and windage drums on the scope were the same and were both adjusted in the same manner with the one tool. The tool was a small barrel which had two locating lugs on its underside which corresponded to the two recesses of the locking ring within the scope's drum. The centre of the tool's barrel contained an inner drum which located on the lug of the central lead screw of the scope's elevation or windage drum. The outer barrel and inner drum of the tool rotated independently of each other, controlled by two cross bar handles. The tool was a struggle to use and was often discarded or lost without replacement due to the absence of a part number

making it impossible to summon a replacement using the VAOS (Vocabulary of Army Ordnance Stores) system which operated at the time. Therefore zero adjustment was often achieved by the use of improvised tools.

The answer provided to overcome the frustrating job of completing the zeroing of one's rifle, which should have been a simple task, was delivered in 1943 in the form of another two tools which were used together, each tool now independently responsible for a component of the scope's drum. The tools often referred to as "key and tongs" were Tool No. 32

ABOVE: Both key and tongues illustrated individually with their respective designation markings visible.

Sighting Telescope No. 1 Mk1, OS 32895 which was the tong's half of the duo and which had leather clad jaws that gripped the range scale of the drum whilst a central arm was located on the central lead screw of the scope's drum. Tool No. 32 Sighting Telescope No. 2 Mk1, OS 32896 was a two pronged key, with the prongs located in the recesses of the locking ring. The new tools were a marginal improvement on the disastrous first Mk1 tool that entered service with the scope.

Once successful zeroing of the telescope was complete the elevation drum allowed the sniper to dial in corrections for bullet drop in fifty-yard adjustments. On the Mk1 scope the drum is simply marked 1 to 10, graduated from 100 to 1,000 yards with an intermediate click between numbers registering the numbered 100 yard increments, split into fifty-yard adjustments. The system was a precursor to the BDC (bullet drop compensation) drums on today's scopes which allow the sniper to quickly engage a target by turning the drum to a pre-marked number referencing a distance. By using the specified ammunition and providing the sniper has ranged the distance correctly he will hit a man-sized target. Although the No. 32 telescope's drums did not work precisely this way the correspondence between the telescope's collimation and specified service Mk7 ammunition was being utilised and shows a synergy with the BDC system that would follow; it was in essence the BDC system at a fledgling stage. The windage drum allowed for the compensation of wind strength, providing the sniper with sixteen minutes of angle adjustment in both left and right directions and in two minute adjustments. The adjustments system on the No. 32 telescope was clearly designed for the job of killing: no fine adjustment

ABOVE: The No. 32 Mk1 telescope's elevation drums adjusted in yards. Although the numbers have lost their white inlaid paint through age the drum. The drum markings are seen here marked boldly and graduated 0–10.

for target shooting, just enough to bring the sniper onto his man.

The trials rifle was equipped with backup sights, or iron sights as they were commonly known, for use when climatic conditions made the No. 32 scope unusable, or if it became unserviceable. The rear sight was a collapsible leaf sight made up of a leaf, adjusting screw and slide with aperture. When the sight was lifted from its folded position and deployed vertically the leaf was held in position by a spring which pushed a ball-bearing up against the underside of the leaf itself which had on its underside two nodules for the ball-bearing to rest between. The leaf was marked with range graduations from 200 to 1,300 yards in fifty-yard increments, however the early four clicks for every rotation of the slider's screw allowed for fine adjustment between the prescribed ranges. The slider which had in it a slightly off centre peep hole for aiming also carried the range scale graticule lines for selection of range which, when lined up, were calibrated for use with the .303 inch Mk7 ammunition. The foresight blade was mounted in a

split block band fixed to the barrel at muzzle end; the block band had a female dovetail in order to receive the dovetailed base of the foresight blade and was retained by a screw that entered the foresight block from the front. The foresight blade was protected by an attractive "waisted" foresight protector which contoured the barrel profile before rising up either side of the blade itself. A very nice component that was expensive to produce. Lateral adjustment of the foresight blade simply involved the retaining screw being slackened and the foresight blade being pushed left or right in its dovetailed block. There was no adjustment of the foresight blade for elevation and it therefore required replacement with a choice of eight foresight blades to choose from, ranging in size from 0.030 inch to 0.075 inch in increments of 0.015 inch.

No. 32 Mk1 Telescope

Technical Specification	
Manufacturer	Kodak Ltd
Length	11in
Weight in the mount	2lb
Objective Lens DIA	19mm
Field of View	9 degrees
Magnification	3 X
Reticle	Post & Wire
Range Graduations	100–1000 Yds
Focus Capability	Fixed
Sunshade	Yes
Lateral Adjustment	16-0-16 Drum
Mount Type	Double
Approval Date	12th February 1942

ABOVE & BELOW: An East African Askari sniper equipped with an RSAF Enfield converted trials No. 4 T. The Askari were recruited by European colonial powers during WW2. Note he is also wearing the beige lightweight hooded smock utilised by snipers in warmer climates. His No. 32, Mk1 scope is equipped with the traditional post and wire reticle.

This Kodak manufactured No. 32 Mk1 telescope is 1941 dated with a relatively low serial number. The scope is the original paired to the trials rifle at conversion and is carried in an unmarked trials bracket complete with sunshade. The scope tube has suffered pitting at some point in its life but it is unclear if the pitting is as a result of poor storage or if it is one of the early telescopes which received a finish that reacted corrosively to moisture.

ABOVE: This 1941 dated No. 8 Mk1 carry case for the No. 32 telescope has a number of paint finishes on top of its original factory applied bronze green. One of the colours is interestingly desert brown which fits perfectly with the date on the tin: the first and earliest sniper equipment was initially sent to the North African desert.

ABOVE: Leather lens caps for the No. 32 scope were manufactured by a plethora of leather working companies. The caps belonging to this Kodak manufactured scope are marked B.H. & Co 1941.

ABOVE: The two No. 8 Mk1 cases illustrated appeared forty years apart. The 1941 case, although difficult to spot in the image, is a Belling and Co. case marked B & Co. The much later 1983 L1A1 case was manufactured by Cook & Perkins Ltd and is marked C&P. The bronze green factory paint finish also remained standard. The bronze green on the 1941 tin is visible through the layers of WW2 applied paint.

The left side of the receiver wall had two "pads" mechanically fixed, the purpose of which was to receive the scope bracket via two sturdy knurled thumb wheels by simply screwing the thumb wheels into the threaded holes in the pads. When the scope was not required, or when the rifle was in transit, the sniper could remove the scope where it would be installed in its own metal carrying tin complete with leather carry strap. The tin was designated Case, Telescope, No. 8 Mk1 and contained two brass bosses into which the thumb wheels screwed to secure the scope in place. Later the left hand boss in the tin would simply be for locating the left hand thumb wheel, the thread being made obsolete; it's written elsewhere that the drilling out of the left hand boss was due to varying tolerances between scope bracket and boss interrupting the closure of the case lid. For whatever reason, screwing the right hand thumb wheel in tight and locating the left was ample for the safe transport of the scope with the lid secured. But it should be noted that No. 8 Mk1 cases with two threaded bosses are still around today and usually dated 1941, a rare find for the collector. The design of the case incorporated a series of metal loops for a long leather carry strap to be fitted, enabling the sniper to carry the case in a slung fashion which suggests its purpose was to protect the scope in field conditions. However there is little evidence that the sniper used it for this purpose.

Arthur Hare describes in the book *The Sniper* how it was common practice in his unit to carry the telescope in one of the large pockets of the Denison smock until it was required. The No. 8 Mk1 case remained the primary case for housing the No. 32 scope for the scope's entire life including that of its L1A1 conversion to the L42A1 sniper rifle. The carry case started life in 1941 as a round cornered case which was expensive to produce with a number of its parts individually pressed into shape. The case design was revised during WW2 and an economy variant was produced with square welded corners.

Post WW2 saw the case return to its original round cornered design which, it has to be said, is a far superior and robust design although serviceable square cornered cases remained in service being passed to the L42A1 sniper rifle's CES and served to the end of the L42's days in the early nineties.

1944 saw the No. 8 Mk2 case arrive, which was a thin metal oblong sleeve covered with a rubberised canvas with a large flap closure. The Mk2 was carried within its own harness constructed from web strapping and may have been produced in response to snipers not really using the No. 8 Mk1 metal case in the field. Although when new it more than likely offered better waterproof protection than the Mk1, or a Denison smock pocket for that matter, it was, like a lot of equipment, produced with a wartime economy at the heart of its design and was therefore not as robust as the metal case and was phased out by the 1960s. Observed markings on the Mk1 cases suggest it was produced in the 1940s, 1950s, 1970s and 1980s.

Each scope now marked TEL STG (telescope sighting), No. 32 Mk1 was beautifully finished with a high quality bluing to the tubes and the brass drums and sunshades were chemically blackened. The blued finish was similar to that found on early photography equipment and was reportedly unstable in wet conditions which caused a reaction that started an aggressive corrosion of the tubes. The bluing process was quickly dropped and replaced

ABOVE: The No. 8 Mk2 carry case for the No. 32 telescope looks to be a soft rubberised canvas case on first impressions whereas it has actually been made rigid with a thin metal liner that was susceptible to crushing. The case arrived in the latter stages of WW2 and was phased out through the sixties with many being sold out of service during the disposal process, after which the trusty Mk1 case was reinstated. Note the method of adjustment label pasted to the canvas and situated under the flap closure for protection.

with a Brunofixed finish similar to the finish the rifle body received but as the war progressed such a time intensive and lavish finishing could not be sustained and a painted finish was ultimately applied.

The telescope was permanently paired to its chosen rifle in that the telescope's serial number was physically applied to the rifle. The preparation of the receiver wall to take the pads was done with the use of an engineering jig which controlled the extent of the milling and made the process repeatable, or exact, every time. I do not conform in any way on this point with the findings others have stated in other publications on this subject. Others would suggest a telescope was individually handcrafted to one specific rifle, ruling out the accuracy of a different telescope should it be fitted intentionally or otherwise and over the years in the course of my collecting and shooting these very fine weapons I have on many occasions used a rifle with a mismatching telescope and I have yet to find one that doesn't perform

well. Furthermore, at the end of hostilities when many thousands of No. 4 Mk1 T rifles went through refurbishment, many received a telescope and/or bracket upgrade, trading in their war-battered Mk1 or Mk2 telescope in exchange for the then current Mk3 telescope. These telescopes, in the old or even new brackets, were quite simply fitted to the existing pads that received no adjustment and were zeroed to the rifle. An impossible task if the "permanently mated to one rifle" theory is to be believed, not only for the post WW2 refurbishment but for the later L42A1 conversion as well, which would have become even more convoluted when you consider the night vision device which has very limited windage and elevation adjustment built in that was subsequently mounted on the L42A1 rifle via the same components.

However, accuracy could, and did, differ significantly when scopes were swapped between rifles as any given telescope was zeroed specifically to one rifle. In fact the same issue still largely exists today

and overcoming this age old issue would play a major part in the success of Accuracy International who overcame this problem on a mass produced weapon.

Later, in an effort to overcome this, the production rifles were numbered rigidly to avoid the wrong scope being packed with the wrong rifle; after all, the last thing a sniper needs after being deployed was to find his telescope he carefully zeroed to his rifle was somewhere else, but to be clear, the mismatching telescope could simply be zeroed to the rifle if needs be. The scope serial number was stamped on the flat of the butt stock wrist just behind the cocking piece, however the rifle serial number was not stamped on the scope bracket until much later in the post-war years. The trials rifles, during their trials, didn't even carry a manufacture mark to the bracket, nor did they display many of the inspection, selection and completion markings that are standard on the production rifle.

1941 saw the trials No. 4 Mk1 T subjected to lengthy field endurance

LEFT: Front and rear pads typical of both the No. 4 T and L42. Note the number of stake marks to the screws of the front pad which had a tendency to work loose in comparison to the rear which commonly carried a single stake.

tests and it was found the No. 32 Mk1 telescope, scope pads and bracket, on average, were capable of around 3,500 rounds without major malfunction and the accuracy of the rifle was maintained to around 5,000 rounds, however the front pad which was sweated into place and secured with three screws could work loose quite unpredictably. The armourer's solution was to stake the three securing screws at the point of the screw head's slot which slightly deformed the metal and prevented them turning, a common feature of most examples today.

The sniper equipment was much needed and the test results were found to be acceptable given it was a single shot rifle and was not designed for rapid fire, therefore the 1,400 trials units were completed. It was also at this point it was realised that there was no transit chest designed or built to house and transport the new rifle, so Bren gun chests were hastily converted for these initial sets, a solution that would be repeated sporadically during the war years when a transit chest was required quickly.

RIGHT & BELOW: The Bren gun chest was initially converted to house the first sniper equipment, however the practice continued sporadically through the war when supplies became slow or disrupted. This chest carries a 1943 date and the inside looks to have never housed a Bren gun, suggesting it was converted straight after its manufacture.

Complete Equipment Schedule

Each rifle was packed with a CES (complete equipment schedule) which consisted of the three draw Scout Regiment Telescope, leather American 1907 loop pattern sling, usually of First World War vintage and fitted with brass claws, chamber stick from the Bren gun kit and No. 4 rifle cleaning kit.

The No. 32 telescope if considered in its own right was packed in its No. 8 Mk1 carry case complete with leather protective lens caps, adjustment tools and leather carry strap for the No. 8 case. A khaki cotton handkerchief was also made available for use as a lens cloth. Later at unit level CESSI (complete equipment schedule supplementary issue) equipment would be drawn by the sniper which usually consisted of a GST (general service timepiece) watch, two airborne soldier's camouflaged scrim scarves/nets as well as a compass and binoculars. The WW2 sniper was also issued the Denison smock originally designed for airborne troops and commandos.

A Waltham manufactured general service watch with black face carrying a serial number and broad arrow on its reverse. Issued to snipers during and after WW2, the GS watch was manufactured by some prestigious manufacturers such as Rolex.

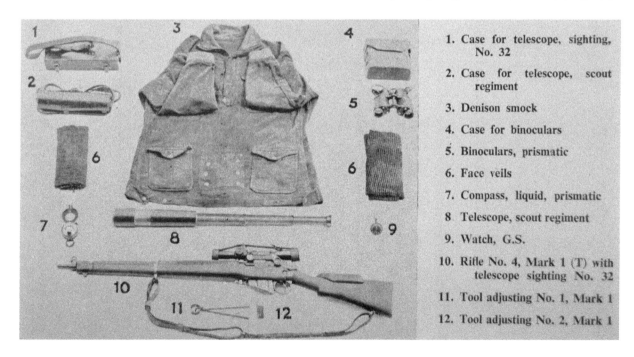

1. Case for telescope, sighting, No. 32
2. Case for telescope, scout regiment
3. Denison smock
4. Case for binoculars
5. Binoculars, prismatic
6. Face veils
7. Compass, liquid, prismatic
8. Telescope, scout regiment
9. Watch, G.S.
10. Rifle No. 4, Mark 1 (T) with telescope sighting No. 32
11. Tool adjusting No. 1, Mark 1
12. Tool adjusting No. 2, Mark 1

Taken from the 1951 Pamphlet No. 10, the complete equipment schedule which accompanied the No. 4 T rifle was by today's standards quite sparse. Note the GS watch and the telescope's adjusting tools.

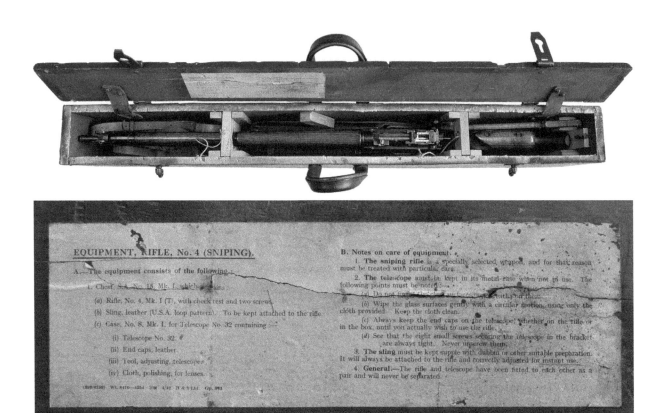

EQUIPMENT, RIFLE, No. 4 (SNIPING).

A.—The equipment consists of the following:—

1. Chest, S.A. No. 15, Mk. I, which contains :—

   (a) Rifle, No. 4, Mk. I (T), with cheek rest and two screws.

   (b) Sling, leather (U.S.A. loop pattern). To be kept attached to the rifle.

   (c) Case, No. 8, Mk. I, for Telescope No. 32 containing :—

      (i) Telescope No. 32.

      (ii) End caps, leather.

      (iii) Tool, adjusting, telescope.

      (iv) Cloth, polishing, for lenses.

B. Notes on care of equipment.

   1. The sniping rifle is a specially selected weapon, and for that reason must be treated with particular care.

   2. The telescope must be kept in its metal case when not in use. The following points must be noted :—

      (a) Do not finger the surfaces, nor breathe on them.

      (b) Wipe the glass surfaces gently with a circular motion, using only the cloth provided. Keep the cloth clean.

      (c) Always keep the end caps on the telescope, whether on the rifle or in the box, until you actually wish to use the rifle.

      (d) See that the eight small screws securing the telescope in the bracket are always tight. Never unscrew them.

   3. The sling must be kept supple with dubbin or other suitable preparation. It will always be attached to the rifle and correctly adjusted for instant use.

   4. General.—The rifle and telescope have been fitted to each other as a pair and will never be separated.

ABOVE: The illustrated label is commonly found pasted to the inside of the No. 15 Mk1 chest lid. The label lists information regarding care of the rifle, telescope and sling alongside an itemised list of equipment concerning the rifle and telescope. Note item iv of the scope equipment is listed as Cloth, Polishing for lens; this item on a later revised label is listed specifically as Handkerchief Mk1. The alternative label also lists both No. 8 carry case Mk1 steel, and No. 8 carry case Mk2 canvas.

RIGHT: Private J. Donald, a sniper with "C" Company, 4th King's Own Scottish Borderers, Holland, 11th December 1944, enjoying a well-earned cigarette. Note his Mk1/Mk2 scope has the sunshade still intact. He has one of his camouflaged scrim scarves draped over his helmet for camouflage.

ABOVE: A contemporary layout of the No. 4 T with all the equipment associated with its use. A place for everything, and everything in its place. Chest, Small Arms No. 15, Mk1 provided very little storage space for anything other than the rifle's accoutrements.

Observation and Spotting Equipment

The main observation instrument of the WW2 sniper was the Scout Regiment Telescope, or the three draw telescope, almost unchanged from that which his forebear of WW1 had used. The Mk1 SRT was approved for service on 24th April 1939 and was granted approval for modification just months later in August before the outbreak of war. As shown in the List of Changes, the leather covering was approved to be changed to vulcanised rubber as instruments passed through Woolwich for repair, a modification which advanced its mark to 1*. Of course we know today the vast majority of telescopes wear a leather covering far outweighing those with a vulcanised rubber covering. The decision to upgrade covering material was a pre-war decision which perhaps lost its relevance under the strains and raw material demands of war.

There is good reason why it was still the principal instrument; the benefits it provided over a pair of binoculars have been praised and published many times, and the praise has sometimes come from high places such as Major Hesketh-Prichard and Captain C. Shore. The twenty power magnification telescope provided the sniper pair with the ability to see into the shady places the enemy will have deliberately chosen to conceal himself, and the quality of the lenses also had good light gathering ability in poor weather or dawn and dusk conditions. Arthur Hare mentions in the publication *The Sniper* how he carried binoculars and his partner carried the Scout Regiment Telescope when out stalking the enemy.

When in observation posts for extended periods the sniper pairs often took a customised MkIV

ABOVE: The Scout Regiment Telescope is illustrated both packed as well as mounted in the short MkIV signaller tripod. The WW2 sniper used the short variant of the tripod when manning a position for long periods. Being supported aided better observation and eliminated fatigue. Note the brass draws of the telescope still have their subdued finish. Both telescope and tripod are easily slung when carried on patrol.

RIGHT: This image is from 1951 Pamphlet No. 10. The instructor shows how using the rifle a well-supported position could quickly be adapted for observation when no other means of support is to hand.

Sniping from buildings

ABOVE: This illustration taken from the 1946 Pamphlet No. 28 provides guidance on observing from a building. Note the sniper is set back in the room using shadow and has a mattress folded in front of him as protection from incoming fire and shrapnel.

signaller's telescope tripod. The standard tripod stood at around one metre high and was ideally suited to hold the SRT. The sniper would reduce its height to around 300 millimetres to give a low profile when in the prone position or so it could be secreted low down amongst the rubble or foliage with a scrim scarf draped over it for camouflage. The telescope could then be set up and trained on a particular feature or traversed without the fatigue that would take over when having to support the telescope freehand for hours at a time.

The binoculars Hare mentioned would have been a standard No. 2, or No. 3 6x30 prismatic type binocular with a ranging reticle in the right hand lens. The origins of the 6 x 30 prismatic binocular most definitely lay in the Great War but although the Great War binocular was x6 magnification the objective lens was not 30mm. The 6 x 30 came about between wars and would be the most common binocular within the British Army, being issued at a rate of one set to almost every officer and NCO in a number of marks and constructed by a host of manufacturers.

The solid construction was of mainly brass with a black leatherette covering on the body. The two halves were joined via a barrel hinge

BELOW: The Scout Regiment Telescope was easily stripped and was straightforward to maintain. Its long service life was certainly aided by its simplicity.

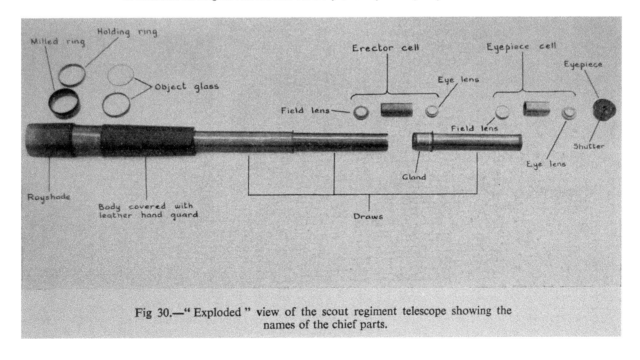

Fig 30.—" Exploded " view of the scout regiment telescope showing the names of the chief parts.

ABOVE: This sniper heavily clad in Denison smock and camouflage headdress demonstrates the correct use of the prismatic binocular. The image also seems to advocate the adage "less is more" when applying camouflage cream to the face and hands.

which allowed the user to adjust the angle to suit. The eyepieces were also adjustable so the focal length could be adjusted to the eyes of the user. The 6 x 30 Prismatic Binocular remained in service until the 1990s, remaining as a constant as the British Army went through many changes including the enrolment into NATO when the binocular, like every other item of kit, received its own unique NSN V6/1240-99-962-3737.

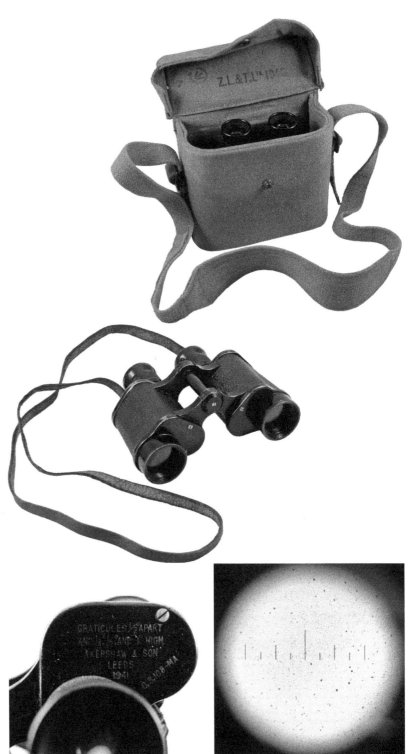

ABOVE: The prismatic binocular was a robust and reliable instrument which also enjoyed a long service life, and the WW2 sniper employed this binocular routinely as a secondary observation tool. The 1941 A. Kershaw & Son manufactured binocular is shown with the correct 1937 pattern case. Details of the graticule markings are also visible next to the right hand eyepiece. Note the black spots in the graticule picture; these are not the more common mould spots but wear to the lens which is completely unapparent until photographed and stand testament to its heavy use.

The Sniper's Garments

The Denison smock was first developed solely with airborne forces in mind and on the arrival of the first pattern in 1942 its issue was extended to Royal Marine Commandos, Special Operations Executive and Snipers. The smock offered an oversized fit so it could be worn over battle dress and came with four roomy large pockets with Newey press stud fasteners as well as being camouflaged. Harry Furness made a modification to his smock which involved the fitting of a pocket over the left buttock which carried his Scout Regiment Telescope. The first pattern smocks were sandy beige with green and brown tones applied to the fabric by hand in large brush strokes which brought about the unique pattern, the colour tones of which are said to have suited the North African and Italian theatres perfectly.

The Denison smock was equipped with a crotch flap which when passed between the legs from the rear fastened at the front with a choice of six press studs for the best comfortable fit and was effective at preventing the garment from riding up when stalking. The first pattern was superseded in 1944 by a second pattern that added Newey studs to the rear of the smock so the crotch flap could be stowed and the wool cuffs were removed and replaced with a simple button adjusted cuff. As the war developed the British sniper found himself operating in all climates around the world where the Denison smock was in some situations unsuitable.

The heavy, thick twill fabric and baggy oversized fit as well as the camouflage that was best suited to a temperate zone were traded in for a range of hooded smocks with

BELOW: Front and rear views of the Denison smock. This example is a second pattern dated 1944.

ABOVE: The main features of the smock included the crotch flap, or beaver tail as it was dubbed, shown here at the rear retained by two Newey press studs when not in use. The six press studs at the front gave the flap three options of adjustment. The cuff lost the wool comforter with the second pattern and received the button adjustment instead.

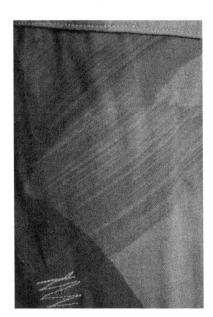

ABOVE: The twill fabric used to construct the first pattern smocks was camouflaged by hand with non-colour fast dyes with the use of a large brush, hence the brushstroke-like pattern. The second pattern like the example here kept the now famous Denison camouflage, however the fabric was screen-printed which suited mass production techniques better.

ABOVE: A sniper wearing his baggy Denison smock lines up a shot whilst using the side of a chimney breast for support; the mantelpiece of the fire surround offers his elbow a convenient rest. He's deep within the room of this battle-ravaged building making good use of shadow.

ABOVE: Front and rear views of a hooded lightweight smock utilised by snipers in hotter climates. The drab coloured smock came with matching trousers. This example is dated 1942.

ABOVE: Later during the war a windproof suit was produced in the same pattern as both the drab and snow suits. However the material was thicker and although the camouflage pattern was similar to the Denison smock the colour tones were very different. This example is dated 1944. The windproof suit was also used extensively in Korea, then later many were modified receiving a full-length zip and became synonymous with the Special Air Service.

matching trousers all of the same design and were tailored more towards a specific environment. In hotter climates such as southern Italy a drab coloured smock of lightweight material for comfort in the heat was utilised as well as a white version of the same outfit for winter snowscapes. From around 1943 onwards a windproof suit, again of the same design, was made available in a similar camouflage pattern to the Denison smock but with different colour tones. The fabric was thicker and was used as a winter windproof suit where snow was not present but a bitter winter wind chill was, and proved successful beyond WW2 in Korea.

The Denison smock remained in service with the sniper post war and received a further revision to its pattern in 1959 which incorporated the return of the wool cuffs as well as a full length zip being installed. The smock lost its generous proportions and became more fitted and was produced all the way to 1972 in several variants that mainly changed the colour tones.

The first of the new sniper equipment was sent to join the North African campaign where the No. 32 Mk1 scope was found to be increasingly unreliable in real world conditions, suffering issues such as cracked lenses, loss of zero and complete failure of windage and

elevation drums. There were also many complaints concerning the cumbersome means by which the scope had to be zeroed.

It's fair to say the desert environment was brutal and disrupted any kind of effort to commit snipers to the fight. It's not recorded as to whether German forces deployed snipers in this environment and it's presumed they did not.

Bill McMillan, service No. 2763697, who served with the 1st Bn The Black Watch was called up for service in July 1940 and recalls his experience as a sniper as follows:

"My first introduction to sniping was after a few months at Perth

ABOVE: The Army Illustrated Magazine, or AIM for short, reported on a more personal level telling stories of unit or individual successes. This edition dated 24th July 1944 actually tells the reader the magazine rams the subject of sniping down their necks, and makes no apology for it and then proceeds with two accounts of sniping in Italy, quite a robust style of writing. *(Courtesy Nigel Greenaway)*

Barracks where I shot five bulls eyes on the target with .22 ammo, which at the time was good shooting. Much later I was taught about camouflage etc, even to see how near I could get to some sheep without being detected. Later again with .303 ammo on the range I scored a two inch group on the bull from two hundred yards. The officer in charge pulled me back to three hundred yards and you may not believe me but I got four shots on the bull, for my last shot I received a flag, which meant I missed the target completely. How could I have missed the target I thought, but on closer examination at the butts it was changed to five bulls and another two inch group, two shots almost on the same mark.

Much later with a stalker at hand we went shooting deer around the Dornoch area with telescopic sights, you couldn't miss!

When we went abroad to the Western Desert during 1942 our last thought was using snipers, but a good while before Alamein I was chosen to zero quite a number of the battalion sniper rifles, some of them wouldn't have hit the side of a house, also primed loads of hand grenades.

Unfortunately I was hit on both legs and right arm during a night patrol."

Courtesy of Nigel Greenaway

The next major theatre for deployment was Italy, a much kinder environment to the equipment and a much more suitable theatre for the sniper pairs to operate with rolling and sometimes hilly terrain peppered with small villages and towns, often battle damaged or destroyed, a perfect landscape to secrete oneself. The Mk1 scope was also improved and its service life extended although as a whole it was quite short. Reliability was achieved by the tightening of manufacturing procedures and inspection, or quality control in today's speak. Along with upgrading the quality of the scope's internal components the revised measures collectively served as an acceptable short-term solution. British snipers with improved equipment would in this theatre prove to be far more effective and when detected the enemy would draw in a lot of resources to end the threat.

Harold William Baldwin recalls an experience he had whilst serving as part of a sniper section in Italy:

We had orders to go to this farmhouse as the platoon of infantry was getting a lot of bother from enemy snipers. We left at 04:30 in the morning and got there at 05:30 and gave the pass-word which was Water Spout.

Once inside we went upstairs and knocked two bricks from the corners of the walls, you always kept away from windows. Anyway we had a good morning and scored quite a few hits and the enemy stopped being as brave as they had been. About 02:00 AM we were subject to the biggest load of shell fire and mortar fire. I had known the Germans had eight barrelled mortars and they were very clever with them.

We were all lying downstairs and hoping for the best. I was lying alongside the fireplace and there was a figure of the Madonna on the mantelpiece and the blast came in through the window and blew it in half.

We managed to get back to H.Q. and were detailed to go there again. When we got there they would not let us in because as snipers we would draw a lot of fire down and the farmhouse may have had a direct hit.

I won't try to tell you what they called us, as I said before we were not very welcome. So we had to make our way back to H.Q. before it got light and we really had to make it fast.

Courtesy of Nigel Greenaway

Whilst Europe was erupting events were also unfolding in Burma and Southeast Asia, another theatre that did not suit telescopic sights very well. The robustness of the SMLE ensured its continued use as the infantry rifle in the Burmese jungle although the receiver and barrel required a liberal coat of khaki paint to protect against rust which on an unprotected rifle would spread like a cancer due to the high humidity. The humidity made the No. 32 scope completely unreliable as it would generally fog up; coupled with this the dense jungle environment made sniper work almost close quarter, making open sights more practical for quick target acquisition.

A Royal Welch Fusilier describes how, armed with an SMLE, he sniped the Japanese at Kohima at relatively close range:

At Kohima from a forward O.P. one hundred and fifty yards away the Japanese were holding positions slightly downhill from me. Observed for quite some time a head would appear and search the ground. This was observed by me and reported at the time. I was given a free hand to engage. This took place over a number of days. Generally all that was exposed was the Jap helmet top to the nose and I fired when the target maintained his observation.

Some days later after our infantry attacks the Japanese having withdrawn and our advance proceeded it was found there were around a ladder forty bodies. All had been hit squarely between the eyes. It made me realize just what a formidable enemy we were facing.

Courtesy of Nigel Greenaway

Rifle No. 4 Mk1 (T)
Holland & Holland Conversion/No. 32 Telescope

By now the early trials No. 4 Mk1 T sniper rifles were being joined by the No. 4 Mk1 T production rifle, the rifle now being produced in a factory set up on a production line. The conversion to sniper configuration was tasked to the famous gun company Holland & Holland, London. Although H&H had accepted the contract to carry out the conversion they were far from ready to do the work and needed time to ready themselves and get on a war footing, however sniper equipment was needed and the programme could not be put on hold.

The first of the production rifle conversions were carried out by RSAF Enfield 1941 and 1942, and examples have surfaced telling a different story from that which was previously understood. Rare examples of these rifles when encountered are identified by the absence of the Holland & Holland marks with just a select number of Enfield marks instead coupled with the factory selection TR stamp on the wrist which separates them from the trials rifles. Several have been noted to have been fitted with an EFD marked front pad much like the trials

rifles. It has also been suggested these rifles were fitted with beech woodwork. The handful of examples that are still around today have in subsequent years been subjected to post-war refurbishment as well as service replacement of many parts but the unique set of markings these rifles possess identifies them as special rare survivors of the fledgling 4T conversion programme.

It is to be noted that these rifles were not trials rifles and were supplied from production facilities. The Enfield conversions were in all likelihood as a result of

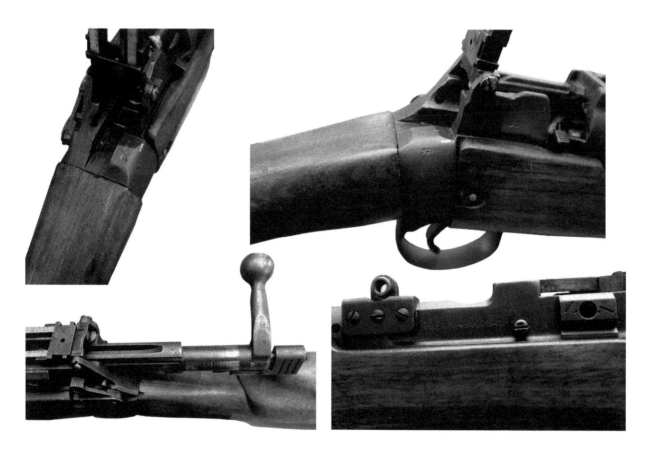

ABOVE: RSAF Enfield converted the very first of the production No. 4 rifles. This 1941 Maltby production rifle is one of those early Enfield conversions. The rifle would have originally had a beech wood set. It does not bear any of the selection, inspection or completion marks one would associate with a Holland & Holland conversion but does carry a select few Enfield marks.

ABOVE & RIGHT: This example of an early Holland & Holland conversion is on a very early BSA production rifle and although it is an H&H conversion the rifle illustrates that both the H&H and BSA system of marking for selection, inspection, and completion was not yet established and was very much a work in progress. Note the early BSA manufacturer code of "B" and the very coarse finish on the receiver indicating the urgency of the requirement for these weapons. Also note the beech wood set and early birch wood cheek rest.

their experience of already having completed a similar number of trials rifles and being ready with the equipment, knowledge and manpower and it was nothing more than a temporary arrangement until H&H were ready to go.

Prior to the Holland & Holland conversions commencing the RSAF converted rifles were selected from BSA and Maltby as well as a small number of Fazakerley production, although with the exception of a small number of early examples Fazakerley-produced rifles appear to have been excluded from the conversion programme. The lack of Fazakerley rifles converted to sniper

configuration does not appear to be recorded although it is reasonable to assume they were not manufactured to as tight a tolerance as the BSA and Maltby produced rifles, much the same as the No. 3 Mk1* T was only converted on Winchester manufactured platforms. Rifles coming off the production line in the summer of 1942 were now being converted by Holland & Holland and were paired with the revised specification No. 32 Mk1 telescope.

The marks installed on each rifle began at the production facility when completed rifles were test fired for accuracy and those achieving a higher than average group would be

stamped with TR (telescope rifle) on the left side of the wrist strap and low down near the trigger guard. The selected rifles were then sent to Holland & Holland where before the conversion process could begin an intake inspection of the rifles checked they had been supplied with the correct foresight block, five groove barrel and Mk1 rear sight. It has also been suggested the rifles were then subjected to Holland & Holland's own accuracy test but it should be noted that this theory is supposition as no record exists to support it, however it does carry some credence.

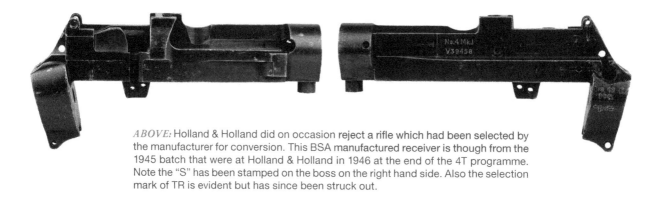

ABOVE: Holland & Holland did on occasion reject a rifle which had been selected by the manufacturer for conversion. This BSA manufactured receiver is though from the 1945 batch that were at Holland & Holland in 1946 at the end of the 4T programme. Note the "S" has been stamped on the boss on the right hand side. Also the selection mark of TR is evident but has since been struck out.

There are a good number of No. 4 Mk1 rifles still in existence today that bear the TR stamp but had never received the conversion, having been rejected by Holland & Holland for one reason or another, but rifles that bear a pre-1945 date should not be confused with the receivers that do carry a 1945 date; it is widely accepted that these examples were in Holland & Holland racks waiting for conversion when the No. 4 T conversion programme ended in April 1946 and were not rejected during wartime production due to an incorrect component having been fitted at the production facility.

Holland & Holland began by completely stripping the rifle back to just its body, with barrel still intact. The fore-end was marked with the rifle serial number so as not to end up on another rifle; after all it is all the component parts of this one rifle that made it special.

The butt stock was a standard "normal" size of which the knuckle was stamped with the Holland & Holland war time code of S51 as well as being fitted with a cheek rest of ash, beech or birch wood. The rear sight of Singer manufacture, marked SM and/or N67, the company's

LEFT: The fore-end marked with the rifle's own serial number in typical fashion as one would expect. Also note the acceptance, maker and inspection marks that accompany it.

ABOVE: S 51 is the Holland & Holland wartime manufacturer code and is not always present. Butt stocks fitted at manufacture were generally marked "N" for normal and remained as so through conversion. Butt stocks were very often changed at unit level to either long or short to better suit the sniper.

ABOVE: American black walnut became standard for the No. 4 rifle with alloy butt plate in favour of brass. The cheek rest on this example is ash wood.

ABOVE: The inspection "S" mark is visible here denoting the correct Mk1 rear sight is present. The leaf of the Mk1 rear sight is itself marked with the Singer Manufacturing wartime code of N67 whilst the slider is marked S.M.

wartime manufacturer code, was marked to the rifle it came off and sent to the machine shop where the aperture, or battle peep sight, was ground off so as not to foul the telescope when fitted. The small flat section just forward of the extraction port on the right hand side of the receiver was then stamped with an "S" indicating the rear sight was correct and sighted to the weapon.

The left side of the receiver wall was then prepared to receive the pads by which the scope would attach to the rifle. The area on the receiver wall to which the pads would fit needed to be milled perfectly flat in both vertical and horizontal planes

to the bore, and is more than likely why this process was completed with the barrel still attached to the receiver. The receiver was held in a purpose made piece of tooling called a jig which both held the receiver and controlled the extent of cutting, as the surface only required to be skimmed of all the high points.

The holes for fixing the pads were also bored at this stage, and required precise placement so they would marry perfectly to the fixing holes in the pads. In all likelihood this was achieved by a further piece of tooling which would have bolted onto the jig, utilising its fixed position on the milling machine. It

is also likely the pads were bored with blank unthreaded holes and when sweated in place and held by solder the pad and receiver wall were tapped, or threaded, as one component. Holland & Holland received scope brackets from the manufacturers marked JC and KD, the wartime code marks for Rose Brothers, as well as brackets marked N92 of Dalgleish & Son of Glasgow.

The brackets were finished to Holland & Holland's strict standards and the machining of the two contact points between bracket and pad was also complete at this stage, as well as the sequential numbering of

LEFT & ABOVE: The illustrated No. 32 scope brackets show the Dalgleish & Son wartime code mark as well as the Rose Brothers JC and KD wartime code marks. Note the N92 mark here is the faded remnant left behind after conversion on an L42 bracket.

the scope rings both top and bottom to prevent them being swapped, an error which would almost certainly affect collimation. The scope's serial number was recorded and stamped on the top flat section of the butt stock's wrist just behind the cocking piece, and the rifle serial number also stamped just forward of the scope's serial number but hidden by the socket into which the butt stock fitted. The final inspection saw the rifle receive the completion stamp of a small "T" on the left wall of the receiver at the end of the rifle's engraved designation and

often close to the ejector screw, indicating the fitting of the telescope was complete.

It should also be understood that both BSA and Holland & Holland markings were not standardised until late 1943 and the "full set" of markings which one expects to see on a rifle today were developed through the conversion period of the first twelve months. Early H&H converted rifles stand testament to this today as examples missing the small "T" or the "S" are encountered and were previously considered spurious. During the period between

1941 and 1943 BSA developed their own wartime code which started with a "B" and by the end of 1943 had morphed into M47 and then finally M47 C.

The magazine commonly fitted to the production rifle was purpose made as opposed to a converted SMLE magazine found on the trials rifle. The commonly fitted magazines were often either marked M56 or M6, these being the codes of manufacturers Cheyney & Son Ltd and Aluminium Bronze Co Ltd respectively.

ABOVE: The No. 4 T carries the serial number of the matching telescope on the butt stock's wrist behind the receiver. Note the serial number of the rifle is also present but hidden when fitted to the rifle.

ABOVE: The wrist markings here show the evolution of the BSA wartime manufacture code, also note the early 1941 example is missing the TR selection mark entirely, not uncommon on No. 4 T rifles produced at the fledgling stage of production.

Rifle No. 4 Mk1 (T) Holland & Holland Conversion/No. 32 Telescope

Technical Specification	
Calibre	303in
Magazine Capacity	10 Rounds
Overall Rifle Length	44.5in
Barrel Length	25.2in
Twist Rate	5 Groove, LH 1 in 10 Twist
Combat Weight	11lb
Iron Sights	Graduated to 1300 Yds
Conversion Approval Date	12th February 1942
Converted By	Holland & Holland
Scope Mounted	Overbore
Quantity Converted	26,000 H&H approx

LEFT: The wrist markings show the rifle to be BSA manufactured in 1944. Note the U.S. import mark of ENGLAND which was mandatory pre-1968. This country of origin mark shows the rifle was more than likely one of the many sold into the U.S. in the late fifties and sixties through Interarms and Kline's. The TR selection stamp is typical and significant as the first mark to be applied to the rifle at the beginning of its sniper conversion journey.

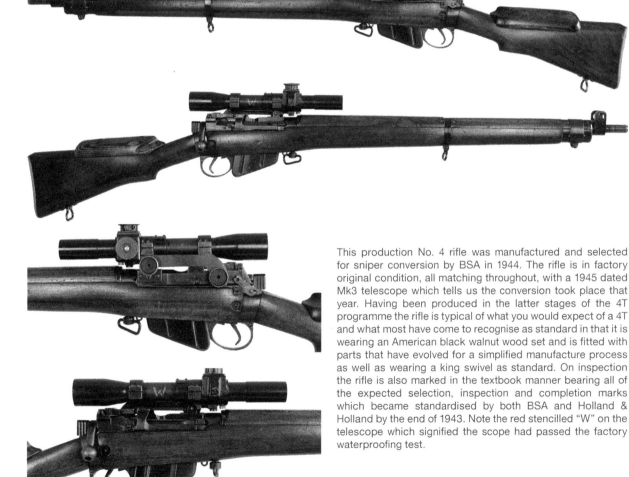

This production No. 4 rifle was manufactured and selected for sniper conversion by BSA in 1944. The rifle is in factory original condition, all matching throughout, with a 1945 dated Mk3 telescope which tells us the conversion took place that year. Having been produced in the latter stages of the 4T programme the rifle is typical of what you would expect of a 4T and what most have come to recognise as standard in that it is wearing an American black walnut wood set and is fitted with parts that have evolved for a simplified manufacture process as well as wearing a king swivel as standard. On inspection the rifle is also marked in the textbook manner bearing all of the expected selection, inspection and completion marks which became standardised by both BSA and Holland & Holland by the end of 1943. Note the red stencilled "W" on the telescope which signified the scope had passed the factory waterproofing test.

ABOVE: British paratroopers during WW2 pose for a picture during combat operations somewhere in Europe. Note to the right of the picture the group is joined by a U.S. paratrooper. The three central figures appear to be snipers; the guy on the right kneels proudly, displaying his No. 4 T rifle. To his right a sniper wearing a camouflaged scrim scarf as headdress is also kneeling with what looks to be a No. 8 Mk1 scope tin with carry strap on his knee. To his right a further individual wears a camouflaged scrim scarf as headdress.

All that was left to do was to mark both the No. 8 Mk1 carry case and the now Chest Small Arms No. 15 Mk1 as opposed to a converted Bren gun chest with both the rifle and the telescope's serial numbers before being packed with the respective equipment.

It is also worth noting that later in the war when the pressure to supply complete sniper equipment had eased Holland & Holland supplied a significant number of scopeless T rifles which had received a complete conversion but

without the fitting of a telescope, therefore they never received the small "T" completion stamp on the left wall of the receiver, or obviously a scope serial number on the wrist of the butt stock. These rifles were supplied in a No. 15 transit chest marked "Less Telescope" and were a kind of blank issued to units who had lost rifles through the attrition of war. The circumstances in which a replacement rifle may have been required would have often been the scrapping of a rifle, or of one which went out with a sniper who

never returned. The unit armourer would have fitted the telescope on the replacement "blank" and marked the scope serial number to the wrist. The "T" completion stamp was never applied to these rifles and sadly today a great many now bear a spurious "T" stamp applied by unscrupulous dealers and the inexperienced collector, making unmolested scopeless T rifles that ultimately received a telescope and saw action a rare find.

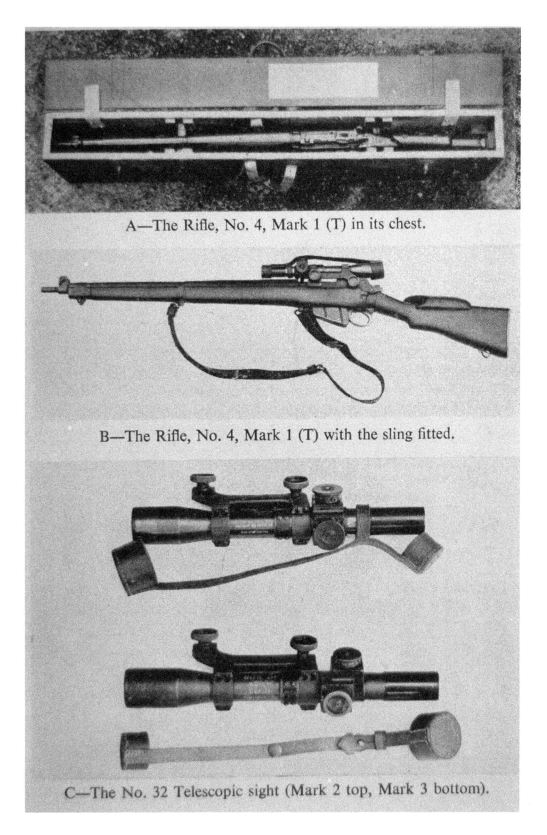

A—The Rifle, No. 4, Mark 1 (T) in its chest.

B—The Rifle, No. 4, Mark 1 (T) with the sling fitted.

C—The No. 32 Telescopic sight (Mark 2 top, Mark 3 bottom).

This extract taken from Pamphlet No. 10, 1951 illustrates the items that make up the Rifle No. 4 Mk1 (T) equipment. The equipment pictured is the principal items on the schedule list pasted to the lid of the transit chest.

Telescope, No. 32 Mk2 and Backup Sights

Whilst the Mk1 soldiered on, the Mk2, which had been designed to overcome all of the Mk1's shortcomings, was starting to reach front line units in 1943. On appearance the two scopes looked the same with the elevation and windage boxes offset from each other, but both the elevation and windage adjustment had moved positively towards a minute of angle value enabling the sniper to make adjustments to elevation in one MOA graduations; the windage remained the same with sixteen MOA in both directions, also adjusting in one MOA corrections.

The task of zeroing still required the adjustment tools, however reliability from the off was much better and although they looked identical the sniper would notice the functionality was also greatly improved. The operation of the Mk2's drums is smooth with a positive feel to the adjustments as opposed to the sometimes sticky and clunky operation of the now seemingly primitive Mk1. The quality of the lenses was also improved, overcoming the Mk1 failure issues of the glass. Waterproofing of the Mk2 was also markedly more reliable with examples being received from manufacturers stencilled in red with a "W" on the right hand side of the scope tube.

The iron sights fitted to the production rifle were essentially the same as those found on the trials rifle, and a cursory look would not tell you anything was different: it was still graduated in the same way, 200 to 1,300 yards with a slider that carried the range scale graticule lines and aperture for aiming, but look closer and one or two

ABOVE: A direct comparison of the production rear sight against the trials rear sight shows little in the vertical deployed position; the most obvious indicator of change is the head of the plunger sitting flat against the bottom of the production rifle sight. Note the Enfield EFD stamp on the trials leaf; also note the base of the peep sight on both sights is still visible after being ground off.

ABOVE: With the sight laid flat, as it would be carried with the scope fitted, one can see on the trials rifle the ball bearing sitting on the right slightly under the sight. Immediately above the ball bearing two very prominent nodules are visible which the ball bearing rests between when the sight is deployed vertical. Also note the base of both sights has a slight radius which when the sight is stood vertical allows the bolt to be removed.

LEFT: This example of foresight shows a solid block band with split foresight blade, regarded early in the war as undesirable to the specification of the conversion and was rejected routinely by Holland & Holland. Note the absence of the foresight blade retaining screw at the front.

things are glaringly different. The adjustment screw of the production rifle completes one full rotation with six clicks as standard. The trials rifle, particularly examples from the 1931 batch, received leaf sights with an adjustment screw that achieved one full rotation in four clicks, however the 1933 trials batch introduced the finer adjusting six click screw which went on to become standard on the production rifle. When the leaf was deployed from its folded position to the operational vertical position it was held in place by a spring that pushed a flat headed plunger against the bottom of the leaf, the two nodules and ball-bearing of the trials design now gone.

The picture surrounding the foresight is less straightforward; outwardly the components from one example to the next look the same but when a broad spectrum of examples spanning 1941 to 1945 are more closely scrutinised the block band, foresight blades and foresight protectors fitted would appear to be of the two most common variants. It's written elsewhere, several times over, that the Holland & Holland conversion strictly fitted a split block band with screw, and solid foresight blade, and anything else was rejected, but that is not entirely true. Many examples of Holland & Holland converted rifles do have a mixture of both split block band/ solid foresight blade and solid block band/split foresight blade (it should be noted the latter has no foresight block retaining screw). It is true Holland & Holland set out observing and implementing strict criteria that governed the conversion process, which after the effects of years of

war fell victim to some compromise, as for some time prior to 1944 the solid block band was sporadically making it through the intake inspection of the Holland & Holland examiners. I suspect this was during pinch points in supply of the desired components when the flow of converted rifles needed to continue, but by 1944 newly selected rifles arriving at Holland & Holland fitted with the solid block band were being routinely accepted.

Early production No. 4 T examples will be encountered wearing an Mk1 foresight protector which for all intents and purposes is very similar to the trials "waisted" protector. This part was superseded by the Mk2 foresight protector which is more commonly found on the No. 4 T as well as being the standard part fitted to the L42.

RIGHT: This early example of foresight is fitted with the original components specified in the conversion specification, the split block band with solid foresight blade. This design used an integral screw at the front of the block band which when tightened compressed the split block band against the solid foresight, locking its zeroed position. Note the waisted foresight protector which although pleasing aesthetically involved a more convoluted process to manufacture.

No. 32 Mk2 Telescope

Technical Specification	
Manufacturer	Vickers Instruments Ltd
Length	11in
Weight in the mount	2lb
Objective Lens DIA	19mm
Field of View	9 degrees
Magnification	3 X
Reticle	Post & Wire
Range Graduations	100–1000 Yds
Focus Capability	Fixed
Sunshade	Yes
Lateral Adjustment	16-0-16 Drum
Mount Type	Double
Approval Date	23rd April 1943

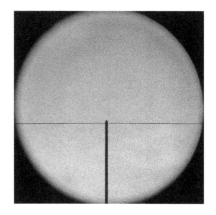

The No. 32 Mk2 telescope, although it looked identical to the Mk1, was vastly improved. The mechanics of the scope were made to be more reliable and felt better when the drums were operated. The post and wire reticle is present and the lenses were improved. This particular example is a rare model manufactured by Vickers Instruments Ltd. Note the very low serial number.

ABOVE: A sniper from "C" Company, 5th Battalion, The Black Watch, 51st (Highland) Division, in position in a ruined building in Gennep, Holland, 14th February 1945.

ABOVE: An extract from Pamphlet No. 10, 1951 showing the correct positioning of the sling around the arm. Note the instructor is utilising the king swivel to demonstrate.

ABOVE: The wartime American leather 1907 loop pattern sling became standard issue to the No. 4 T and was invariably a Great War example, often dated as so with blackened brass claws. Dubbin was issued to the sniper for its maintenance and upkeep.

The production 4T saw a further change to specification in 1944, allowing for a sling swivel to be fitted in place of the main trigger guard screw. The swivel allowed the sniper to make further use of the American 1907 loop pattern sling which became the standard issue sling to the No. 4 Mk1 T sniper rifle.

The next advancement of the No. 4 Mk1 T was the introduction of the No. 32 Mk3 telescope which arrived post invasion of Europe, late 1944. By this time a plethora of manufacturers since 1941 had worked to get the No. 32 telescope to this point. These manufacturers were:

Cooke Troughton and Simms
Vickers Instruments Ltd
William Watson & Son
Kodak Ltd

ABOVE: The task of installing the 1907 pattern sling can be confusing and indeed when visiting the range this particular sling is often seen installed in an array of incorrect fashions. This step by step sequence ensures the correct fitment. Note the last image has the sling set up the same but the rear section has been brought forward from the butt to the king swivel.

ABOVE: The elevation drum of this Mk3 telescope is equipped with a slip ring carrying markings for bullet path correction. The nipple designed to take the tip of a round in order for the ring to be slid back and forth is clearly visible. Also note the intermediate graticule between numbers.

A Kershaw and Son (formerly Kershaw Ltd)
Taylor Hobson & Co.
Houghton Butcher Manufacturing Co.
Research Enterprises Ltd. Canada

The Mk3 telescope incorporated all the modifications the Mk2 had and overcame the need for the adjustment tool with each drum being equipped with a range scale slip ring. The ring carried the markings for correction, the same as the previous model with one minute of angle corrections to both the elevation and windage, however each correction now had a graticule line under and in between each number which corresponded to a small black triangle at the bottom centre of each drum, the top of which pointed sharply to the corresponding graticule line. The slip ring was equipped with a small hollow nipple which, when the rifle was zeroed, allowed the sniper to use the tip of a bullet to push or pull the slip ring back to zero.

The waterproofing had also been further improved with scopes being subjected to a waterproofing test at the factory. Waterproofed scopes continued to wear the red "W" stencil on the right hand side of the scope tube. The reticle of the Mk3

remained unchanged as it continued to use the post and wire pattern. On appearance the elevation and windage drum boxes were now aligned as opposed to the Mk1 and Mk2 boxes that were offset from each other, and interestingly the windage drum remained on the left hand side of the scope, not ideal for the sniper to operate. It is rumoured the drum owes its position to its very earliest purpose, in that it was

originally trialled as a scope for the Bren gun. The appearance of the flat top face of each drum also differed due to the adjustment tool no longer being required.

One feature of the Mk1 and Mk2 scope that was dropped from the specification of the Mk3 was the brass sunshade. The No. 32 scope has quite a short eye relief so extending a sunshade greatly increased the risk of getting

ABOVE: The No. 32 Mk3 telescope had the elevation and windage drums brought in line, however the windage remained on the left hand side of the telescope, a throwback from its original intended role of an offset optic for the Bren gun. Note the larger simplified drum face now no longer needing adjustment tools.

ABOVE: The offset casting of the drum housing of the No. 32 Mk1 and Mk2 telescope is shown here. Note the busy drum face comprised of central lead screw and locking ring in comparison to the Mk3.

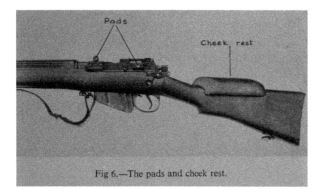

Fig 6.—The pads and cheek rest.

Fig 8.—Adjusting the elevation drum.

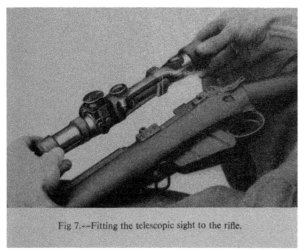

Fig 7.—Fitting the telescopic sight to the rifle.

ABOVE & LEFT: A sequence of instructional images taken from Pamphlet No. 10, 1951 which illustrate the telescope's relevant components fixed to the rifle, fitting of the telescope, and its adjustment when fitted.

thwacked on recoil and receiving a nasty cut above the eye, and even without the sunshade deployed, because its upper rim extended slightly beyond the rim of the ocular lens housing, if one was fatigued and maybe not paying as much attention as one would if fresh, one could get caught out by the protruding brass shade which would cut like a knife on recoil. The Mk1 and Mk2 scopes still around today are predominantly without a sunshade due to their being made obsolete in 1947, however many were probably removed by the sniper and thrown away during the war years. Post WW2 and in late 1945 the lenses of the Mk3 were further improved when they received a special coating known as blooming. This was a coating applied to improve the lenses' light gathering ability in poor light situations, buying the sniper just a few minutes' extra at last light when the enemy is more likely to move freely in the open. Scopes with the bloomed lenses are marked with a blue "B" stencilled on the left side of the scope tube opposite that of the red "W" waterproof mark.

RIGHT: The No. 32 Mk3 telescope was adjusted in MOA unlike the Mk1 which adjusted in yards. The range and MOA scale illustrated here was used to function test the elevation drum of this mark of telescope.

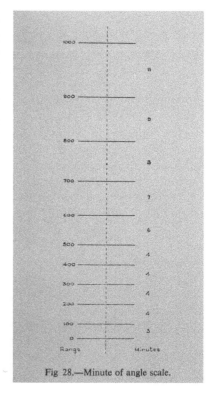

Fig 28.—Minute of angle scale.

Telescope No. 32 Mk3

Technical Specification	
Manufacturer	AK & S
Length	11in
Weight in the mount	2lb
Objective Lens DIA	19mm
Field of View	9 degrees
Magnification	3 X
Reticle	Post & Wire
Range Graduations	100–1000 Yds
Focus Capability	Fixed
Sunshade	No
Lateral Adjustment	16-0-16 Drum
Mount Type	Double
Approval Date	7th October 1944

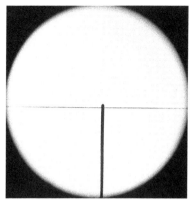

ABOVE: The ever-present post and wire reticle of the No. 32 Mk3 telescope.

The No. 32 Mk3 telescope was being fitted to newly converted rifles from October 1944. This example is dated 1945; its excellent factory finish would suggest this scope never saw any action, in fact very little service at all. The Mk3 was the design peak of the No. 32 telescope, taking it as far as it would go in service with the exception of several minor improvements in the L1A1. This particular example appears to have passed the factory waterproofing test but does not bear the "B" stencil denoting bloomed lenses.

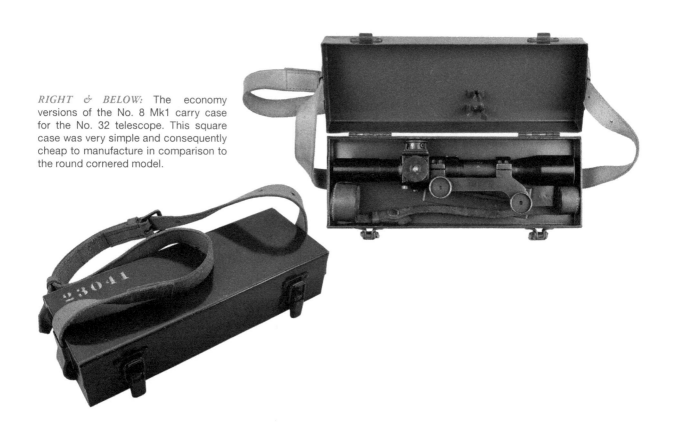

RIGHT & BELOW: The economy versions of the No. 8 Mk1 carry case for the No. 32 telescope. This square case was very simple and consequently cheap to manufacture in comparison to the round cornered model.

The celebrated sniper of WW2, Harry M. Furness, who served with the York and Lancaster Regiment, decided in 2014 to put some of his personal experiences into writing. Harry was an extremely active sniper during WW2 and equally one of the most successful at plying his trade. Harry describes his D-Day landing, the task of moving inland once off the beach and writes further about a 600 yard shot he made as his battalion were breaking out from Normandy. He wrote,

No, I did not return to Normandy like so many N.V.A. veterans; I have no fond memories which would ensure a happy return visit. I did go back for the 50th anniversary of our attack, but my feelings were quite different from many others who seemingly enjoy looking back, exciting times and drinking French Calvados. In the coach which took us to Caen, they were all excited and looking forward to planned ceremonies………….. whilst I just felt a dread chill looking and remembering at the passing Bocage, the dreaded hedgerows through which I once crawled very carefully bypassing the glass prongs of S-mines, and the boxed Schuman anti-personnel mines which couldn't be seen, you had to gingerly prod for them. My FS dagger proved extremely useful and wasn't ever used on any human.

My L.C.A got stuck on a sandbank quite a way out from the beach, and as we were then a sitting target we scrambled off fast as possible, I was 5ft. 5" and struggled mightily with my 80lb pack of supplies into the sea which was neck high, and could only make slow headway, the seabed was uneven and the Naval ships all firing every gun meant that we were hit by high waves. The noise was incredible. Even screamed orders couldn't be heard all of which just about finished me. As I got to the shoreline (Gold Beach, King Sector) I was ripping off the waterproofs of two groundsheets I had hoped to keep my rifle and TS reasonably dry, of course it didn't. I was soaked through and didn't know how the sea-water would affect my rifle. Before wrapping it up I put one-up-spout and just pulled safety on.

Condoms were knotted around my TS lenses and barrel, also my compass and watch. It was about 07:30 hours my L.C.A was signalled in, previously we all assault craft circled until we were strong enough to attack. But I was surprised that there were already a lot of soldiers on the beach as I thought we would be first, we weren't.

Engineers were blowing paths through the excessively close meshed barbed wire which was also mined, and signallers were running with cable drums on their backs laying RT cables (everyone knew in the havoc that Morse code would come out mutilated.) The 80lb or so pack I carried had supplies we'd need to keep going.

With my waterproofs torn off I fired into the sand as I was passing an Officer in battledress but wearing a naval officer's peaked cap, he had a megaphone up to his face but I never heard what he was shouting, he was pointing the way off the beach through the heavily coiled barbed wire. With my load and drenched I was only able to stumble off the beach towards the sea front. I only saw dead and wounded but no enemy soldiers until much later. The mortaring and fast-firing Spandau machineguns seemed all around, and I vividly recall holding the legs of a dead German soldier around my head at one point as protection. It had been impressed on all of us that we HAD to get off the beach and get inland as quickly as possible, otherwise the assault would falter as heavy German reinforcements with very many tanks was expected to counter-attack, we were too few ashore to hold off the expected massive attacks. It was complete and utter massively organised chaos, nothing going to plan. The first objective for my battalion was to secure a road running parallel with the beach, so that following Allied tanks could avoid using the

mined (?) ditches. It didn't happen. A fighter-bomber came in low and dropped a small bomb......... which blew a crater in the middle of the road, so the expected tanks would have to use the ditches anyway. I remember that down a way on our right there was a very large house with a circular drive, probably used as some sort of headquarters, I'd seen it marked on a map we had been given on the ship going over.

All day I seemed to be running around, I wasn't firing like mad as you might expect. At first I saw only dead or dying British and enemy as we cleared buildings, it was awhile before I actually saw running figures in grey/green. On D-Day I only fired my rifle three times, the first shot into the sand as I came ashore to see if the seawater had affected it, and during the day two more shots, each time dropping NCO's who were both moving targets. I used "Kentucky Windage" aim off and I know my eyes were wet through with water when I "fired in anger" for the first time. I was always unsure if it had been sweat pouring down my face, or seawater still dripping from inside my helmet as my eyes was very watery. I actually jumped over one poor sod I had dropped a little later as we advanced. I have no happy memories like many support troops. The weather turned really hot, and the indescribable stench of fast decaying bodies of those killed, lots of them ours and theirs, meant we had the really rotten task of putting the dead into any available slit trenches, we wrapped each body up in the blanket we each carried, then stuck a rifle into the ground as a marker for those following. A few days later we had poor weather, but it remained hot. A Spitfire pilot later told how he could even smell the many dead as he flew over. It was first at dusk that rollcall was taken, and we realised just how many casualties the battalion had

lost, K.I.A., W.I.A. and M.I.A. Whilst I never had any premonition that I would not make it, I did accept that the odds were against me surviving, we all did in the P.B.I.

My battledress dried on me by the end of another day, but I didn't manage to take my boots off my bleeding feet for about a week. So we all had "trench foot" and dysentery from the huge flocks of flies feeding on the dead. It was noticeable that it was always the German soldiers who appeared with a red cross flag first for a short ceasefire whilst the wounded and dead were collected. The first day was certainly grim, but really the heaviest close-quarter fighting came by dawn on the 7th June as German reserves which were held back to see if our attack was a decoy for a main attack elsewhere. Then we were up against elite combat experienced divisions, and our losses vastly increased. It's all a long time ago now, and obviously there is a blurring of what happened all the time, but in spite of memories playing tricks on us, it can never wipe away some of the vivid recollections of which imbedded themselves deep in our psyche, life threatening times never fade. Like most former Infantrymen I can find nothing glorious about war. And I really don't see anything glorious about seeing dead either. I have no pride in doing what seemed right at the time, and no sense of guilt either, it all really happened and I was most definitely there amongst it all as it happened, part of history I guess.

My own personal memories most definitely scarred me, that's for sure, because I'm no Rambo, and shortly after the war, I was full of it, and started to write it all down, warts and all. Erni read my many pages and was upset, my parents were shown what I'd written and my Mam told me to burn it and forget it. She was right. However my regimental museum when they found out I'd got things off my chest wanted me to try and re-write it, but, I didn't want to do it. Military snipers do have rotten tasks, but I have to admit it is wholly a grim necessity in any war, and if somebody/anybody's fate means they'll lose it in combat, then perhaps a sniper's bullet will without violent pain. I used to think so.

Courtesy of Nigel Greenaway

ABOVE: The 4T is pictured with the Scout Regiment Telescope and prismatic binoculars; all are dressed for business. Straight edges and shiny surfaces subdued and broken up with hessian and loose scrim.

OFFICIAL WAR OFFICE CROWN COPYRIGHT PHOTOGRAPH. ARNSBERG KASERNE, SUMMER 1945. ARCHIVES: THE ARMY FILM & PHOTOGRAPHIC UNIT. (REPRINT PHOTO AND CAPTION 1946.)

This photograph was from a series taken to illustrate frontline combat soldiers who had served with distinction throughout the campaign in North-West Europe, 1944/45. SERGEANT HARRY FURNESS, who served as a specialist-trained Operational Sniper with THE YORK AND LANCASTER REGIMENT. In his role as a Sniper he was in constant action from Normandy, across France, Belgium, Holland, and into Germany. Twice wounded by enemy mortarfire, he quickly returned to combat duties after initial treatment behind the lines. Field reports on his sniping activities went up to Army Level, and resulted in being MENTIONED-IN-DESPATCHES. In this photo he is shown wearing his sniper's camouflaged smock, worn over his khaki battledress uniform. The sniping rifle is a special issue No:4 Mark 1 (T) Lee-Enfield military rifle, fitted with a No:32 Mark II telescopic-sight. These special rifles were prepared by Holland & Holland under a Government contract, each was built to exacting standards to ensure extreme accuracy. Sergeant H. Furness went through specialised Sniper training courses at Bisley, Hythe, and Llanberis. Soon after ceasefire in 1945 reports collated by Brigade Intelligence credited Sniper-Sergeant H. Furness as being one of the most active Snipers in his Division. With the end of the war in Europe, Regimental Sniping Sections were closed down, and Sniper N.C.O. Furness was appointed in promotion to Regimental Musketry-Sergeant, and as such became responsible to teach Advanced Weapons Training Techniques. At the same time he was appointed as the Team Captain of the Regimental Shooting Team which very successfully competed in the Army Shooting Championships held at Haltern in Germany 1946. In addition to winning team events, Sergeant Furness won outright three individual shooting trophies which included the major event of the three-day ALL COMERS SNIPING COMPETITION which was open to Combat Snipers of all Allied Regiments. For the last part of his Army service he held the appointment of Regimental Intelligence Sergeant based in Berlin. This A.F.P.U. PHOTO was taken to illustrate the Sniper's face, but in combat he usually wore more camouflage, darkened face and hands, with boots covered by rough hessian, and the entire rifle and telescopic-sight in rag scrimmage.

CREDIT A.F.P.U. OFFICIAL PHOTO ON ANY PUBLICATION.

ABOVE: This Army Film & Photographic Unit photograph was taken of Harry Furness in 1945. Note his prismatic binoculars which he carried as sniper, and his attire which is the camouflaged hooded windproof suit. Harry was gifted; his abilities behind a sniper rifle were outstanding in both combat and in competition. He was also ruthless as a sniper yet compassionate as he strived to kill instantly with one shot. Harry never got gratification from taking a life, or the power he held over it. The overview written on the reverse of the photograph encapsulates Harry's exploits and achievements as a British Army sniper. At the point of writing he is in his nineties and has written over the years about British military sniping to raise the profile of his forebears who did so much in the service of sniping to make British snipers better than their foes. A history in which he himself now firmly has a place, and in turn is written about. *(Courtesy Nigel Greenaway)*

A Sniping incident I won't ever forget.
Harry M. Furness, Hallamshire Battalion

Over many years I have been asked by several military historians what really happened and the after effects of a sniping incident in which I was so very lucky to escape death myself when enemy laid down a tremendous retaliatory barrage to wipe me off the face of this planet, I got away, but only just...................

It happened just as we were breaking out of the Normandy bridgehead in 1944. The C.O. had sent me forward to report back any enemy movement and if I could spot any dug-in tanks or artillery before we put in a battalion strength attack. The situation was at the time very fluid as I left our forward companies who were in slit trenches on the frontline. As I very carefully moved around crawling to get to get ever better concealed positions, I used my x20 telescope to get better clarity of where the German soldiers were likely to be concentrated. Soon I found something very unusual, a group of the enemy were partly hidden behind a hedgerow with trees near them, they were very obviously all officers, so priority targets. As I looked at them intensely with my higher-powered scope, I could see quite clearly that the officer in the centre of their group received deference from the others as they often looked at him as he was looking towards our positions through field glasses. To spot such a rare grouping was an opportunity I couldn't possibly let pass by and I had to be fast. I put down my x20 and picked up my 4T rifle, I was lying prone, and quickly estimated the range which I thought was around 600-yards. Fortunately I had loaded some long-range special ammo I had managed to get from the 2nd Battalion of the Kensington's who were supporting the Hallamshire's with Vickers machineguns.

Previously I had zeroed my rifle for high-precision hits with this type of ammunition, so when I fired I was confident I had secured a good solid hit as the officer in the centre was dropped. I knew that he must have had high rank as he held that Order-Group, but was too far away to identify rank insignia or much else. As I fired I lost my sight picture through the rifle recoil, but was quickly back on target, he was down and the officers surrounding him were in uproar I could see with arms pointing, and I knew then they must have spotted my muzzle flash as most of them had been looking towards our frontlines, and I was concealed in their line of sight. I started immediately to try and crawl out of the way, I didn't attempt to stop any longer to shoot at the other officers, I knew I had to get away fast. The sheer speed of their retaliation was staggering, it seemed to be almost immediate. Which I expect followed so fast in view of all their units receiving immediate fire orders from senior officers. Their aim was excellent as all around me were explosions from shellfire, mortarfire, and machineguns were sweeping the ground to find me. All I could do to protect myself was to lie flat as I could on the ground, and I held my mouth open as we had been warned that explosions and blasts near any of us could perforate and ruin eardrums, and I held my hands over my neck under my steel helmet. But as soon as I could I crawled away towards our frontline. It seemed every type of weapon was being used against me, and several times as I attempted to crawl back I was lifted by the blast of the many explosions. I couldn't hear after the first near tremendous explosions, and I became very confused so I wasn't sure anymore which way to

go, my nose and ears were bleeding and I found it hard to breathe. I don't know how long it took me to get back to our forward lines, and when I did manage it I couldn't hear anything that was being said to me. Stretcher-bearers took me to our Battalion Regimental Aid Post where the medical officer gave me some treatment. It was in the R.A.P. that I was first de-briefed by our 'I' Officer. When the intense barrage had first started, the C.O. informed Brigade HQ at once that the battalion was 'stood to' as it seemed likely that a strong counter attack was coming in, experience had shown that attacks were preceded by heavy stonk.

The 'I' Officer had known I was in their line of fire and thought I was probably already dead; they were surprised that I got away. As I was still bleeding after a while I was sent back to the nearest Field Dressing station to be assessed for further treatment, but returned to the battalion the next day, when I made out my logbook report and de-briefed again for any more information. In the following days any P.O.W.s were first questioned to find out if they knew of any high-ranking officers who had been visiting their units. I was never told any of the results. It never happened that snipers sending back field intelligence reports to rear HQ were ever informed how significant it was.

I was told later by my battalion C.O. that they all had definite opinion that I had targeted and killed a very senior ranking officer for such a massive barrage to be laid down against me as a sniper, as it did not proceed any large-scale enemy attack that day as they would have expected. Whilst it was also a possibility that I had killed a very popular officer, the scale of the retaliation pointed more towards a high-ranking officer who was in the middle of his Order-Group. Which in turn very likely changed their Order-of-Battle at that time? My shot must have caused chaos to the enemy battle planning.

The integrity of my field report was upheld as completely valid by the Brigade Intelligence Staff, it was positively confirmed by the sheer duration and massive intensity of the enemy retaliation barrage laid down against the position where I had until then lay concealed with camouflage.

In retrospect, over all these years since, I have often thought about that particular incident very late at night when I couldn't sleep. During the campaign I had sniped and dropped many enemy soldiers, most of whom were considered priority targets as officers or N.C.O.s, I was always very careful to avoid attracting attention to my concealed positions so I didn't shoot very often at ordinary soldiers unless I considered them a real danger to me, I reserved fire for better targets and when privates moved around it encouraged higher ranks to risk exposing themselves, their mistake.

I never did find out the rank or possible identity of that senior officer I targeted, nor did I ever want to know. It doesn't do any good to know such personal details for any

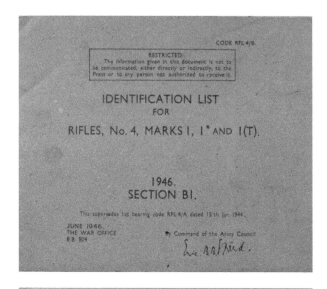

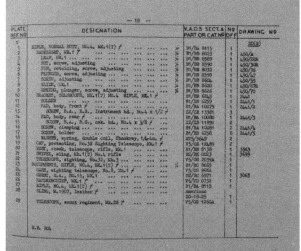

RIGHT: This publication dated June 1946 entered service just two months after the No. 4 T programme ended. The booklet identifies and lists the components for all marks of the No. 4 rifle to that date including the T specification. The components list pictured is far more detailed than the schematic lined drawing which features a very early specification rifle. The illustrated telescope appears to be an Mk1 complete with sunshade, which would be made obsolete in the following year, 1947. Not odd in itself, and it could be an Mk2, but if one looks carefully the cocking piece is illustrated as being retained, a feature mainly connected with the trials rifle. Furthermore the telescope is listed as Mk3. The rear sight leaf is also illustrated complete with battle peep sight intact. Although the parts list is accurate the inclusion of the outdated illustration seems somewhat lazy. An indication of a lack of interest in sniping now the war has ended, maybe.

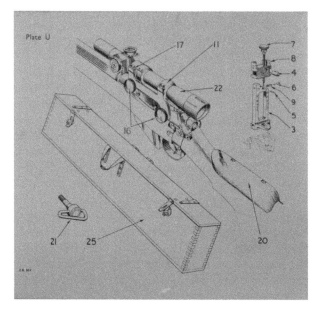

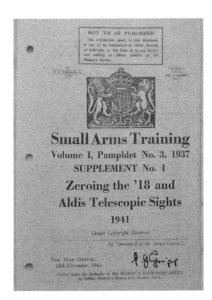
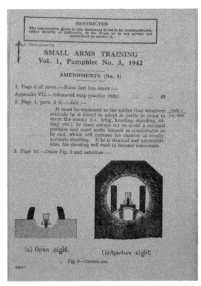
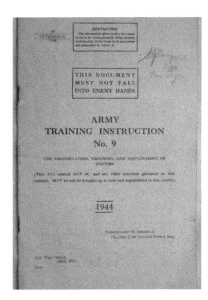

ABOVE: The pictured training literature illustrates amendments applied to the already existing training pamphlets of the day. Pamphlet No. 3 which was a generic small arms training pamphlet contained within it a section dedicated to the sniping rifle. Amendments leaflets for inclusion to the prescribed pamphlet were issued periodically as best practices changed. *Army Training Instruction No. 9* was a booklet in its own right, however it was not a pamphlet and bridged the weapon specific information from that of Pamphlet No. 44 to Pamphlet No. 28, Sniping, 1946. (Image of Pamphlet No. 9 *Courtesy Nigel Greenaway*)

Operational-Sniper, it was a rotten job but a necessary one in war.

Harry M. Furness. Sniper-Sergeant, Hallamshire Battalion, York and Lancaster Regiment, North-West Europe Campaign, World War Two

Courtesy of Nigel Greenaway

The No. 4 Mk1 T fitted with the No. 32 telescope served reliably and robustly doing sterling work right up to the end of the war in September 1945, the rifle's evolution culminating in a tool perfected for the deadly work asked of it. However the end of World War 2 would not be the end for the No. 4 Mk1 T sniper rifle as the next generation of British military snipers would pick up the 4T and once again take it to war. But of course in 1945 military planners could not have possibly known where the next bout of hostilities would take place and with whom. They did though know that the training of men to use

such weapons needed to continue to evolve and improve. Through the war years *Pamphlet No. 44, Notes on the Training of Snipers* was the only complete training pamphlet written and made available concerning sniping although *Small Arms Training, Volume 1, Pamphlet No. 3, Rifle*, which contained a small entry

dedicated to the sniping rifle No. 3 Mk1* T as laid down in *Pamphlet No. 44*, did from time to time carry amendments to this section. In addition supplements would be circulated updating training doctrine to the most current as the situation on the ground demanded it.

ABOVE: Both armed with No. 4 Mk1 T rifles, a sniper demonstrates the superior "Hawkins" prone firing position (right) next to a colleague in the standard prone position at the 21st Army Group sniping school near Eindhoven, 15th October 1944.

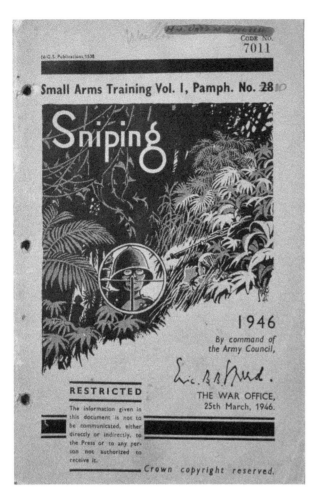
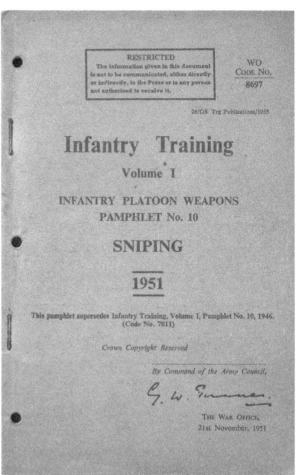

ABOVE: The official and most comprehensive training pamphlet covering the No. 4, Mk1 T did not appear until five years after the rifle entered service, and in the following year after the war ended, but was compiled after a plethora of wartime amendments to Pamphlet No. 44. Pamphlet No. 28 would be further amended and revised in the form of Pamphlet No. 10 in 1951.

It would not be until immediately after the war that a revised pamphlet would be available for the training of snipers. 1946 saw *Small Arms Training, Volume 1, Pamphlet 28, Sniping* replace the wartime literature. Six years of war in which the British Army fought with snipers from beginning to end taught snipers a considerable number of lessons, which by the end of the war enabled a new comprehensive pamphlet to be written containing the most current best practice for instructional training of snipers as well as being weapon specific for the 4T, and given the pamphlet was approved for service on 25th March 1946 it must have been formulated and written during 1945 which suggests boldly that the British Army was most definitely in full swing and not at all slowing in any way with the end of the war in sight. *Pamphlet No. 28*, War Office code 7011 was in service for five years before the next generation of training pamphlets circulated the then modern British Army.

In 1951, a year into the Korean War, British Army training literature received a new image and was rebranded. The infantry's pamphlet title became Infantry Training as opposed to Small Arms Training and they were packaged in new blue colour front and rear cards. *Pamphlet No. 28* became *Infantry Training, Volume 1, Infantry Platoon Weapons, Pamphlet No. 10, Sniping*, and was War Office approved for circulation on 21st November 1951. The training pamphlet No. 10 was further assisted by other mediums by which to train snipers such as film strips which would often feature

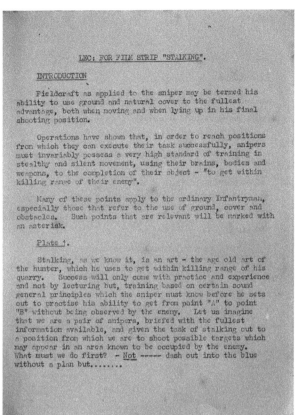

ABOVE: Pamphlet No. 10 1951 lists within it a number of training films which can be used in conjunction with the pamphlet. The film pictured is FS 849, STALKING, and is one of the film strips recommended.

and concentrate on a particular skill requirement of the sniper such as stalking, or concealment.

The use of film and its application to training was in the post-war era a technological advance in training technique and was set to stay with training film strips becoming the norm as film and the technology around using it became better. Indeed today in the digital age snipers are taught with the aid of high definition glossy films that have become the most effective way of communicating certain aspects of the training package to the student. With the end of hostilities in 1945 a great many snipers' equipment returned to stores. Arthur Hare writes in *The Sniper* how in Germany at the end of hostilities he entered the stores where he handed in his sniper

rifle, which had been his closest companion as he fought across Europe, to the armourer, never to see it again. If we could have tracked Arthur's rifle from that day it more than likely sat in stores for several years waiting for refurbishment. There was a breathing space of less than five years; by June 1950 Great Britain committed forces to the Korean War where once again the No. 4 Mk1 T did deadly work during the three year conflict and again in this conflict as in WW2 individuals like Harry Furness came to the fore and displayed natural ability for the sniping game.

One such individual who skilfully plied his trade in this latest campaign was Sergeant Tom Nowell MM of the Duke of Wellington's

Regiment which was part of the 29th Commonwealth Infantry Brigade.

In the 1990s Tom decided to put several of his experiences as a sniper in Korea onto paper. As he wrote:

The Pest Exterminators

During our periods of getting to the front of the forward enclosures, we alternated between the different parts of the battalion frontage. It was in Korea, and winter was behind us, and the weather was improving. We held a line of hills, and at the other end of the valley, the Chinaman laid claim to a similar range of hills. The area between was considered No-man's land and this area was always subject of who should have it, or control it. Hence the area between hills was always the subject of patrolling and confrontation.

It was our custom to vary our movements and our stay in any one particular Company area. The Company, and the local Platoon Commanders were a little nervous of our presence in their locality as it would appear that if we decided to open up and fire at any particular enemy target that we wished to engage, there was always the risk of retaliatory fire from the other side. That is, if they had spotted our position. Understandably, the Platoon Commanders didn't want any extra work put their way, so we were treated as a sort of leper squad in that respect.

It was the done thing to arrange visits, or to let people know that we were working in their area. It was also safer too for us, the risk of being shot-up by our own trigger happy troops who might think that we were the enemy out there in front of them. They in turn had visions of capturing the odd Chinaman in order to qualify for a couple of extra days leave, and a bottle of whisky for bringing in a Chinaman on his arm. One had to be careful of his rear, so to speak.

The other side of the coin was when the forward troops were being sniped at by the enemy and they could not discern from where the sniping was coming. The casualties, although not severe, were mounting up and this particular section was getting a bad name as being not too comfortable to be in. The movement to and from this section of trenches was considered a hazard and the lads couldn't make out where the sniping was coming from. Every time they ventured out down that section of trench system, they were being "got at". We were called in to see if we could help in this situation. My pair, Seymour and I went down to meet the corporal and his lads involved in this neck of the woods we heard the story from the corporal and some of his lads and they were of the opinion that all snipers ought to have their fingers cut off so that we could all fight fair. One thing was for sure, they were referring to enemy ones and not to their beloved Seymour and his lovely Sergeant.

If we could sort out the Chinky who was causing them all this aggravation, then they would be ever so grateful. Thank you very much. Suddenly, the place cleared as if by magic. Seymour and I were left on our own, in the trench and close to the area where the shots were arriving. The nearest hoochie, or weapon pit had a lintel made of sturdy wood. We examined this timber and found shot holes in its front area. It was obviously a case of being sniped at. I put a pencil into the shot holes and the majority of them confirmed that they had come from a certain direction. That gave us a starting point so we were able to concentrate in that direction. According to the information that the lads gave us, it was when they did this and did that, and when they operated at a certain time that they were getting this troublesome strafing. It was going to take some time to find the culprit, or culprits. The section of the trench was now ours, we were not unduly troubled with sightseers, wanting to come down and see how we operated. They were quite content to leave us in peace and for us to discover who was doing this thing to them.

We spent all that day, until dusk came down, observing and noting the places we thought it was possible that the enemy sniper might be operating from. It seemed a long day with nothing really happening, so we called it off until the next day. There wasn't going to be any more sightings now that the sun was going down. The lads of the forward sections would soon be out and about, mounting the patrolling activities in front of their Company positions. So, back to base then and get something to eat and rest up. We decided to get down there, the first thing in the morning, before daylight broke and take over from the lads as they came in from their night patrol work. The usual activity at this time was for the lads to clean down and then get some rest. There were duties to do such as cleaning out the place and tidying up a bit. Making sure that the risk of infection from unwanted and discarded tins etc. was kept to a minimum. Health and hygiene being most important in that God forsaken land. There were plenty of opportunities to catch infection, without adding to them.

At last, after the normal "stand to" and "stand down" had been observed, both Seymour and myself found ourselves alone in this little spot of real-estate that was troubled by the enemy snipers. The dawn was now well underway and we could see most of the valley through the morning haze and we had rigged up our scopes and camouflaged the rifle, ready for any eventuality. It was a case of being patient and covering the ground in front in a systematic manner. Trying to search into anything that even looked like cover for the Chinaman. If the Chinkies were anything like our own forces in their method of operations, then they would presumably have a night shift going off and a fresher day shift coming on.

That might suggest some sort of liaison and change-over routine that we might be able to spot. Sure enough, one such incident occurred and we were fortunate enough to discover the whereabouts of the hide, and the possible routine to and from this hide. Eyes down then, look in, as the saying goes. Let us see if we can catch them on the hop. Now that we had located a possible source of the trouble, it only remained for us to keep them observed until we could put him/them out of action. With Seymour on the powerful telescope as back-up-observer and myself on the sniper rifle we waited our chance. The range was something like six hundred yards, pretty close

as ranges went in the distances well beyond that in the valleys between hills in this neck of the woods.

The hills rising up and becoming dominant features overlooking the rest of the valleys below. The Chinaman had moved into the no-man's land between two adjacent hills and had presumed to take advantage of the nearness and the surprise, to take his toll on our front line forces in their trenches.

A murmur from Seymour to indicate that the enemy was visible and I was already in the aim at the centre of the opening in the hide. I let a shot go and we both saw someone, or something fall back into the recesses of the hide. We waited quite a while after that, not wishing to let another shot go so

as not to alert anyone as to where we were operating from. That last shot may have proved sufficient. There was no movement from the enemy position but we continued to observe the hide just in case there were any other developments.

At the end of that afternoon, when the lads started to appear and were getting prepared to carry out their evening tasks, we contacted them and told them of what we had found, and done to it. We suggested to the Corporal that he could take some further action against the hide whilst his lads were out on their standing patrols. We gave him the location and he said he would have some action taken against it. The lads, when they heard the news of the demise of the trouble, thanked us

ABOVE: Sniper Lance Corporal Alec Jamieson, 1st Battalion, The King's Own Scottish Borderers, maintains his lonely vigil over enemy hills with the Scout Regiment Telescope.

both and we were promoted to their "Pest Exterminators". We were not sure whether this was a compliment or not. Since we could do no wrong down that neck of the woods after that episode, the moans and feelings

of being lepers subsided somewhat. My pair, Seymour was going to get himself set up with a few free beers when the regiment got back to reserve for a rest.

All that remained now was to sign off, out of the area and make our way back to Int. H.Q. and make the usual report and add that an enemy sniper and hide had been dealt with.

Courtesy of Nigel Greenaway

Shooting at Long Range in Korea

Due to the nature of the terrain that we experienced in Korea during the war with North against South, it was a case of hills and valleys, with the ground in between being low lying and terraced for what used to be the peasants rice paddy fields in calmer, peace time. The country was mostly hilly and it was a case of who held the highest hill around was in the prime seat and was able to dominate the surrounding area. As the war stabilised and there was a semblance of a front line, then these hills were important and there was always a fight going on for one hill or another. Some of these battles for these hills got to ferocious proportions as the war dragged on. It was quite usual for the intervening ground between hill and opposing hill to be anything up to twelve hundred yards or more. Some hill features that were closer than this always seemed to be the subject of taking possession of and then losing it only for another attempt to re-take it again.

The intervening ground being considered as no-man's land and was up for grabs by both sides trying to dominate this area by sending out patrols of varying strengths and trying to cause as much discomfort to the nearest holders of the adjacent hill.

Because of the distance across the valleys at some points, it would appear to the average soldier that here he was and twelve hundred

yards over on the other side was Chinky and there didn't appear much that they could do about it. From an observational point of view, however, with observer telescopes and large efforts that the tanks and gunners had at their disposal in their Observation Posts, the enemy was revealed quite large and menacing. Even the enemy on the other side of these wide valleys had this same facility of being able to see at long range and were not slow to give us a taste of their mortars and shelling when we on our side got a little complacent about not being seen. So, we ended up at these points as long range participants in this long range observing and shooting. Some soldiers at these points were often surprised to be told that the enemy were watching them and they hadn't even seen a Chinky, all the time that they had been in that locality.

When observation contact had been made in these sort of areas and distances, there were one or two alternatives that one could take. To restrict the enemy from the use of his O.P. thereby giving we at this side a quieter time of it, was the main objective. If we could stop him from seeing what we were doing, their own intelligence would be the poorer.

We could use our tanks and their weaponry, or we could call down a stonk of our own mortar fire plan on them. We could also use 25 pounders artillery if the situation called for it. All this would seem to

be rather expensive and over the top when all you needed was to take out a single enemy O.P. that you had found and wished to eliminate. I remember a typical situation on one feature opposite us on a nice bright, calm morning in May time. I/we had spotted some movement in a position about two thirds up towards the top of the crest of the hill feature "Pheasant", from our Yong-Dong side. It appeared to be some canvas, or other material covering a doorway or trap door. There was an occasional movement when the occupants were either changing position, or it was part of a communication system with this as a central point with it being made into an O.P.

The sides of the hill were pretty bare, what with all the shelling and all. The soil was sandy in colour as sandstone rock is after it has been pulverised. It showed up well in the morning light, which at this time of the day was shining into the enemy's eyes and would have been giving them some problems with seeing out and across to our side. It reminded me of the "Stop Butts" at Bisley in England when the shot arrival was clearly seen as a spurt of dust and a darker patch where the shot had turned over the fresh soil. We decided to engage these Chinkies with sniper rifle fire from the position where we were on the forward slopes of Charlie Company. We set the sights to the maximum that we could get on the scope and estimated what windage there could be at that time and we proceeded to let off a shot, my oppo working on the spotter scope saw the arrival of the shot and called it. It was quite a ways off to the right and low. I made some corrections and went away again. This time I was on target, but still a little low. This went on for a few shots and we did not seem to be getting any response in the way of further movement or retaliatory fire. The thing to remember about a shot coming in from long range is that the recipient does not hear the crack of the shot unless it has gone by him, whether close at hand, or at a distance. Any shot that falls short then, and in front of his position, he would possibly not be aware of.

We seemed to be having no effect on this position, although we had determined that we were reaching with our shots. I was getting just a wee bit frustrated by all this and was wondering what next we could do to liven things up a bit, when I spied a Sergeant colleague of mine from Charlie Company coming down our way on to his patrol area. We had

a few words and I bemoaned the fact that I wasn't having too much luck in sorting out this Chinky O.P. He suggested that I enlist the help of the tank Sergeant on the top of the hill. He was in contact with him on his radio frequency. He got me through to this Sergeant and I outlined my problem and gave him some directions to get on target. He came back on the air after a short while and said "Yes, I can see what it is that you are after, what do you want me to do with it?" Funny man isn't he? I said a nice single shot down their front doorway would do them a world of good. I had in mind he would have a ranging shot or two to get on target and then he would be able to sort it out. We were observing across on to the opening in the O.P. when there was a bang from up and behind us and a shot from the tank went into this observation post through the front doors to speak.

It scattered the front elements quite a ways and that was the end of that. I got on to the tank Sergeant

to thank him for his assistance and to compliment him on his excellent shooting. He said, "That's quite alright and thank you, will that be all, just give us a ring."

I was able to report later that an enemy observation post over on "Pheasant Hill" had been silenced, thanks mainly to the Centurion tank Sergeant on top of the hill. Whilst it was quite feasible to shoot at long range with the sniper rifle, the standard of accuracy and the grouping capacity with the scope attached was well in the limits of what it could do, there were times when a more direct approach was called for. It could be more effective to at times. The use of the sniper rifle at this range, and sort of target proving more of nuisance value than anything else, was on our side the sort of situation we had to contend with and we as snipers had been able to help in the discovering and the silencing of these "pests".

Courtesy of Nigel Greenaway

A Funny Happening Whilst in Korea

I was operating in a part of the Commonwealth Front in Korea just north of the famous river Imjin. Over the other side of the valley from where I was stood the hill feature "Pheasant". This was the code name given to one of the hill features opposite our front line positions. People got to know the features by these code names and made reference to them as such. From where I was positioned on one late afternoon, in the dry weather, I observed a party of Chinamen acting as a working party and carrying supplies up the side of the feature called "Pheasant" and to all intents

and purposes, they were working away, thinking that they were out of sight of our forces and would be safe to do what they were doing, unobserved. The materials looked to be ammunition and petrol, or diesel. Some of the containers looked like mortar bomb cases. They were obviously stocking up for another go at our defences. I thought that the target was large enough for a concerted attack by our gunners, or mortars. There were about ten, or a dozen involved in this operation and if they were to continue with their work uninterrupted, they could have had quite a sizeable amount of stores brought up to the upper slopes by night-fall.

I was a fairly long way away from where they were working but from where I was they were quite in full view to me. I decided to enlist the efforts of the local tank and mortar forces in our area. They wanted to know the location and map reference to this point and I wasn't able to give them a good reference as I had not a map with me. We did carry one or two tracer type bullets that we used for target identification on those times when trying to point out a target was proving difficult. It was arranged that I would fire a tracer into the area of the target and let the gunner O.P. pick out the grid reference and get on to it. The target was more than a thousand yards away from where I was, but

ABOVE: Some of Sergeant Tom Nowell's snipers pictured here in Korea. This short sharp conflict would be the last hurrah for British snipers before a twenty-year absence from the practice would begin. *(Courtesy Nigel Greenaway)*

had been used to firing at these sort of ranges before. If I got a shot anywhere near to where the work party was, then the gunners could encompass that little lot in their ranging and consolidate fire power. On the word, I let a tracer go at the centre of activity and I observed the tracer going across the intervening valley and on to the target. The most unusual thing happened.

The shot struck one of the people carrying petrol and it ignited. It spilled out into a ball of flame and the luckless Chinaman fell to the ground and went rolling back down the hillside. His comrades that were with him downed tools and went after him, grabbing him by the legs and trying to put his burning clothes out by throwing dirt and anything else that they had to hand on to him to put him out. It was a pure lucky shot and the ball of flame that erupted served as a fine target pin-pointer for the gunners.

Courtesy of Nigel Greenaway

Post WW2 saw rifles and scopes returned from war in a pitiful state even though they were a much cared for weapon by the sniper who relied upon it to function without fail regardless of weather and environmental conditions; the weapon inherently suffered a hard life. The sniper will have stalked over rough stony ground; he may have operated in a destroyed urban environment and crawled over rubble where the rifle would have been dragged whilst in the leopard crawl; he may have lain on the weapon frozen whilst listening for enemy activity whilst his body weight pressed the rifle and scope into broken brick and glass. Then there were the hours spent observing and waiting for an opportunity to present itself in a position where sniper, spotter and their equipment

were exposed to the elements. Hot sun, rain and freezing snow and ice all took their toll on the sniper rifle.

Wood furniture, particularly the fore-end, took an enormous amount of rough treatment, returning with harsh gouges in the wood as well as chunks of wood plucked out which kept armourers busy patch repairing everything they could whilst only the very worst would be discarded for new.

Scopes came back scratched and rusty. The action body of the rifle also suffered badly, whether factory blued or Brunofixed by Holland & Holland. In the end, this was in many cases insufficient in its protection against rust, however, let's not forget the conditions these snipers' equipment operated in were often extreme to horrendous and this is not a slur on the outstanding work done by BSA, Maltby and Holland &

THE MILITARY MEDAL

No. 22249555 Sergeant Thomas Nowell,
The York and Lancaster Regiment

In December 1952 Sergeant NOWELL carried out a very bold reconnaissance behind the enemy lines. It was necessary for him to move out and back across no man's land and between strongly defended localities in darkness and having reached his point of vantage, to remain motionless during the hours of daylight. This he did, although the temperature never rose above freezing point. When daylight came, he found himself within twenty yards of two Chinese sentries. Notwithstanding this, and in spite of the intense cold, he managed to carry out his appointed task. As night fell, an enemy standing patrol joined the two sentries and Sergeant NOWELL was surrounded by seven or eight enemy soldiers. With great skill and daring, however, he managed, although numbed with the cold, to extricate himself and to return to his own lines bringing back vital information which subsequently enabled plans to be made for several successful operations against objectives in rear of the enemy front line positions.

Some time later he directed a fighting patrol in a night attack against an enemy tunnel which he had noticed during his previous reconnaissance. Unfortunately the patrol was observed and on reaching the tunnel they saw the enemy in flight. Sergeant NOWELL, however, entered the tunnel and obtained invaluable information as to its construction and defences. On this information was planned a subsequent raid which achieved complete success.

Sergeant NOWELL, who is the Battalion Sniper Sergeant, has, over a long period, obtained information of the utmost value. He has moreover, by his excellent marksmanship, effectively silenced many snipers opposite him. Much of his work has entailed exposing himself to great danger. His courage and initiative have been quite outstanding.

Citation dated	**London Gazette**
5th June, 1953	**8th December, 1953**

ABOVE: Tom's military medal citation dated June 1953. The exploits told in the citation are, I am sure, just a snapshot of his service in that conflict in which his military medal could have been earned a dozen times. Although the citation clearly describes the importance of the information his skills as a sniper obtained, and would possibly only have been obtained by such a highly skilled individual, the then MoD still saw fit to cease all army selection and training of snipers. *(Courtesy Nigel Greenaway)*

ABOVE: These images from Pamphlet No. 10 show how the sniper typically carried his weapon during a stalk and go some way to explaining the condition of these rifles when returned to stores after the war.

Holland. Weedon Royal Ordnance Depot, Northamptonshire played host to tens of thousands of 4T rifles in the post-war years and is where Arthur Hare's rifle probably ended up. Thousands of rifles surplus to those still issued as well as those serving in Korea at that time sat for years in racks at Weedon as it was here many thousands were put through the refurbishment process; these rifles are identified today by the Weedon ordnance stamp which is a five-pointed star with "W" in the centre. The stamp can more often than not be found on the underside of the wrist of the butt stock.

The level of refurbishment depended largely on how the Weedon inspectors graded the condition of the weapon; for the worst it was decided the refurbishment of the action body should incorporate a thorough bead blasting followed by a hot carbonising dip and then a final finish of black paint, most likely Suncorite. The carbonising process usually involved the replacement of the telescope fitting pads due to the destructive nature of the heat process. The original Holland & Holland fitted pads were mechanically fixed, the front via three screws and the rear via two but were also sweated or soldered into place and it was this soldered material that was destroyed by the heat which was considerable. The action body was heated and then dipped into oil which resulted in a tough textured carbonised finish which travelled several thousandths of an inch into the metal but where the solder failed it allowed oil to ingress the joint and potentially sit behind the pad, resulting in new scope pads

ABOVE: These two rifles pictured are both 1944 BSA manufactured examples. The example on the left is still in excellent post-conversion condition with its original blued finish entirely intact, and the original No. 4 Mk1 designation engraving can still be clearly seen. The telescope also is still in its original factory finish condition. The example on the right is in pristine post-war refurbished condition having been subject to bead blasting and a Suncorite paint finish; the designation can now barely be seen. The telescope and bracket have also been subject to complete refurbishment and are also finished in black Suncorite paint. Note the scope markings are now picked out in white; this became standard in the post-war years. Also note the "B" stencil mark on the scope tube.

being fitted. Late BSA converted rifles are often encountered with the front pad bearing a broad arrow mark; these should not be confused with refurbished rifles that have had replacement front pads. For the rifles with actions not graded as being in the worst category the refurbishment was limited to bead blasting and a Suncorite paint finish.

It is also worth remembering at this point the 1,400 trials rifles that went into service in 1941. A number of these rifles were during the war subsequently sent to Longbranch, Canada for the Canadian sniper rifle trials which initiated the Canadians' own 4T production. The Canadians initially back engineered these rifles and copied the trials parts which were obsolete on British production rifles. Those today searching for trials rifle parts often encounter LB marked items as opposed to the much rarer EFD marked parts. Those trials rifles that survived had been part updated along the way as they needed the attention of an armourer receiving new wood or an updated scope as well as the replacement of small parts, but many served reliably and ended the war in their original trials trim. It was at this refurbishment stage that these rifles received a FTR (factory thorough repair) being brought up to production rifle specification. However, that said, the examples I have personally encountered have been completely FTR'd, having been marked as so on the wrist just above the TR stamp, which was also stamped as part of the FTR because as mentioned earlier trials rifles had none of the selection, acceptance or completion marks of the production rifle so starting life as a trials rifle the TR stamp would not have been present. In addition examples have been noted to have retained their trials four click rear sight and several have also retained their trials magazine cutoff, but in all

other respects had been upgraded to the latest Mk1 T specification.

With the vast majority of refurbished rifles put into stores, the rifle No. 4 Mk1 T continued its service as the British Army's front line sniper rifle and despite Britain's membership of NATO and its adoption of the 7.62 x 51mm rimless ammunition in 1953 with the introduction of the L1A1 self-loading rifle, or SLR as it was popularly abbreviated by the troops that used it, the .303 inch ammunition remained in service with the 4T until the introduction of the L42 in the seventies, having been made officially obsolete in 1960 after some seventy years in service.

The .303 inch ammunition was first adopted as the British service cartridge in 1889 and served the Lee Metford rifle officially designated Cartridge, S.A. Ball, Magazine Rifle, Mark 1.C. Solid Case, .303inch. The first variant was a 215 grain bullet

with a Cupronickel jacket propelled by a Black Powder charge. In 1891 Cordite replaced the Black Powder charge in proportions of 58% Nitroglycerine, 37% Nitrocellulose and 5% Mineral Jelly formed into tubular rods, although the propellant also took the form of tape, flake as well as being sliced. Over the next twenty years different propellants were toyed with and although Cordite remained a propellant in the military cartridge well into the 1960s, Nitrocellulose was used extensively, particularly through WW1 and WW2.

In 1910 the MkVII round was developed. The lighter 160 grain bullet with a design that had much emphasis on long range was, however, a complete failure as it disastrously failed accuracy testing which resulted in its manufacture being immediately suspended. The embarrassing episode resulted in the 174 grain bullet that went on to serve for the remainder of the

ABOVE: The serial numbers on the wrist of both of these examples bear a prefix letter "A" identifying them as originally trials rifles and are indeed examples from both the 1931 and 1933 batches. Note the FTR and TR marks. The TR was in all likelihood applied during the Factory Thorough Repair.

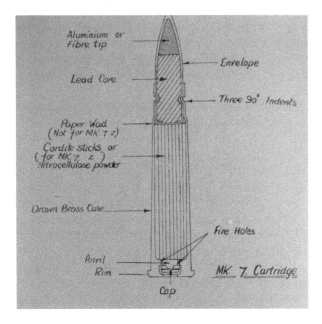

ABOVE & LEFT: A later specification drawing of the Mk7 .303inch cartridge. Note in comparison to the earlier WW1 vintage drawing Nitrocellulose powder and Cordite sticks are listed as propellants. The accompanying image shows a 1943 dated round broken down into its component parts. Note the Cordite sticks and the Cupronickel jacketed bullet which by the end of WW2 became a gilding metal jacket.

cartridge's service life. The new cartridge was approved in November 1910 being designated Cartridge S.A. Ball .303 inch MkVII (note the mark VII was not changed; many suspect this was to avoid drawing attention to the problems first encountered with its development). British military ammunition was on a very slow transitional path to the copper jacketed ammunition we are familiar with today. From 1911 the Cupronickel jacketed bullet (which although silver-grey in appearance was a copper alloy with a large copper content in its makeup) was produced as standard until around 1943 when a change to gilding metal began which had an even greater copper content, making its appearance more like what we recognise today. In the seventy years the cartridge was employed by the British military it was manufactured in twenty countries and existed in almost 200 military variants. During WW1 British production of MkVII ammunition peaked with over 300,000,000 rounds of ammunition being produced per month, culminating in over 7,000,000,000 rounds of ammunition manufactured in total.

In the immediate years that followed the Korean War the British Army began reverting to type: yet again withdrawing its interest in sniping, always the first victim of cost cutting, it would seem. By the late 1950s the British Army was no longer maintaining continuation training of trained snipers at unit level, although unofficially I would imagine it continued to some degree with weapons that were almost certainly sitting in the armoury. The formal training of new snipers at the traditional schools of Bisley, Hythe and Llanberis was abandoned but even so the 4T went into action again in the Aden Emergency in 1963 and again in Northern Ireland in 1968. In the absence of trained snipers within the infantry unit the sniper rifle would have been the responsibility of an "old sweat" who had previously been sniper trained or in all likelihood the section's best

ABOVE: The Radfan Campaign: The combined Federal and British Army Force engaged in operations against Yemeni supported tribesmen in the Wadi Taym district of the Federation of South Arabia, 40 miles north of Aden. Private Mugleston of the 1st East Anglian Regiment is armed with a No. 4 T rifle. It is unclear if Private Mugleston was a trained sniper; this being a period long after the British Army had ceased training snipers would suggest not. The poor fitting of the sling and it being carried so badly would also suggest the rifle is in the hands of the "best shot". Note the No. 8 Mk2 carry case for the No. 32 scope.

ABOVE: Troops in Northern Ireland sheltering behind a wall. Their rudimentary riot equipment suggests they are involved in quelling a disturbance. As they had not yet been issued DPM combat clothing, their uniform is the plain green 1968 pattern. This places them in the late sixties, early seventies pre-L42A1. Note the guy who is prone is armed with a No. 4 Mk1 T rifle and has bare elbows! No. 4 T in anger whilst on operations in Northern Ireland

shot who had attended one of the sharpshooter courses which began to appear as the absence of trained snipers began to be felt, particularly when deploying on operations. The sharpshooter course was by no means sniper training and was more or less an introduction to the weapon and its No. 32 telescope. We had not travelled far from the days of the Great War when the first sniper rifles were handed to the best shot before the sniper schools got to grips with things.

Through the 1960s the Ministry of Defence committed thousands of the stored 4T sniper rifles to disposals through UK companies which sold considerable numbers of rifles in the UK as well as further afield to the U.S. There large American surplus companies such as the Interarms Corporation based in Virginia and Kline's of Chicago mass purchased and distributed across the U.S.A,

ABOVE: This old advert was placed by Klein's in 1959. A complete No. 4 T kit for an eye watering $38.88.

and Hercules Surplus based in Toronto imported considerable numbers into Canada. The surplus 4T, wherever it ended up in the world, was largely used for hunting and cheap plinking, and thousands of rifles met a very unceremonious end, being sporterised in the garage by do-it-yourself riflesmiths, fore-ends chopped, barrels cut down and receivers drilled to take modern scope mounts. Today the U.S. collector is waking up to the importance of the Enfield rifle, recognising its place as the finest sniper rifle fielded during WW2, and it is fast becoming highly collectable throughout the U.S and Canada. Many wrongs are now being put right as sporterised rifles are being found and restored although at the point of writing original 4T parts are becoming extraordinarily rare and when they surface command huge prices, ultimately condemning some rifles to be left to fall by the wayside.

Although the L42A1 sniper rifle's conversion from No. 4 Mk1 T went into production in 1970, the army would not be directly involved with sniping again until 1973 and therefore the No. 4 Mk1 T could still be found serving with units well into the seventies. As RSAF Enfield methodically produced batches of the newly converted L42A1 rifles and dispatched to central stores, Donnington, the 4T slowly disappeared from 1973 onwards.

Chapter 4
Legacy of an Icon

The 1960s saw the fate of the No. 4 T sealed. As early as 1963 it was recognised that complete conformity to the NATO 7.62 x 51mm rimless cartridges was now necessary. That decade saw peaks and troughs of activity as an exploratory conversion programme started with a view to converting the No. 4 rifle to the 7.62mm calibre with a designation of L8A1. With the L1A1 self-loading rifle already pushing towards a decade of service it's presumed the converted No. 4 rifles were destined to be issued to lower echelon units, Territorial units and the Commonwealth in support of the main body of British forces armed with the L1A1 SLR. In a complete contradiction to what was happening within the army regarding sniping, several No. 4 T rifles were removed from stores and entered into the programme with a view to conversion to L8A1 T and were test fired at RSAF Enfield in their 4T guise, the results of which

ABOVE: The rimmed .303inch cartridge pictured next to its successor, the NATO rimless 7.62mm cartridge.

were recorded for later comparison. The rifles then went through L8 T conversion after which they looked outwardly no different with the exception of the magazine profile, but of course under the wood was a very different story.

On the whole the L8 programme was a complete failure with L8 test groups fired at RSAF Enfield achieving ever so slightly better results than the .303 No. 4 rifle, not much in the way of reward for the development work put in. The L8 T performed no better: the test results of grouping shots fired conflicted with the recorded 4T results from the same pre-converted rifles and with inconsistency running through all the examples converted at all distances test fired. The programme was scrapped with only the magazines being worthy of rescue and they were packed for long-term storage and retired to stores for future use. The newly designed ten round capacity box magazine which accommodated the 7.62 x 51mm rimless ammunition, part numbered CR141A with numbered follower CR1256, was simply an improved box type magazine with feed lips front and rear that retained the follower platform and its spring. The rear left lip also incorporated a small slightly oblong plate spot welded into place which acted as the ejector, the 1965 engraved date being a tangible link to the failed L8 programme.

The secret to the new era of British military sniping lay in an unforeseen place, civilian shooting. At that time many NRA competition shooters were enjoying huge success with No. 4 rifles converted to 7.62 x 51mm calibre. Their rifles

ABOVE: The L42A1 rifle's magazine was the only thing salvageable from the failed L8 programme, its 1965 date giving a clue to this. Note the small square plate on the rear left lip. This replaced the ejector screw used on the pre-conversion 4T receiver.

wore cut down, sporterised fore-ends to accommodate the heavy free floating match barrels they were using. The civilian conversions experimented with various barrel lengths and rifling twist rates which delivered an impressive level of accuracy at all distances. The civilian shooters' success with a rifle RSAF Enfield had already attempted to convert to sniper did not go unnoticed by the army and it became increasingly difficult to ignore. After a short collaboration between the army and the UK's NRA (National Rifle Association) a number of No. 4 Mk1 T rifles were removed from stores in 1969 and sent to RSAF Enfield for conversion to such an incarnation and designated XL42E1, the XL denoting experimental and 42E1 denoted the specification. The

PREVIOUS PAGE: Squatting in a frozen stream, this sniper is clearly having a bad day whilst training in horrendous winter weather. Note the fore-end of his L42 is an Mk2 fore-end retro converted back to Mk1 specification.

ABOVE: Pictured is a 1970s 20 round packaging box of Green Spot 7.62mm L2A2 ammunition.

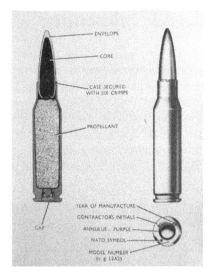
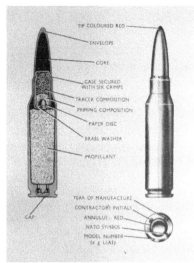

ABOVE: Illustrative diagrams of the 1970s were high quality and detailed. These illustrations of the 7.62mm ammunition feature the L2A2 ball and L5A3 tracer rounds.

new specification closely resembled the rifles of the NRA competition shooters with the inclusion of the No. 32 Mk3 telescope unchanged in how it mounted to the rifle but altered to allow for the flatter trajectory of the NATO 7.62mm ammunition.

Enfield's log shows thirty rifles were converted to XL42E1 specification and it's presumed these rifles were delivered to ITDU (infantry trials development unit) in batches, the first of which was in February 1970.

XL42E1 required full evaluation and in the hands of ITDU the rifles were put through their paces with various barrel lengths and

rifling twist rates in combination with the R.O.F. Radway Green manufactured ammunition designated L2A2. Manufactured to NATO specifications, the bullet was 144 grain (9.33 grams). Later an L2A2 cartridge was produced to tighter tolerances and marketed as Green Spot; this ammunition was used exclusively by snipers, and the name derived from the NATO black spot symbol for standard ball ammunition but was branded Green Spot by Radway Green to denote its higher performance. A replacement scope was also pondered but nothing could, at the time, come near the robustness and reliability of the No.

32. Several of the XL42E1 rifles are in collectors' hands today and some are easily identified by the remnants of the trial designation's engraving still being partly visible while others are more commonly identified by the deep scalloped area where the old trial designation has been removed quite robustly with the new L42A1 designation engraved over the same area. Another clue to the XL42E1 is the small "T" near the redundant ejector screw hole on the receiver wall which is often barred out but still visible on a number of former trials rifles.

ABOVE: The image on the left shows a rare XL42E1 receiver and its designation. Note the old completion "T" mark has been struck out. Also note the ejector screw is still intact. The image on the right shows barrel types trialled by ITDU. The muzzle and foresight arrangement on the left closely resemble that of the final specification.

Rifle 7.62mm L42A1/L1A1 Telescope

The trial and development period was short, mainly as the No. 4 Mk1 T receiver ITDU started their work with was already excellent proof, should it be needed, in the fact that none of the wartime conversion work done by Holland & Holland was altered. The gestation period of the new weapon was relatively short, around six months from start to finish, which is really all it needed to be given. The civilian competitive shooter provided a proven concept for ITDU to transfer into an already existing sniper rifle, and of course the magazine was already manufactured and sitting in stores. The new hand operated bolt action rifle, which was also magazine fed, was given designation L42A1, and was approved for service in August 1970 being allocated the NSN (NATO stores number) B1/1005-99-963-3786.

Technical Specification	
Calibre	7.62mm
Magazine Capacity	10 Rounds
Overall Rifle Length	46.5in
Barrel Length	27.5in
Twist Rate	4 Groove, RH 1 in 12 Twist
Combat Weight	12lb
Iron Sights	Graduated to 1300 Yds
Conversion Approval Date	24th August 1970
Converted By	RSAF Enfield
Scope Mounted	Overbore
Quantity Converted	1020 approx

LEFT: The wrist markings of this L42 show a 1943 wartime dated No. 4 T of BSA manufacture was converted. Note the early BSA wartime code and TR selection marks.

The two L42A1 rifles pictured demonstrate how much the wood sets can vary. One of the rifles still has its original American black walnut No. 4 T wood altered at conversion with an ash cheek rest whereas the other retains its original American black walnut butt stock whilst the fore-end and hand guard are beech. The cheek rest introduces a third wood type which is ash. Note the beech fore-end is an Mk2 retro converted back to Mk1 specification.

ABOVE: The attire of this sniper places him around the mid-1980s. He appears to be wearing a paratrooper's smock, not the very similar looking sniper smock and lightweight jungle DPM trousers. Note his L42 and telescope is shrouded in green sniper tape, an interesting image as this practice is most commonly associated with the L96A1 rifle. Note the GPMG sling improvised to slip over the barrel.

With the new specification rifle approved, RSAF Enfield were not slow to commence production as thirty 1970 dated conversion rifles left Enfield in that year, but they were not delivered to the MoD as you might have expected, but proceeded straight into a Metropolitan Police trial and evaluation process instead. The arrangement with the police was finalised on 26th November 1970 when it was agreed the delivery of the rifles would be made by road no later than 14th December 1970, one week after the production completion date of 7th December 1970. The rifles are recorded as being packed in L39 transit boxes, lightly oiled and ready for use, and on receipt the police had their own armourer conduct an intake inspection and found faults of one description or another on all of the weapons which were listed as:

1. Breech bolt head fouling magazine platform. – All weapons.
2. Front pads loose. – Five weapons.
3. Loose screws in cheek rest. – Five weapons.
4. Hand guards loose and Front lands loose. – Four weapons.
5. Split cheek rest. – One weapon.
6. Badly fitted magazine. – All weapons.
7. Burr on front pad. – One weapon.
8. Butt out of alignment. – One weapon
9. Sticky backsight slide. – One weapon
10. Striker loose. – One weapon.
11. Scale of backsight leaf blurred. – One weapon.
12. Backsight fouling breech charger guide. – One weapon.
13. Foresight protector loose. – One weapon.

14. Telescope – full scale adjustment not available. – Seven weapons.

At the request of the police RSAF Enfield sent two senior armourers to Old Street Police Station to investigate the faults which they did on 13th January 1971, and subsequently many of the faults were dismissed as being acceptable or within specification. The RSAF Enfield report which was later written on 16th February 1971 reduced the faults to a select number of rifles identified as serial numbers X33648, T39794, K3104, T39795, G30582, D37784, M36982, T39853, X31731, R32165, C33151 and P33114. The report went further and blamed the extensive list of faults as being due to the Metropolitan Police armourers not being familiar with the standards specified for the conversion programme and their inexperience as to the methods of

ABOVE: A close-up image of the rifle's designation shows this example carries a 1971 conversion date and although it looks relatively simple fraudsters find recreating these markings very difficult. Note the ejector screw has been omitted; also note the number of stake marks around the screw in the front pad and the bracket's Rose Brothers wartime code just in shot.

sight adjustment. It would appear there was much toing and froing thereafter; the police clearly had much higher expectations and consequently rejected the rifles and terminated the trial.

These rifles next appear in the records as being delivered from RSAF Enfield to Donnington central store in January 1971 which would suggest the police rejection took place almost immediately after the RSAF armourers visit to Old Street Station, after which they then entered military service, almost definitely with the Royal Marines. It's worth noting at this point that one L42, serial number N36862 with scope No. 26138, was sent to

Australia to enter their own sniper rifle trials but subsequently the Australians adopted the Parker-Hale M82 in favour of the L42. The lion's share of the MoD contract was fulfilled in 1971 and the vast majority of examples today carry a 1971 conversion date.

Post 1971 saw smaller batches of converted rifles being delivered to Donnington in 1972, 1974, 1975 1977, 1978 and 1979 and spuriously 1980, but records so far do not support this conversion date. Enfield's own handwritten log shows a total quantity of 1,050 L42 rifles produced but it should also be noted the thirty XL42E1

rifles were entered into the log and then it appears they were entered again after they were converted to full L42A1 specification, so the true number of converted rifles would appear to be closer to 1,020.

The barrel selected was manufactured by Enfield and is 27.5 inches long with a one turn in twelve inch twist rate of rifling, meaning the bullet completes one full rotation as it passes along every twelve inches of barrel. The L42 barrel can be found marked with part number CR1470, is fully tapered in profile and is produced via a cold hammer forging process which resulted in a finish that has been described as being "snakeskin" like.

This was an expensive barrel to produce and was a commercial learning curve for Enfield as several years after the introduction of the L42 the 7.62mm calibre Enforcer was launched and adopted by the UK police. This rifle used a heavy chordal barrel which on first appearances gives the rifle an L42 look about it. In an effort to bring the L42 unit cost down rifles produced after 1971, which is when the main body of the MoD's contract was fulfilled, received the new revised chordal barrel. These barrels were produced from the same highest quality steel but were produced on different

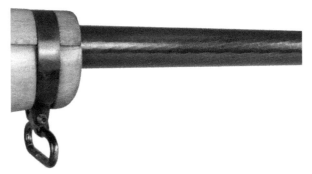

ABOVE: The snakeskin marks of the original Enfield barrel created by the cold hammer forging process.

ABOVE: The curious snakeskin pattern now gone with the introduction of the Chordal barrel. Note the step in the barrel's diameter as it leaves the fore-end created by the machining process.

machinery which could not produce a continuous tapered profile. These barrels are easily recognised by a step in their profile which is situated just as the barrel emerges from the fore-end. The wider diameter length of barrel was hammer forged and the narrow length from the step to the muzzle was machined. The rifling in these barrels is known as chordal and was cut differently with the edges being slightly radius as opposed to a sharp square edged cut of the previous design and was thought to better aid accuracy, particularly long range accuracy, as the chordal style of rifling did not score the bullet as harshly as the alternative style did, which heavily striated the sides of the projectile. The changes to the barrel manufacture process did not have a detrimental effect on the L42's accuracy in any way; it performed the same and the barrel life was comparable to the previous design.

The No. 4 receiver and bolt which had gone through conversion, and which was rated for the eighteen and a half tons pressure of the .303 ammunition in its former life, had to now conform to a new pressure test of nineteen tons for the more powerful 7.62mm ammunition. The pressure bearing parts of the L42

are marked with the acceptance, or certification mark, of 19T which can be found on the bolt head, bolt handle and at the rear of the receiver on the flat to the right of the entrance to the bolt chamber. The wood of the L42 was in the specification meant to be its original walnut as worn in its 4T guise and indeed many still are today, but the re-machining of the inner chamber to accommodate the new magazine and the alteration to the barrel channel in the fore-end to allow the new barrel to be fully floating was in many cases too much for the old walnut to bear and many failed.

A cheap and hastily arranged solution was found in beech wood which, as at the beginning of WW2, was at the time a cheap hardwood in plentiful supply and being hard wood was capable but not ideal, as I wonder why it was never stained to subdue its extremely pale appearance. The lack of effort to improve its aesthetics only attracted the attention of those at the time who argued that as it is as pale as new pine it should never have been selected and a vocal disapproval was heard of how the L42 programme was being done on the cheap. There must have been

some justification in the complaints as it is the one weapon with so much emphasis on camouflage and concealment and yet new beech wood is almost white in appearance when new. It was common for the L42 to be a mismatch of several different wood types. Some L42s kept their entire walnut wood sets, the fore-end and hand guard being cut half of one inch in front of the stock band and all kept their walnut butt stocks commonly fitted with an ash or beech cheek rest. The odd elm cheek rest was occasionally encountered, however there were many that received "blond" beech fore-ends and hand guards and by the late eighties many wore a mixture of all of the above.

Three styles of hand guard were fitted. The hand guard from Rifle No. 8 of which the finger grooves for grip travelled the entire length of the guard, a smooth hand guard with no grooves cut for grip, and the more common style that carried finger grooves that stopped before the stock band. The early to mid-eighties saw a severe shortage of replacement wood sets for the L42A1 sniper rifle, particularly replacement fore-ends, which was remedied by the Mk2 fore-end found on the L39

 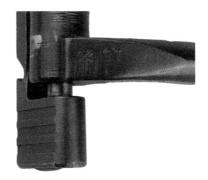 

ABOVE: The 19T with cross flags certification mark can be seen here on the bolt head, bolt handle and receiver. Note the cluster of marks on the bolt head which tell of the rifle's history. The large hand engraved cross flags are a .303 certification mark which, coupled with the low bolt head size number (out of shot), indicates this is probably the original 4T bolt head modified at conversion. The 19T can be seen accompanied by a neatly engraved cross flag mark that is relevant to the 19T mark. Stamped slightly over the 1 of the 19T, the London Proof House mark can be seen with its crown sitting over the letters CP denoting Crown Proof. This proof mark was applied when the rifle was sold out of service; the Birmingham proof mark of BNP is more often encountered.

LEFT: Even though the walnut fore-ends may have failed there was no requirement to change the butt stock, therefore American black walnut butts are commonly found on the L42 regardless. Note this very pleasing ash cheek rest which in all likelihood came with the butt stock at conversion.

ABOVE: Pictured are the two most commonly encountered hand guards on the L42. Both featured are beech wood, however original walnut examples are also regularly encountered.

ABOVE: Common markings found on the underside of the hand guard. C. Moon & Co, the manufacturer, as well as the Enfield EFD stamp and date, 72 in this case.

target rifle retro converted back to Mk1 specification. By the mid to late eighties and with the introduction of the L96A1 sniper rifle looming there were no new, second hand, or Mk2 retro converted fore-ends left in the system. It has been suggested that in the final days of L42 service rifles with heavily worn fore-ends were patch repaired with the use of an epoxy bedding material, however only one rifle to date has emerged with such a material around the receiver area within the fore-end. It is also reported that several rifles examined at the point of disposal were fitted with unmodified Mk2 fore-ends.

In 1971 Donnington central stores was holding a significant number of newly converted L42A1 sniper rifles and yet the army had long disengaged itself from sniping. Clearly there was a plan being played out from on high but whichever way things would be played out, the situation arrived at

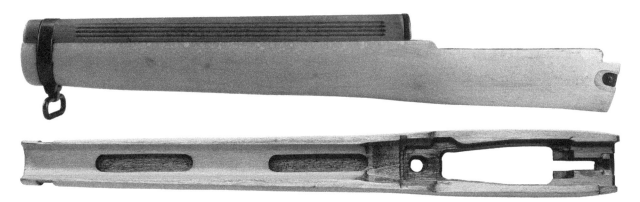

ABOVE: A replacement beech Mk2 fore-end retro converted back to Mk1 specification. A view complete as it would appear on the weapon and a view internally illustrating the degree of machining necessary for the 7.62mm conversion.

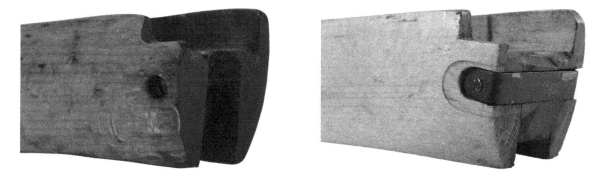

ABOVE: A detailed view at the rear of both an unmodified and modified Mk2 fore-end. Note the modified example has been in-filled at the rear as well as externally to accept the tie strap and rivet. When fitted to a weapon it is these external in-filled areas behind the oval ends of the tie strap that give it away.

ABOVE: Spot the sniper. Although this sniper is well camouflaged his uncamouflaged weapon and scope can clearly be seen. Note the very pale fore-end and hand guard. The trained spotter would be looking for geometric shapes and colour change.

ABOVE: Snipers on the range in complete darkness training with the IWS night sight fitted to their L42s. Training at night under realistic conditions of darkness was wholly necessary as when darkness falls everything changes, even the simplest of tasks taken for granted in daylight.

ABOVE: A 1979 copy of the SASC sniper instructor's course notes. *(Courtesy Nigel Greenaway)*

the same point, which meant there was some catching up to do as no trained snipers existed and neither did any instructors to train them within the army. Whilst RSAF Enfield methodically produced batches of newly converted rifles which filled the racks of central stores, the army turned to the navy for a solution.

The Royal Marines had never ceased or wound back their sniper capability and still ran a tough annual sniper cadre as well as continuation training of their trained snipers at unit level. The army became fully active in sniping again in 1973 with a sniper training wing established at Warminster, Wiltshire on the edge of Salisbury Plain, with all of its senior instructors having been trained by the Royal Marines at CTCRM (Commando Training Centre Royal Marines) in 1972. This newly trained core of instructors went on to devise a six and a half week course to train the infantry's regimental instructors. The course involved an intensive live firing week in Otterburn where the students got to grips with judging distance and

wind by day as well as at night in the pitch black of Otterburn training area with night sights as well as the conventional No. 32 telescope under illume provided by flares.

The students who passed this course would return to their respective units where they would, in turn, be responsible for the training of their battalion's own snipers at unit level. A second course was also established at Blair Atholl, Perthshire, Scotland exclusively for members of the Special Air Service (SAS) and Special Boat Service (SBS) and ran predominantly through the 1970s. New life had once again been breathed into army sniping; a new infrastructure and a new weapon was a good start, although there were serious issues with the standard of shooting within the army.

Selection of candidates for sniper training was being hampered by the poor standard of individual marksmanship, the standard being compared to that of the IRA's at the time. The issue had the Army Rifle Association scratching its head

and asking how the army shooting team could be winning all available competition silver all over the world and yet the general standard of shooting was so poor. 1974 saw members of the Army Eight shooting team, the best eight shots in the whole of the British Army, brought in to address the problem and assist in finding a solution. The shooting team found the pressures applied to them in competition shooting had parallels to the pressure one would experience during operational shooting so the solution to raise the standard lay in more competition style shooting events at unit level as well as the APWT (Annual Personal Weapon Test) being tailored to present the shooter with a more challenging series of practices during the test.

Overall and going forward the training the soldier was subjected to when training with live ammunition became more challenging; timed exposures of targets as well as moving targets which were engaged from different distances and firing positions were built into

ABOVE: Snipers of the 3rd Battalion the Royal Green Jackets pictured just after winning the UKLF sniper concentration in 1988. Note several rifles are fitted with a GPMG sling.

the continuation training within the infantry in order to apply the desired level of pressure on the soldier.

In the years that followed, sniping was at unit level a victim of priorities within any given battalion. Regiments such as the Royal Marines and Parachute Regiment who were headquartered in the UK and who had at least one battalion based in the UK at any given time in Spearhead readiness maintained a full and robust sniper training programme. However, it was not uncommon for regiments such as those operating in a heavy mechanised role as part of BAOR (British Army of the Rhine) to relax their commitments to sniper training and to the use of snipers. Such decisions were made by the units themselves and I suspect the level of sniper activity from one unit to another could, and did, vary. An example of this is the Third Battalion the Royal Green Jackets who whilst serving as a mechanised infantry battalion in Celle, Germany, ceased training snipers for nearly four years. The last course ran in 1983 and the next took place in January/ February 1987 before the battalion was re-rolled with a move back to the UK, whereby the battalion recommenced regular training of the battalion's snipers and went on to win the UKLF (United Kingdom Land Forces) sniper concentration held in Catterick, UK in 1988.

Telescope, No. 32 Mk3, L1A1 and Backup Sights

The No. 32 Mk3 telescope and bracket was largely unchanged, the bracket still bearing the WW2 manufacturer code and often a faded No. 4 T serial number not quite cleaned away by the bead blasting at conversion, replaced by the newly stamped or engraved serial number of the L42 rifle it was being paired with. The scope itself was subject to a complete refurbishment with improved waterproofing and was engraved with the new markings that incorporated the instrument into the NATO stores system. The elevation drum is marked with "M" denoting the telescope has been altered to the metric system allowing for the trajectory of the 7.62mm ammunition. The old OS number, OS2039A, is now barred out and the NSN, 1240-99-963-2063, TEL. STRT. STG L1A1 and new OS2429GA number applied. Zeroing of the sight was done at 100 metres with the elevation drum set at 1.

The rear leaf sight, it would appear, was never considered for complete change during conversion to account for the effects of the

trajectory of the new ammunition; in fact the 1971 User Handbook which accompanied the rifle in its transit chest informs the prospective user that the sight is graduated in fifty-yard increments from 200 to 1,300 yards marked every 100 with even numbers on the left and odd numbers on the right of the leaf. The User Handbook goes on to inform the user that the leaf is unchanged in any way from that of how it served the No. 4 T rifle and was calibrated in yards to suit the .303 inch Mk7 ammunition, making accurate placement of the MPI (Mean Point of Impact) with 7.62mm ammunition unachievable at all ranges marked on the leaf. Therefore to minimise the effects of this it was recommended the sniper zero the backup sights with an accurately placed MPI at 400 metres which would guarantee a hit on a man-sized target from 200 to 500 metres with an MPI range of half an inch low to two and a half inches high of his point of aim. To make this possible the slider on the leaf which carries the aperture for aiming and graticule lines that

enable the sniper to select a target range on the leaf were altered so when set to 400 the prescribed zero method could be achieved. The left side of the slider body is marked with a bold letter "M" denoting the metric alteration has been carried out to accommodate the new 7.62mm round. Why at this juncture the rear sight was not completely remodelled, or the existing ground and recalibrated, is unclear.

Maybe the naysayers were right and the conversion was an economical one, or maybe there was data collated from Korea and WW2 that told another story regarding the sniper's use of his backup sights and the resultant arrangement was an acceptable compromise.

The foresight fitted to the L42 was that of the No. 4 T although in a more standardised fashion, in that every rifle received a split block band equipped with a solid foresight blade. The block band fitted onto a section of barrel at the muzzle end that was reduced in diameter to accept the Mk2 foresight protector

ABOVE: The No. 32 scope in its L1A1 livery. The letter "M" on the elevation drum denotes the telescope has been calibrated for the metric 7.62mm ammunition. Note the markings on the scope tube applied at conversion. The NSN and new L1A1 designation are engraved on the opposite side of the tube to where the original WW2 marks are found.

originally used on the narrower No. 4 T barrel.

The lens caps remained the same. The ocular and objective lens caps connected by a single leather strap marked with the caps' own NSN, V5/1240-99-961-7423, and with a small Sam brown stud which allowed a little adjustment for releasing the cups from the scope, however, anyone who has any experience of these lens caps with either the No. 4 T or the L42 will know they require no adjustment as the leather of the lens caps suffered the same stretching with use as the 1907 pattern sling and often fitted so poorly it would not stay on the scope when carried from A to B.

ABOVE: A sniper armed with his L42A1 sniper rifle takes aim. He uses the shadow of the trees and takes advantage of the erratic nature of the cover around himself to blend in.

ABOVE: The Poole manufactured slider has been engraved with a letter "M" which denotes the rear sight has been metric modified. Also note the CR part number. All of the L42A1 rifle's parts have a Carbine/Rifle part number. The foresight arrangement of the L42 was that which Holland & Holland originally specified on the 4T.

ABOVE: The rear sights of both the 4T, left, and L42, right, are illustrated here. Note the leaf of both are numbered in yards however the engraved graticule lines that correspond to these numbers are different. The revised L42 lines are much lower on the slider.

L1A1 Telescope, NSN 1240-99-963-2063

Technical Specification	
Manufacturer	AK & S
Length	11in
Weight in the mount	2lb
Objective Lens DIA	19mm
Field of View	9 degrees
Magnification	3 X
Reticle	Post & Wire
Range Graduations	100–1000 Yds
Focus Capability	Fixed
Sunshade	No
Lateral Adjustment	16-0-16 Drum
Mount Type	Double

ABOVE: The L1A1 converted No. 8 Mk1 carry case. The conversion allowed for the inclusion of a metal pocket in the lid and for a sprung steel clip between the scope bracket mounting bosses. Neither were ever used, and neither were they omitted from the specification of the case as they were still present in cases being manufactured well into the eighties. Note the 44 pattern carry strap: this example has a shoulder pad which closely resembles the shoulder padding on other equipment from the 1980s. Its design has elasticated loops allowing it to slide onto the strap.

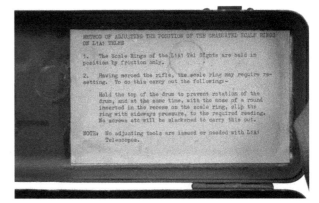

RIGHT: Notes to the adjustment of the L1A1 range scales on the elevation and windage drums. The illustrated label is typically hand typed and glued to the metal lid.

The L1A1 conversion took place using Mk3 No. 32 telescopes and with the exception of the metric recalibration it is the same telescope with improved waterproofing. Note the scope bracket on this example is a Dalgleish manufactured bracket, given away by its flat surfaces and square edges. Also the traditional post and wire reticle is still going strong in the L1A1 telescope.

ABOVE: Typical markings commonly found on the leather lens caps manufactured for the Telescope Straight Sighting L1A1.

ABOVE: A sniper from a Gurkha battalion gets behind his L42 to offer the media a photograph opportunity.

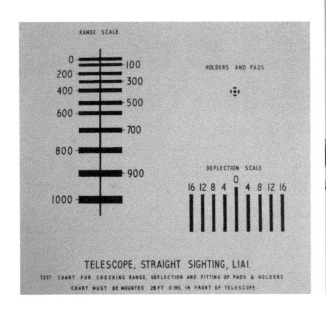

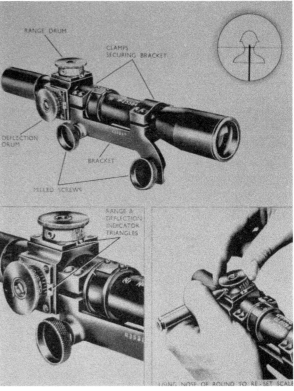

ABOVE: As with the No. 32 telescope fitted to the 4T, a range and deflection scale was used to function test the telescope. Note the instruction to place the scale 28ft away from the telescope.

ABOVE: A 1970s educational illustration lists the key components of the L1A1 telescope and bracket. The drawing illustrates the use of a round of ammunition to slip the graduated scale.

The No. 8 Mk1 carry case received an internal modification to allow for lens tissues and a small brush to be installed, however the CES of the rifle allowed for a plastic screw cap bottle which housed a soft brush for lens maintenance. The internal modification was redundant from day one; even so the L1A1 scope tin continued to be manufactured right into the eighties unchanged, still including unofficially obsolete components.

The modification changed the designation of the case to Telescope Straight Sighting Cased L1A1 but having said that, there were plenty of L42A1 rifles in service with standard unmodified No. 8 Mk1 cases carrying their telescopes and many of the examples still around today stand testament to this.

The leather carry strap for the No. 8 case was also joined by an officially accepted alternative web strap which was actually a 1944 pattern utility strap and was generally around sixty inches long.

Towards the very end of the L42's service life when supplies of both the leather and 44 pattern straps were becoming exhausted, the nylon GS Aerolex strap could be found on the L1A1 carry case.

Complete Equipment Schedule

In 1970 the 1907 American loop pattern sling and Scout Regiment spotting scope passed from the 4T straight into the transit chest of the L42, and the sling remained until superseded around 1975 when the sling, small arms, nylon, NSN 1010-99-132-3199 was introduced and became synonymous with the rifle. The new sling, even though it had its critics, was far superior to the aging leather 1907 pattern which stretched when pulled taut and most annoyingly could become extremely slippery when subjected to a good downpour or a stalk through wet foliage. The nylon sling was much wider and constructed from extremely tough woven nylon. It was in two pieces like the former leather sling but adjusted by the use of a sturdy clasped buckle designed to be easily operated with cold numb fingers. The sprung steel clasps at each end for clipping onto the rifle were coated in plastic in order to eliminate any metallic noise the metal clasp and sling swivel might make against each other during a stalk.

The CES included a plastic screw cap bottle which actually belonged to the CES of the Carl Gustav 84mm anti-tank weapon cleaning kit which is Swedish in origin although the NSN, M3/1005-12-142-8021, on the ordnance stores label often carries the two digit NIIN (National Item Identification Number) as 12, denoting Germany as the NATO country of origin. The plastic bottle housed a soft sable hair brush for dusting the lenses of the scope and it was common practice to keep a small piece of lens cloth in the bottle with the brush. Both brush and bottle are today rare and command hefty prices when they surface. The brush has since been reproduced by Heckler & Koch as part of their SA80 upgrade and these brushes are in appearance the same but lack

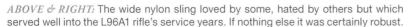
ABOVE & RIGHT: The wide nylon sling loved by some, hated by others but which served well into the L96A1 rifle's service years. If nothing else it was certainly robust.

LEFT: Lens brush bottle, lens brush and small patch of lens cloth illustrated here laid out. Note the RAOC stores label still present on the bottle.

RIGHT: A shortened lens brush illustrated next to an original uncut example which belongs to the IWS schedule of equipment.

a certain quality of the old original brushes which were in fact lens brushes produced for the IWS night sight. The handles of these brushes were long and to fit the bottle were chopped short without any finesse; they just needed to fit the bottle. So when found today they can be recognised by the varying lengths and rough cut finish.

The cleaning kit of the L42A1 rifle was a slightly improved No. 4 rifle cleaning kit. The pullthrough, NSN B1/1005-99-960-0113, was the Mk7 introduced with the SLR and incorporated an angled cut end which could be used as a tool for the removal of carbon deposits. The half fluid ounce oil bottles, NSN B1/8125-99-961-9248, were of wartime vintage, the screw cap lid incorporating an application spoon, and were often found as black plastic or the later transparent orange type. Not officially part of the L42 CES equipment, a phosphor bronze chamber cleaning brush was also included and was attached to the SLR multi tool for this purpose. Both of these items are not listed in the CES booklet but were included by the snipers themselves and became almost as common as the official weapon cleaning tools the CES catered for. A small wood or plastic handled bristle brush, NSN B2/1005-99-961-7994, was present as was a length of 4 x 2" cleaning

cloth which would have been part of the cleaning kit as standard; all was housed in a modified metal No. 4 rifle cleaning kit tin, NSN B1/1005-99-960-0065, the dubious barrel cleaning gauze and small brush clip in the lid having been removed. The beech wood chamber cleaning stick, NSN B2/1005-99-961-7729, also passed straight from the 4T CES to the L42, an excellent piece of equipment that held a piece of 4 x 2" cleaning cloth in its slotted head, basic but extremely effective in its

role, so much so that it was passed again, this time straight to the L96 CES. The L5A1 bracket, or IWS bracket, for mounting Weapon Sight Image Intensified, L1A1 onto the L42, was also part of the CES equipment of the L42 rifle. In contrast to the brackets used for mounting the IWS scope on the section weapons, these brackets were part of the IWS telescope's own equipment being stored in its transit case.

Literature carried with the weapon was limited to a User

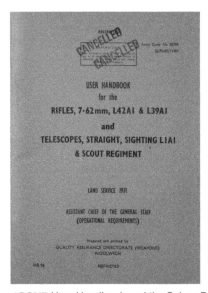

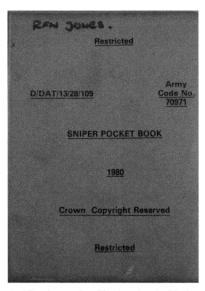

ABOVE: User Handbook and the Sniper Pocket Book remained in the chest with the rifle for reference by the sniper as he required. Note the pocket book is dated 1980. These small books which contain shooting data as well as an aide memoire are often found with a 1973 date. Also note the restricted classification of this example of User Handbook has been stamped with "cancelled".

Handbook which covered the L42A1 sniper rifle, L39A1 target rifle and Scout Regiment Telescope detailing the rifle and Scout Regiment Telescope's basic operating information, use and care. The handbook also covered standard issued equipment that supported the weapon including how to correctly attach the 1907 pattern sling, and is today sometimes encountered with a stapled amendment regarding the sling information that became effective after the issue of the nylon sling. General information regarding the L1A1 scope and ammunition types was also covered. These 1971 dated booklets which were originally supplied with the rifle were on occasions lost, or after years of service were heavily worn and were replaced by administrative copies of which the print quality was not as good as the professionally printed originals. Today this practice is common and the departments responsible have a title, Graphics Department, where any current manual can be reproduced and bound for the end user.

Additionally the sniper was issued a Sniper Pocket Book. The pocket book first appeared in 1973 when sniper training recommenced and remained as standard issue to the sniper long into the future. The pocket book was in two parts; part one enabled the sniper to record his shooting data and part two was a tactical aide memoire specific to the sniper. The CES booklet was also kept with the transit chest as a standard document governing the contents of the chest.

ABOVE: The rifle is laid out and illustrated with all of the equipment the sniper would have used in conjunction with this weapon and additionally it is also illustrated packed in its chest with the official CES equipment. Once the rifle and its immediate equipment was housed in the transit chest there was very little space for anything the sniper may have wished to include. Note the position of the lens brush bottle which was vulnerable to damage against the rifle butt.

ABOVE: Hidden for over twenty years, these markings were a surprise and illuminated a piece of history. The chest is marked with the UIN of 3RGJ and the markings that lay under the paint were expected to relate to the unit identification number. However once revealed it would appear the rifle had been loaned by the 3rd to the 2nd Battalion for exercise Pond Jump West, a brigade exercise that took place in Canada.

The means of carrying the L42A1 sniper rifle is, when you scratch beneath the surface, more varied than you think. The whole ensemble was housed in a robust transit chest, NSN B1/1005-99-963-5800, designed with the input of the Royal Marines and constructed from twelve millimetre thick marine grade plywood. The chest is designed to give safe transport to the rifle and all its CES equipment of which each individual piece has its own storage place within the chest and is laid out in such a manner that if anything is missing it is easily spotted.

There is very little spare space once everything is packed and the only real design fault with the chest was the positioning of the plastic lens brush bottle on the inside of the lid, where it conflicted with the rifle butt stock, and if the lid of the chest was dropped or slammed closed the plastic bottle had a tendency to shatter. After many years of service the chests are often found today in a battered condition and painted, many layers applied by the various regiments who used them.

The suggestion that a rifle was owned and used by one regiment from beginning to end is simply fiction due to many factors, breakages being the main driving factor behind a well-travelled L42 rifle. If the repair was beyond the remit of the unit armourer the rifle and all of its CES would be packed in its chest and sent to a command workshop and a replacement would be supplied to the respective unit who would in all likelihood never see that particular rifle again. L42 rifles that were with units based in Germany will have served amongst the BAOR (British Army of the Rhine) regiments, only being handed to the next regiment taking up residence, and repairs would have been carried out by a command workshop in Germany.

A replacement rifle or rifles being taken over would have the regiment's own markings applied to the transit chests, with the previous unit's details struck out, so removing the paint often reveals the details of the last unit the rifle served with. Commonly lurking beneath the splodges of paint is a UIN (Unit Identification Number) and often a shipping address, amongst others.

The soft carry case of the L42 is a less straightforward picture and appears quite ad hoc in places. The 1971 User Handbook illustrates the rifle laid out with full CES equipment which includes a standard U.S. manufactured light beige Springfield case which was in all likelihood commandeered for the photograph as the soft case which was needed was not yet decided upon. The case which does still exist and has most commonly been associated with the rifle is a modified No. 4 case which further suggests the American Springfield case pictured in the handbook was never issued with the rifle in the first place, well not in the seventies at least, although in 1973 a copy of the Springfield case was produced which was constructed in a green webbing material the same as that of the 1958 pattern personal load carrying equipment of the day. With the exception of the buckle on the flap closure which was typically British, it was a straight copy and was marked with NSN, B1/1005-99-961-9515, and a 1973 date which was also accompanied by a maker's mark and broad arrow. These cases seem to have only been manufactured once in 1973 and are not common, unlike the No. 4 case which is often encountered with the addition of a web shoulder strap

and an extra six inches added to the length to accommodate the L42's longer barrel. This modification appears to be standard and was more than likely done by Remploy.

With the decision made to alter a quantity of No. 4 bags to suit the new L42A1 sniper rifle, it is staggering that the age-old problem first encountered with the No. 4 T rifle of not being able to insert the rifle with scope fitted was not finally being addressed. The new manufactured Springfield case was, one would have thought, the ideal juncture at which a carry case for the new rifle capable of meeting all its needs would have been designed, but even this case did not allow the rifle to be carried with the scope fitted. It would seem, though much later, that the No. 4 case was modified further as a small number have been noted to have been fitted with an additional panel which does allow the rifle to fit with the L1A1 scope fitted, however it is not clear if this modification was done at unit level or on a wider, larger scale with Remploy; the quantity in existence today would suggest

not. Curiously the eighties did see the U.S. manufactured Springfield carry case appear unmodified in any way to accommodate a scope and carried only a U.S. maker's mark; interestingly these cases which were observed as a batch by the author were all formerly cases from RAF Regiment L42 rifles.

An additional transit case exists for the L42 about which little is known, mainly as so few were ever manufactured, but it's widely accepted the cases were produced for SBS and Royal Marine use and the construction does appear to have been an attempt to create a watertight means of transporting the rifle. The robust fibreglass case has four clasps which bring the two halves together against a dense foam seal and contains heavy dense foam moulded panels to accept an L42 rifle specifically with L1A1 telescopic sight fitted. The foam sections are the same material as that found in the IWS case, and bear the same Q.E.D. manufacture mark. This alternative case does not house the CES of the rifle and gives very

limited provision for ancillaries in the form of a single square recess which accepts two military twenty-round boxes of ammunition.

The opposite end of the case has a recess moulded to cater for what is presumed to be a specific type of binocular, the model of which is currently unknown to the author. One heavily used example of this case has also been noted to have had an improvised modification to the foam either side of the L42 moulded barrel channel where it has been removed to widen the channel, and a second recess created for a foresight protector was also created. This particular case was altered to carry a No. 4 T rifle which the Royal Marines were still operating right up until 1973 alongside their L42 rifles. The case bears the handwritten serial number 85044, or 35044, which has been checked against the L42 register where it does not appear, therefore it is assumed to be the serial number of the No. 4 T it was improvised for.

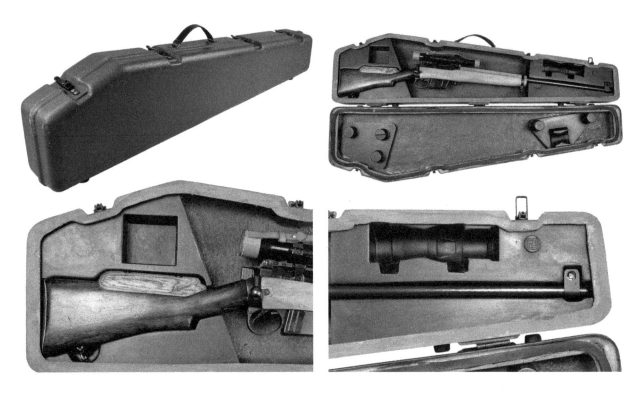

ABOVE: Carrying systems for the L42A1 sniper rifle were very limited and for the field army were limited to the transit case, or soft rifle bag. SF units also had the luxury of this fibreglass case which housed only the rifle and a binocular of some description. Royal Marine units favoured this case the most as great efforts were made in its manufacture to make it waterproof. The SAS also used the exact same case again lined to house a Tikka Finlander M55 rifle. Note the QED manufacturer mark, the same manufacturer who made the IWS case.

Observation and Spotting Equipment

The three draw Scout Regiment Telescope, NSN V5/1240-99-963-0493, remained as part of the rifles CES for the rifle's entire service life with a number being refurbished in the eighties. The refurbishment incorporated the brass tubes being painted black and the body and sunshade had its leather covering replaced with vulcanised rubber,

ABOVE: This example of the SRT is typically marked and was manufactured by KEC (Kodak Eastman Company). Instead of being bound in the plain leather of earlier models this example has a vulcanised grip finish and still bears its black subdued finish.

ABOVE: A 1970s educational illustration identifying the key components of the Scout Regiment Telescope.

ABOVE: A scarce green plastic moulded carry case for the SRT is illustrated next to the traditional leather case and carry strap.

ABOVE: Two NSNs were applied to the case and not to be confused with each other as one referred to the telescope's case itself and the other to the complete cased ensemble.

furthermore many of the leather carry cases were embossed with Case, Telescope, Scout Regiment.

The very early eighties also saw a green moulded plastic case introduced which entered service as the leather cases perished beyond economical repair. The case was marked with two black and silver foil-like stickers at opposing ends, the top marked with the NSN of the actual case, 1240-99-966-0837, and the bottom sticker was marked with the NSN of the complete assembly

and new designation, Telescope Straight, Cased, L1A1. 1240-99-962-2031. These green plastic cases are particularly rare today as late seventies, early eighties plastic moulding technology was not what it is today and they were extremely vulnerable to splitting at the seams that run along each side under the carry strap.

Binoculars made available to snipers were WW2 vintage 6 x 30mm Bino Prism No. 2 Mk3 binoculars unchanged with the exception

of a post-war refurbishment and the removal of the wartime date and maker's mark; details of the right hand lens graticule marks remained with the addition of the NSN V6/1240-99-962-3737 where the date and maker's mark were formerly. The L42 sniper's means of observing and locating his enemy was unchanged from that of the WW2 sniper.

The rifle for the era was an accurate one well supported with a well thought-out CES including

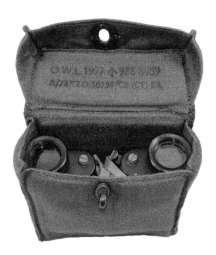
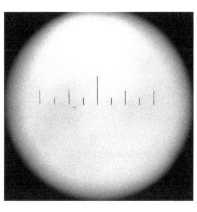

ABOVE & RIGHT: Still in service as late as the early nineties, the 6 x 30 prismatic binocular of WW2 vintage is pictured with the correct 1958 pattern case of the seventies and eighties. Note the ranging graticules are still present and the WW2 date and maker's mark has been removed, replaced with a NATO optical stores number.

ABOVE: A sniper platoon on the ranges putting their L42 rifles through their paces. The images show the firers practising the Hawkins position from a fire trench, as well as in a full prone position. It may just be a range shoot but all are fully clad in their ghillie suits so they are fully accustomed to operating in this type of attire. Note the spotter in the first image is using the prismatic binocular.

ABOVE: Thirty years on and the accuracy of the L42 is still very much evident as illustrated here. This 15-round group on this Hun's Head Figure 14 target was shot at 200 yards.

observation optics which may have been getting on in age, but still extremely effective due to their quality. The end result was a rifle capable of good accuracy which could deliver deadly fire much further out than British sniper doctrine taught or practised; deadly fire out to 600 yards and harassment fire out to 800 yards were taught and adhered to. During the rifle's service it was, on the range, pushed out to and tested at 1,000 yards many times and it was indeed common knowledge amongst snipers that their weapon was capable of more than was taught but the official doctrine remained as it was considered repeatable and what could be performed with consistency by an individual who could pass the sniper cadre. Collectors and enthusiasts today take their L42 rifles to the range and use them successfully at 1,000 yards with no problems whatsoever, putting rounds through a Figure 11 target; although at this range the No. 32 L1A1 scope with its x3 magnification is a handicap, with a little practice it is perfectly achievable.

The L42A1 sniper rifle did not have to wait long before its services were called upon, seeing service in Dhofar in the early to mid-seventies after which its existence was largely involved with the endless training connected with the Cold War until its deployment to the Falklands conflict with Argentina in 1982. The latter conflict was the rifle's finest hour but possibly brought about the beginning of the end for the L42 and although the L42A1 sniper rifle did deadly work and was a particular specialist at night in combination with the IWS night vision sight, due to the WW2 dated equipment being mainly wood and metal it suffered in the sub-zero temperatures and the persistent inclement wet environment. This led the MoD post-conflict to begin the search for the L42's replacement just twelve years into its service, however the evaluation and procurement process would draw the L42's service life out significantly.

The MoD's decision may have also been influenced by the success the Americans were having with their M40 programme. The U.S.M.C (United States Marine Corps)

used the Remington Model 700, designating it M40, in Vietnam. Like the L42 it was a rifle of wood and metal, however in the early seventies they improved the system by replacing the wood stock with a composite fibreglass stock which brought huge benefits, the main being the composite material is thermally stable and will not shrink and expand in varying environmental conditions unlike a wooden stock which in such conditions will alter the zero of the weapon as the wood moves. The M40 became the M40A1 after the modification and

22 SAS
DHOFAR, OMAN. 1974.

ABOVE: The author's own artistic impression of a famed photograph depicting a Special Air Service trooper with his L42A1 sniper rifle across his lap during the Dhofar campaign in 1974.

an example as such was supplied to Warminster by the USMC for UK trials. It was entered and tested extensively by the Small Arms School Corps, and that very example still resides today at Warminster as part of the SASC collection. I believe the advancements the Americans were making were not lost on the MoD as post the Falklands conflict things moved swiftly towards the L42 replacement.

Weapon Sight Image Intensified, L1A1

The IWS (individual weapon sight), as it was abbreviated, was NSN coded Z7/5855-99-966-1132 and brought a new dynamic to sniping. The night vision telescope entered service in 1970 around the same time the first of the L42A1 sniper rifles were being delivered to central stores so it was paired with the L42 from the beginning, giving the sniper system an enhanced role from that of the No. 4 T it was converted from. However it took a decade before the L42/IWS combination would really prove its worth under the conditions the equipment was designed and built for. The Falklands conflict in 1982 was a short but vicious clash of British and Argentine forces; the most ultimate of human responses to resolve a dispute of territory was sanctioned, which involved everything from basic brutal hand-to-hand fighting with fixed bayonets

ABOVE: The L5A1 bracket otherwise known as the J bracket, or simply IWS bracket. Note all of the contact points on these brackets were not painted and were left with their phosphate finish exposed in order for collimation to remain consistent with wear.

to the use of technologically advanced missiles.

The Falkland Islands has been British territory since 1892 which has been disputed by Argentina for most of that time without military intervention. Argentina was in 1982 ruled by a military junta at the head of which was General Leopoldo Galtieri whose popularity was rapidly fading. In an attempt to boost his ratings and get the people back on side he hatched a plan to retake the Falkland Islands and bring the territory under Argentine rule, and therefore unleashed his forces with an invasion of the Islands on 2nd April 1982. A small garrison of Royal Marines were stationed on the Islands who with limited resources bloodied the nose of the invading force but were ultimately overrun and captured. The British response was the formation of a naval task force which had to carry everything needed to retake the Islands from

8,000 miles away. The battle plan was originally a very modern one designed to swiftly defeat the Argentine forces that by the time of the British arrival had chosen their ground and prepared fixed defensive positions.

The British planned to deliver the fighting units to each battle across the Islands by helicopter where fresh, well-equipped troops would overrun the Argentine positions, regroup and then do it all again, however the old adage "A good plan is a flexible plan" was never more applicable than to the British assault on the Islands. The helicopters that were the lynchpin in the plan, along with vast amounts of small arms ammunition, were being carried on the requisitioned cargo ship *Atlantic Conveyor* when on 25th May it was hit by two Argentine Exocet missiles which sank her along with six Wessex helicopters and five RAF Chinook helicopters before

the retaking of the Islands could even get underway. The plan had to change and quickly reverted to what British infantrymen were so good at: tabbing, or yomping in Royal Marine language. By day troops advanced to contact, covering large distances and carrying everything on their backs, and then when they reached the objective they fought a battle against relatively fresh defending troops. The Argentineans chose to defend a range of peaks across the Islands where they dug in, placing their defensive positions overlooking well selected arcs of fire. The British largely chose to advance by day through Argentine artillery, mortar and sniper fire, reaching their objectives in time to commence a night-time attack. Much of the fighting was done in the dark hours when the L42 equipped with a IWS night vision sight came into its own, doing a great deal of deadly work and proving to be

LEFT: The urban filter prevented damage to the IWS from urban street lighting.

RIGHT: The reticle of the IWS was a multi weapon reticle which was used in conjunction with all the weapons the scope was made available to.

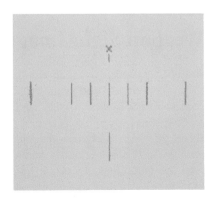

an effective combination which Argentine forces quickly learned of.

The weapon sight fitted to the rifle via the same two scope pads the No. 32 scope used but was mounted on its own L5A1 bracket, NSN B1/1005-99-964-3254, with the use of two STANAG (Standardization Agreement) screws. The IWS bracket then screwed to the scope pads with similar large thumb wheel screws as the No. 32 scope bracket.

The scope was housed in its own rather large transit case that stored the scope and all its associated equipment such as the soft carry case, spare batteries, lens brush and User Handbook, all of which had their own respective storage space within the transit case. The main compartment of the case housed the IWS itself along with four section weapon brackets, enabling it to be mounted on the GPMG L7A1 machine gun, AR 15 Armalite, 84mm

Carl Gustav L14 anti-tank weapon and the SLR L1A1 rifle. Interestingly the User Handbook, Weaponsight, Image Intensified, L1A1 1970, lists the above brackets and makes reference to a bracket for the sniper rifle which reads "A mount for the sniper rifle is now undergoing development" which when it arrived in the form of the L5A1 bracket became part of the L42's own inventory of CES equipment.

The sight unit is powered by a large single mercury battery of 6.75v. On occasions when the IWS sight was deployed to urban areas such as Northern Ireland the objective lens was equipped with an urban filter, NSN Z7/5855-99-967-4180, to protect the internal tube from the damaging effects of street lighting. Street lighting as well as bright natural light could at best leave black burnt spots in the field of view when operated or at worst

could completely burn the internal tube out, rendering the device useless.

For the purposes of zeroing to a weapon the scope came equipped with a heavy rubber lens cover which was not to be removed from the scope in daylight conditions whether the device was turned on or off and is marked to that effect. The lens cover had a pin hole in its centre which was sufficient to allow enough safe light into the device under daylight conditions, allowing the device to be zeroed to a weapon under live firing conditions. The IWS weapon sight was zeroed at a range of 200 metres in order for the reticle, which was a multi weapon reticle, to correspond with the recommended aiming points in conjunction with the L2A2 NATO 144 grain (9.33 grams) round.

Weapon Sight Image Intensified, L1A1
NSN Z7/5855-99-966-1132

Technical Information	
Weaponsight (with Adapter Bracket Fitted):	
Height	18.4cm (7.25 in)
Length	47.6cm (18.75in)
Weight	2.9kg (6.6lb)

Technical Data:	
Battery	6.5v Mercury
Inverter	Canned Unit, Input 6.75v dc output 2.7 kV (nominal) Peak to Peak at 1600 Hz.

Optical:	
Eyepiece Focus	Fixed at -1.75 dioptres
Field of View	180mils (10 degrees)
Magnification	X 3.75

Maximum Reticle Adjustment:	
Horizontal	60mils
Vertical	60mils
Objective Focus	From 10metres to infinity

Weapon Sight Image Intensified L1A1 was by today's standards a sizeable piece of equipment. Housed in its own transit case it came with weapon brackets, soft case and spare batteries.

ABOVE: The IWS was in its day a huge technological advance, and not just in sniping as it allowed all of the section weapons to be used accurately in the dark. This device did, though, enhance the sniper's role, extending his deadly capability into the dark hours which further created fear in the enemy who would have previously felt safe when operating at night.

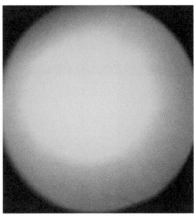

ABOVE: A sniper on a night shoot with the IWS mounted on his heavily camouflaged L42A1 rifle. The sight tended to sit high on the weapon which brought about cheek weld problems, furthermore the sight added over six and a half pounds to the weight of the weapon. The accompanying image illustrates the sniper's view through the device.

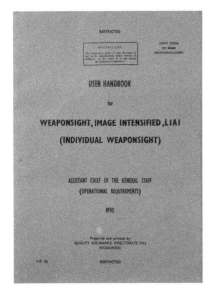
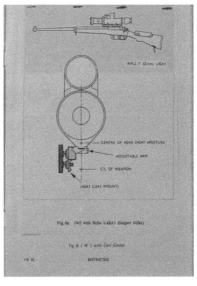
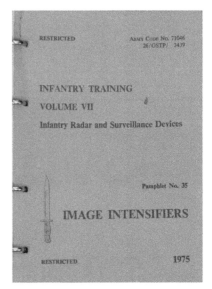

ABOVE: The User Handbook which accompanied the IWS was dated 1970 and predated the production of the L5A1 bracket, therefore the amendment illustrated was subsequently added to the handbooks and usually stapled to a page within.

ABOVE: Infantry Training Volume 7, Pamphlet No. 35 was the training literature that covered this device.

Post Falklands conflict saw the L42 slip back to routine sniper training centred on the prospect of having to fight a campaign against the Eastern Bloc; however since the L42's introduction it had some limited use in Northern Ireland. In the opening years of the "Troubles" the Royal Marines, when deployed to the province, exerted themselves quite robustly and used snipers aggressively to counter the IRA threat (the IRA themselves embarked on a crude sniper campaign against the security forces). The Royal Marines, who had never ceased their sniping activities, initially used the No. 4 T rifle until they were among the first to receive the new L42A1 sniper rifle, deploying it with trained snipers long before the army came back into the sniping fold.

The following accounts are from two marines who deployed to Northern Ireland with 40 Commando RM in 1972.

ABOVE: With what looks like Salisbury Plain in the background this sniper wears his own handmade hooded camouflaged smock. His rifle and telescope are taped and the barrel has been heavily camouflaged with scrim scarf netting.

A 430 Yard Shot

Prior to our '72 tour it was realised that none of the trained snipers in our unit, all being N.C.O's, would be available for that role. The known best shot from each troop from the fighting and support companies (SP Coy would have the role of a fighting company on this tour) were therefore asked to volunteer as snipers. I was the obvious choice in my troop and I joined eleven other marines for six weeks training under an efficient and seasoned sniper instructor. We were detached from the rest of the unit as they trained for N.I. and practiced all the skills that were considered relevant for a city tour.

I think I was probably the only one of the twelve to have had previous service in the Province, and one other marine had considerable experience of sniping in Aden six

years previously. We knew well in advance that our tour was to cover the area from Belfast City centre north, including the nationalist areas of New Lodge (which by this time was a "no-go" area), Docks and Bawnmore, and the loyalist areas of Fort William, Skegoneill and up to Rathcool. The final part of the unit training took place at Lydd and Hythe training areas where as well as ample live firing ranges, an old married quarter's estate had been turned into an I.R.A. enclave. The sniper section acted as 'enemy' for the rest of the unit, setting up sniper shoots and bombings, sometimes running rings round them, sometimes getting caught and interrogated.

The No4 T was in the process of being replaced and were issued with brand new L42's, although one No4 T remained in the unit. (The last No4

T to be used in action perhaps?). There were no brackets to fit the I.W.S. "Starlight Scope" to the L42 so we all also had an S.L.R. and I.W.S. each for night work. This meant that when we travelled to N.I. we had far more kit to carry than everyone else, and as we went to this war on public transport every move was a nightmare. We had to change trains, and platforms, at Birmingham, and our first action of the tour involved a drunken Irishman who decided to assault us with verbal abuse, which didn't last long, my troop Sergeant saw to that!

My company was posted to the northern part of the unit area, the sniper section being split up back to individual troops. We were in a large disused factory (Carmony) that was also used by Army units on short emergency tours. We arrived in early June at a time when the troubles were building up to a civil war situation. There was no trouble at all in our area, and being deployed on the ground for anything up to eighteen hours a day, we had little idea of what was going on only a few miles away. After a few days in my troop I was moved into the newly formed company intelligence section. We operated alone with our own transport, and on our first trip into "town" one evening I was amazed at the amount of shooting that was going on. This short period of about one week, gave me the opportunity to read newspapers and watch television and clearly the level of violence was gathering speed. It reached a climax one day when rumours were rife that there was going to be a short cease fire, and intelligence reports indicated the I.R.A. were really "going to have a go" until the deadline. A company of Fusiliers on temporary attachment with us had been in Lenadoon and came back having had almost fifty percent casualties. One survivor had what was clearly a spent bullet embedded in his flak jacket which we pulled out for him, (he thought he was wounded), a photo of which appeared in the national press the next day.

I can't remember how long this 'cease fire' lasted, twenty four hours I think, however intelligence sources indicated the I.R.A. were going to force the security forces into breaking it and have another "go" at us. I and (Phil) another sniper from my company were sent down to Brown Square Police Station in the very south of our unit area on our first sniper task. As we entered the Police Station in an open Land Rover driven at speed, a group of youths stoned us, however I was gratified to note one youth threw a stone , the size of half a house brick, which hit a lamp post and bounced straight back and hit him on the head. Our briefing lasted

about twenty seconds as I recall – "Go up those stairs, you'll find a sangar on the roof, see you in the morning". It was about 4 o'clock in the afternoon, so as I climbed the stairs I was wondering why the usual "any questions?" wasn't asked.

Our protection consisted of about fifty sandbags piled on a small wall with the sloping slate roof angled up at the immediate rear of the sangar. I think there was a wriggly tin roof, and it was very cramped. There was only enough room for one at the front "business end", the other had to squat on the roof immediately behind. The position faced north and was totally exposed to any hostile fire that should come our way from the hundreds of windows of the Unity Flats on the right and Denmark St Flats (under construction) on the left, that we overlooked. We found a field telephone but when we tried it were told to "Shut up unless you've got something important to say"! We were in the extreme bottom left hand corner of our unit's area, the Shankill Rd running to our left and Divis Flats to our rear. This was an area I was familiar with from my previous tour in '69, and almost below me the place where the first policeman had been killed, which I had been close to witnessing. The unit on our border, to our immediate left and rear did not have a very good reputation and had taken many casualties already. As we were setting up we could hear small arms fire echoing over the city, and being so high up it seemed every shot was being fired at us.

For several hours we took turns in the front of the Sangar, sometimes leaning right out to get a better view of what was happening down the Shankill, or hunched up at the rear with only a small field of view. The small arms fire rarely stopped for more than a few seconds and we quickly learned to recognise the sound of different calibres compared to the Army S.L.R's.

Although the streets were relatively empty it was obvious a lot of people had difficulty getting home from work, and at one stage a group of women became hysterical when they were caught in crossfire in the street below us. Although we had all sorts of small arms fire coming past us including tracers and ricochets, I don't think we were fired at directly and we never saw a single weapon fired from either side, although the gunmen clearly knew we were there. We had only brought our L42's with us and one I.W.S.; we also had no bino's, so we used the 32 scope on our rifles for observation. As it got dark we found out one of the major problems with the I.W.S. After looking through it, one is blind in that eye for a few seconds after, you were supposed to observe through the non shooting eye but that is often impractical.

Being in the position we were, we expected to see a gunman at any moment, but when we did it took us completely by surprise. It was about 1 o'clock in the morning and the small arms fire had slackened to the occasional single shot (probably the members of the army unit next to us having N.D's as they returned to barracks) when we heard the sound of several pistol shots followed by the unmistakable "boom,boom,boom" of an S.L.R. This was directly to our front but behind the old church at Carlisle Circus which was 430 yards away. I was at the front of the sangar with the I.W.S. pressed to my eye looking for any sign of movement when the same pattern of shots occurred again only closer. As the S.L.R. was fired the figure of a man came sprinting round the corner from Carlisle Circus and stood pressed to the wall looking around the way he had come, with a pistol in his hand held up in classic James Bond style, and in full view of me. I almost threw the I.W.S. down and put the L42 to my shoulder. It was *not a good position to fire from and as I had been squinting through the I.W.S., when I put the scope to my eye I couldn't see. I shouted to Phil, who was about two feet away "I can't fucking see!" I think Phil called me a wanker. I stayed on "aim" and gradually I got my vision back, this only took a few seconds but it seemed like an eternity. The man had changed position to what I think was a doorway, and I put the pointer of the sight on his chest and squeezed off a shot. I quickly reloaded and came back on aim but he had simply disappeared. We both thought he may have gone to ground so we emptied our magazines into all the likely shadows and the ground around where we had seen him. Phil's position was not good for*

shooting from and I noticed half way through my "rapid fire" the sandbag my elbow was resting on kick up sand as he put a shot through it. His muzzle was next to my right ear.

We saw no more movement and were relieved at first light. We only gave a very brief report to the Officer in the "ops room" on the way out and were driven straight back to Carmony. I was convinced I had missed the guy as he could easily of ran at the first shot and disappeared behind Unity Flat, however towards the end of the tour the unit 2 i/c interviewed me. He had a list, of I believe some fifty six names of terrorists shot by the unit , and after a short conversation put my name next to that of a man who had been found shot dead with a wound

through the chest near the place we last saw him. Several months later in a conversation with a colleague from the adjoining company, he told me about chasing a gunman who had fired at his patrol, but the chase was rather cut short by a barrage of shots from Brown Square!

Shortly after that most of the snipers were brought together in a central location and also joined by another ex Aden veteran with a consequence we were far more effective although we lacked a certain amount of leadership. I believe about half the names on the 2 i/c's list were accounted for by our section.

Courtesy of Nigel Greenaway

IRA Come Out to Play

As Royal Marines our introduction to the L42 was initially as Company snipers, we never really got deployed properly until John Mottram, the C.O. of 40 Cdo in 1972 used the snipers as snipers, and tasked them to find and occupy sniper hides in the New Lodge area....to very good effect. It scared the hell out of the I.R.A. as they suddenly found they were the ones being shot without knowing where the shots were coming from! I went back over with 40 in 1973 to the same area, and they were so scared of us they didn't come out to play, the most boring tour I've done. I don't know how, or if, the army used snipers, they didn't start training snipers again 'till 1973, they sent some of their small-arms instructors to CTCRM to do the course and they became Sniper Instructors at Warminster, whether they had passed or not, they reasoned that as long as they had the pamphlet they could instruct! The army had stopped training and using snipers in the mid '50s, the thinking was

they didn't need them because of the firepower they had. We were the only British force to continue to train and employ snipers during that time. We trained some army ranks at C.T.C., mainly from the S.A.S. and Paras, but every one of them meant one less place on a course for one of us, so there weren't that many.

As the years rolled on sniper operations in Northern Ireland became less and in the end were not common, the weapon being carried randomly as part of the odd patrol, or "brick" here and there so the soldiers could return accurate fire on a window or some other narrow gap from which they might be sniped at. It served more as a visual threat than a must-have tool in the box. The vast majority of engagements were dealt with the SLR often fitted with the L2A2 S.U.I.T (Sight Unit Infantry Trilux) which was perfect for use within the SLR's own effective combat range of 300 yards, particularly effective in the urban environment. Operations mounted were often done so on

information received from a reliable informant or other intelligence and hasty ambushes were set as well as OPs (Observation Posts) being manned with soldiers for days at a time waiting for an individual, or individuals to show to carry out a murder, arms swap or set up an illegal VCP (Vehicle Check Point). Soldiers, whether in an ambush or a lengthier OP operation, would be tasked with engaging with the terrorist on sight of a weapon or the moment they endangered life, a situation which would often escalate quickly and require significantly more firepower than the L42 could offer. Therefore the SLR was the weapon of choice being used in conjunction with the S.U.I.T sight and IWS night sight.

The following extract titled "The Bryson Incident" is a very good example of how many engagements with the IRA were fought in early 1970s Northern Ireland.

The write-up of the incident is detailed and shows how such an exchange often unfolded with an element of confusion on both sides playing its part in dictating the outcome. 1972 was a particularly violent year during the Troubles which brought about the heavy deployment of many elements of the security forces. The Bryson Incident, which involved the Royal Green Jackets, also occurred around the same time as the previous two accounts when 40 Commando deployed, and illustrates how the army in comparison to the

Royal Marines operated prior to reengaging itself with sniping. The event also illustrates why possibly the L42, which you might think an ideal weapon for such an operation, was not often used in the following years when the sniper was in a pre-selected hide with a dominating view over the area affording the sniper the chance to select his targets at will. However, the terrorist was more often than not armed with weapons

capable of full automatic fire and given the relatively short distances often involved they did not have to be the best of shots to find their target when spraying bullets in the general direction of the army.

The extract was written by Captain R.G.K. Williamson for the 1973 edition of the Royal Green Jackets annual journal.

The Bryson Incident

Bryson was a squat, broad shouldered, evil looking man, with a face that mirrored his violent nature. His nose was misshapen in an extraordinary way and somehow gave his appearance a touch of insanity. During his youth he acquired a reputation for bullying and brawling. His name became well known to the R.U.C. through his criminal activities and when "the troubles" began in 1969 Bryson readily joined the Provisional I.R.A. He came from a fiercely Republican family and was more than grateful for the opportunity to indulge his homicidal tendencies.

During the escalation of insurrection in Belfast in 1971 Bryson developed into a cunning ruthless killer. His reputation was greatly enhanced by a spectacular escape from the prison ship Maidstone when he and six others swam the icy waters to freedom. Although Bryson was known throughout Belfast he operated mainly in the Ballymurphy area where his crude leadership and shooting exploits made him the object of a cult following. He probably reached the peak of his power and notoriety during the truce period in June 1972. He took command of the Ballymurphy Provisional Company and exercised absolute control over the people living in the area. He ruled by a

system of terror which demanded and got universal obedience. He was also extremely active himself and is known to have shot a number of soldiers and policemen personally. The weapon he invariably used for sniping was an Armalite rifle with telescopic sight. When he was finally caught in November '72 it brought considerable relief to the Security Forces. However in March '73 he made an audacious escape from Crumlin Road Court House.

At about this time another Provisional was creating something of a reputation, Patrick Mulvenna, who had been Bryson's adjutant, became the O.C. of the Ballymurphy. In the meantime Bryson went South with a fellow fugitive called Frank Duffy who was also a notorious Ballymurphy Provisional. Whilst in Eire they were both charged with robbing a bank in Dublin and Bryson was subsequently expelled from the Provisional Movement because he recognised the Court. In their absence Mulvenna rapidly began to acquire the same sort of charisma as Bryson by escaping the clutches of the Army on two occasions and shooting several soldiers.

The arrival of 3 R.G.J. in July coincided with embryonic beginnings of a step-up in the ever present friction between the Official and Provisional I.R.A. In the Ballymurphy, which was taken over by "S" Company, the Officials,

under the leadership of Ronald Bunting, the renegade son of Major Bunting, Ian Paisley's right hand man, were particularly militant. The rate of "Security Forces – Not – Involved" shootings rose weekly under the interested attention of "S" Company. "Kneecapping" was the most common outcome of a system of mutual reprisal operated by two I.R.A. wings. "S" Company achieved a very high rate of weapon finds and arrests and generally asserted their presence without receiving the normal acrimony associated with the practice of "dominating" the area.

Besides possessing good sources one of the chief methods used by "S" Company to collect tactical intelligence and maintain general surveillance on the area was the use of O.P.s. There would often be three and sometimes four O.P.s overlooking different parts of the area. On the morning of 31st August a corporal and a rifleman climbed stealthily into the attic of a flat directly above the infamous Bullring. A hole in the roof, caused by some missing tiles, afforded them a good view of the Bullring and surrounding roads leading off it. The position itself was cramped and allowed little movement for shooting. The corporal and the rifleman settled down stoically to their task.

At the beginning of August Bryson, despite his expulsion, was asked by the Provisional Brigade

Staff to return to the Ballymurphy and help redress the balance against the Officials. He accepted the invitation and moved North with Frank Duffy. In similar fashion to Bunting he set about terrorising the local Officials. In one celebrated incident he lined several of them up at gunpoint against a wall, inside a drinking club, and then proceeded to spray the roof with an Armalite rifle on automatic fire. The implications of this were not lost on the Officials who decided that Bryson would have to be executed. They convened a meeting a week later at which they discussed how and who should carry this out. Brian Trainor, anxious to make an impression on his older colleagues, volunteered to be part of the execution party. His offer was quickly accepted but his enthusiasm dwindled significantly when he found that he alone was the execution party.

It was the corporal's turn "on stag". His bones were beginning to ache slightly. Neither he nor the rifleman had seen anything of particular interest; it was now 18:30 hours. During the course of the day he had frequently expected to be discovered by the free ranging children of the Ballymurphy. With a long suffering sigh he glanced out of the hole and mechanically began to take notice of an olive green Hillman Hunter at the bottom of Ballymurphy Road. It was travelling at an even speed towards the Bullring. Suddenly to the corporal's astonishment he noticed three rifles sticking out of the windows. As the car reached the Bullring it began to sound its horn at regular intervals. Frantically the corporal began to report what he was seeing whilst at the same time reaching for his rifle. The car made one circuit and drove off down Glenalina Road before the corporal could even point his rifle out of the hole. He began to interpret the details of the after images still

on his mind. There had been four men, three rifles: One Armalite, a Garrand and something else. He quickly reported further details to Zero hoping to alert other O.P.s and foot patrols.

A short time before this Brian Trainor, the young Official Volunteer, had set out from a house in Ballymurphy with a "grease gun". His orders were to shoot Bryson on sight. Even now he was walking nervously round the bottom of Glenalina Road with the "grease gun" concealed under his "noisy jacket" desperately regretting his earlier rash decision to accept the assignment and hoping against hope he wouldn't see Bryson. The green Hillman was reported by another O.P. as moving round the area followed by a red van. The corporal and the rifleman were tense as they listened to the radio net and strained their eyes for the possible reappearance of the car. They began to be attacked by feelings of self-doubt. Were there weapons or weren't there?

Brian Trainor suddenly stopped in his tracks as the big Hillman Hunter swept round the corner. He made out the unmistakable features of Jim Bryson and saw rifles sticking out of the windows. An instant assessment of the odds and discretion being the better part of valour he darted into an alleyway and tried to erase what he had just seen from his mind. With his pulse racing madly he then ran back to the house he'd set out from faster than he had ever ran before.

What in fact was happening was that Bryson, Paddy Mulvenna, Bimbo O'Rawe and Frank Duffy were driving around Ballymurphy partly to show their disregard for the Army and partly to humiliate the Officials.

Despite his vigilance the corporal was taken by surprise when the car coasted quietly across the Bullring followed by the red van.

They stopped at the junction of Ballymurphy Road and Whitecliffe Parade. The occupants casually got out and Bryson began to direct them to ambush positions. The corporal gingerly pushed one of the tiles in front of him to one side so as to get a better view and also to enable him to create a cramped fire position. Suddenly one of the loose tiles clattered across the roof and crashed to the ground alerting the attention of the ambush group, one of whom fired in the general direction of the O.P. The corporal immediately returned four rounds, although he could scarcely aim. He was forced to pull his rifle in when it developed a stoppage. During this interval the ambush party must have returned to their cars and left because when the corporal looked again there was no one there. Having given their position away the corporal and rifleman set about enlarging the hole by kicking other tiles out. The corporal put his head out to try and get a better view of what had happened. He withdrew it sharply as two rounds hit the roof. He fired three quick shots at a gunman he caught a glimpse of behind one of the houses to his front, but missed. It now seemed clear the car and the van had gone. The riflemen hurriedly packed their kit. Just as they were leaving the corporal was amazed to see the green Hillman Hunter emerging from Whitecliffe Parade and returning right on to Ballymurphy Road. Ironically Bryson had become confused by the problem that had so often enabled him to escape unscathed from his own sniping attacks in the past, that of determining where the fire had come from. He had thrown the car into a wild "U" turn in Whitecliffe Parade because he thought it was leading him towards danger. As they turned into Ballymurphy Road, Paddy Mulvenna fired two shots from his Armalite rifle. The corporal pressed his eye to the telescopic sight of his S.L.R. and began firing rapidly at the back of the accelerating Hillman Hunter. He had to compensate for the first shots which went low left and then fired seven more shots at the retreating car trying to incapacitate it before it reached the corner.

Inside the car the four gunmen were writhing in hysterical panic. O'Rawe, who was sitting behind Bryson, the driver, was slammed into the front seat as a bullet ripped into his left shoulder. Duffy, sitting behind Mulvenna, grovelled on the floor at the back. Looking up he saw the sight which haunted him for weeks. Bryson's head was jerked forward with a dull thump as a 7.62 entered the back of his neck. He slumped forward over the steering wheel as the car careered into the garden of 99 Ballymurphy Road. The three others cowered in the bottom of the car temporarily immobilised with shock.

The corporal and the rifleman observed the crashed car two hundred metres away for a moment and then jumped down from the attic

into the flats below, where they took up fire positions to cover the car. By this stage "S" Company foot patrols were closing in on the gun battle. Impulsively Mulvenna flung open the door of the car and rolled onto the ground. He was now aware of where the shooting was coming from and fired a long burst on automatic at the O.P. with his Armalite. Duffy raised the M.1 carbine given to him earlier by Bryson and began to fire from the back of the car. Mulvenna then decided to get up and go. As he did so the corporal fired three shots, two of which hit, and Mulvenna died instantly. As he changed his magazine he saw Bimbo O'Rawe clutching a Garand running towards the front door of 99 Ballymurphy Road. Again he fired three shots, hitting O'Rawe as he pitched forward inside the house. Meanwhile Duffy had scrambled out of the car and was sprinting towards the alleyway between 95 and 97 Ballymurphy Road. The corporal fired a final three shots but missed.

When the "S" Company foot patrols reached the car accompanied by the corporal and

rifleman from the O.P. they found Mulvenna dead, Bryson deeply unconscious and O'Rawe badly wounded in the back garden of 99 Ballymurphy Road.

The Ballymurphy was stunned by what had happened. As they crowded round the scene they stood mesmerized by the sight of the bodies being taken away. An unannounced amnesty seemed to exist whilst lifesaving actions were carried out on O'Rawe and Bryson. Violent animosity against the Army was inexplicably absent until voices were heard saying "The Stickies done this". Mulvenna was buried a week later, Bryson died on 22nd September and O'Rawe, despite being hit five times, recovered. The obituaries of the first two referring to "Enemies of Ireland" rather than "Crown Forces" underlined the popular notion that they died as a result of an Official I.R.A. ambush.

The achievement of "S" Company was in itself highly valuable. It destroyed arguably the best Provisional A.S.U. in Belfast and disposed of two of the most wanted and dangerous men in

ABOVE: Both the L42 (Top) and SLR rifles pictured together. The spotter was armed with the SLR which was capable of bringing to bear heavy hitting rapid fire if required. Note the two weapons are comparable in length.

Northern Ireland. The effect of these deaths was to deal a severely demoralising blow to the Provisional Campaign. Total war between the Provisionals and the Officials was only avoided by strenuous combined efforts of restraint by the Brigade Staffs of the two respective wings. It initiated a highly charged confrontation which lasted several weeks. This caused the I.R.A. to become acutely introspective and therefore ineffective against the Security Forces at a time when Government, engrossed in the delicate negotiations to form an executive from the Assembly, were anxious not to be seen to be giving leeway to the Army to help it fight the terrorist.

In Ballymurphy one of the first blows in the ensuing "O.I.R.A./ P.I.R.A. Feud" came shortly after the shooting. Information was supplied by a Provisional source which led to the discovery of a "grease gun" and a Thompson machine gun. Also in the house where they were found was a certain Brian Trainor. His immediate arrest completed for him, a very bad day.

Luck certainly was not on the side of the gunmen that day, as of all the OPs to debus in front of, the OP they did was most unfortunate. The corporal featured in the incident was one of the battalion's keenest shots and went on to become a gifted sniper, winning many trophies in competition. He also went on to run the battalion's sniper platoon and oversee the training of up and coming snipers in the battalion through the eighties.

With the resurgence of sniper training within the army in 1973 the Sniper Wing was established at Warminster, Wiltshire on the edge of Salisbury Plain training ground. The training pamphlet used to initiate training was essentially *Infantry Training Volume 1, Infantry Platoon Weapons Pamphlet No. 10, Sniping, 1951*. It was a short-term measure with weapon specific information changed from 4T to L42 only and bridged the gap until a training pamphlet written for the L42A1 rifle in its entirety was produced in 1975 and distributed the following year. Once again the army rebranded and gave the training literature a bit of a facelift; although Infantry Training was still the title Skill at Arms was also in there. The blue cards became pale and the pamphlet size was increased to more generous proportions, and *Pamphlet No. 10* became *Infantry Training Volume 1, Skill at Arms (Individual Training) Pamphlet No. 4, Sniping 1976*. *Pamphlet No. 4* was the sole edition of training literature produced for the weapon and remained the British Army's official sniper training document into the fledgling years of the L96A1 sniper rifle.

ABOVE: This bridging pamphlet carried across the weapon specific information from the 1951 Pamphlet No. 10 that covered the No. 4 T and was a temporary measure until Pamphlet No. 4, 1976 (also pictured) could be written encapsulating the L42 with all other relevant information.

The Sniper's Garments

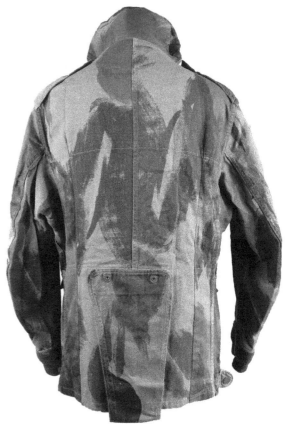

ABOVE: This Denison smock largely known as the 1972 pattern would be the final Denison after the smock and its camouflaged pattern had seen a thirty-year reign. Being the only issued garment that offered a camouflaged pattern at the time it was also favoured by snipers when it came to making a ghillie suit. Even after the new DPM sniper smock superseded it the '72 pattern remained popular.

At around the same time *Pamphlet No. 4* was issued a purpose made sniper smock was produced in the very first pattern of DPM (Disruptive Pattern Material) camouflage which had been adopted by the British Army in 1972. The smock was built in the sturdy combat clothing 1968 pattern and was the first of its kind. Prior to Smock, Snipers NSN 5413-99-132-4791, the sniper's issued garment was the Denison smock as first issued during WW2 with several variants being used in the post-war years, the colours as well as the last two patterns having full length zips being the main features that separated them. The most common smock being utilised at that time was the 1972 pattern Denison which was tri colour, very pale in its tones and seemed to be favoured the most by snipers when it came to making their own handmade ghillie suit even after the sniper smock was issued.

The sniper smock was designed purely for the purpose of sniping, a specialist garment by its very own features. The four pockets are large cargo type with press stud closure; the two lower pockets are situated on the sides of the garment so the sniper can access them in the prone position. The smock continued the rear crotch flap in exactly the same way as the Denison and came with comfortable woollen cuffs and a full length zip plus excellent padding of the two shoulder areas to reduce fatigue from the rifle's recoil as well as ample padding of the underside of the forearms which made stalking over rough ground more bearable. The padded forearms also provided good protection when in a firing position off the elbows. Both of the upper arms carried a sturdy metal hook so the sling could be secured around the arm when being utilised in a fire position and the collar had buttons so the 1968 pattern hood

ABOVE: With the adoption of the Disruptive Pattern Material camouflage in 1972 a purpose made sniper smock was not long to follow. This example is a first pattern sniper smock. The DPM pattern is arguably the best of all the DPM patterns that would follow.

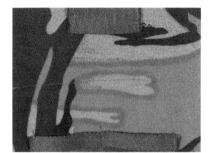

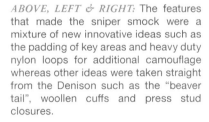

ABOVE, LEFT & RIGHT: The features that made the sniper smock were a mixture of new innovative ideas such as the padding of key areas and heavy duty nylon loops for additional camouflage whereas other ideas were taken straight from the Denison such as the "beaver tail", woollen cuffs and press stud closures.

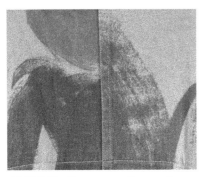

ABOVE: The three camouflage patterns used by the sniper armed with the L42A1 rifle. The 72 pattern Denison, first pattern DPM and second pattern DPM. Note the second pattern DPM became darker and lost the speckled edges to the pattern.

could be attached. The smock also had the unique feature of nylon web loops stitched on the back, upper arms and upper chest so strips of hessian and natural foliage could be attached to break up the sniper's shape and assist in blending into the immediate environment.

The sniper smock is still in service today, still being the dedicated garment issued to trained snipers and is largely unchanged although the build quality has fluctuated over the years, the 1985 pattern probably being the worst. During the L42's era

LEFT: The sniper knee pad was used to customise a standard issue combat trouser when making a ghillie suit by hand. The examples pictured have been produced in the second pattern DPM.

BELOW: A selection of dated camouflage head nets are illustrated. This form of camouflage has been issued to the British sniper for some decades. The earliest date I have encountered is 1966 and the latest is 1991.

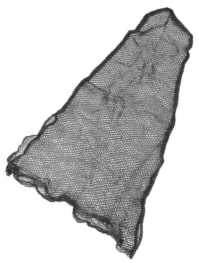

there were three variants only; the first of all the smocks allowed for the attachment of a hood and has since been made obsolete. The second was still the 1968 pattern built specification but the camouflage changed, losing the speckled detail to the edges of the DPM pattern and becoming darker. The third was the 1985 pattern which saw a stark difference in the build quality and was produced in the same second DPM camouflage pattern.

In addition to the smock, large ten inch by eight inch knee pads were issued in a similar gauge of dense closed cell foam as found in the padded areas of the smock. The knee pads, NSN 8415-99-132-5004, were issued in the same DPM camouflage with a wide fabric web so they could be quickly stitched in place. Another item to aid concealment which first appeared in the post-war years and remained still being issued with the L96A1 sniper rifle was a head and shoulder concealment net which when worn was tucked into the smock. The green net material eliminated any fleshy colours and enabled the sniper to break his head and shoulder shape up by adding natural foliage to the mesh netting.

There is some controversy amongst collectors today, some of whom argue that later, after the L42 had been withdrawn from front line service, it saw service again in the first Gulf War, the rifle having had a new scope bracket produced to carry a Schmidt & Bender 6 x 42mm telescope, or L13A1 as designated on the L96A1 sniper rifle. The argument suggests Special Boat Service and Special Air Service units wished to deploy additional sniper rifles to this particular theatre and in order to do so brought a number of L42A1 sniper rifles out of war stores and equipped them with a new bracket and scope.

There is no argument as to whether the bracketry to carry and mount the Schmidt & Bender scope existed; indeed it does but its purpose and the extent to which it was used is questionable. When the L96A1 sniper rifle first entered service it ran into problems which delayed its rolling out across the whole of the army, which in turn led the MoD to look at ways of extending the L42's service life. The weakest component of the L42A1 system was its telescope. The No. 32, or L1A1, was by this time very old and tired, and it's fair to say it became the Achilles heel of the weapon due to its breakages; if replaced the weapon could have served on and filled the temporary void should it have been necessary. In 1988 14 Maintenance Advisory Group of Woolwich, London ran a feasibility study with a view to evaluating an economic solution by firstly exploring the possibilities of converting the L39A1 target rifle of which there were plenty by the use of commercial scope mounts fitted to the top of the receiver. The programme also looked at mounting the Schmidt & Bender L13A1 telescope onto the L42 by the most cost effective means so two new brackets were produced commercially and two No. 32 scope brackets were also modified: their 25.4mm rings were widened to accept the 26mm tube of the 6 x 42mm Schmidt & Bender telescope. The June 1988 report also speaks highly of the Schmidt & Bender scope's excellence, recommending it to be installed on whatever sniper rifle, new or old, the MoD decided upon, stating the advantage of continuity it would also provide in the training of snipers by radically improving the performance of old stocks of sniper rifles.

The commercially produced bracket was recommended in the report and it is at this point that a

rather large gap appears in the sequence of events. It appears the evaluation took place, the findings of which were published in the 1988 14 Maintenance Advisory Group report, and a solution was found and was waiting in the wings should the L42 have had to step into the breach for any period of time. History now tells us it didn't as the L96A1 rifle's issues were resolved quite swiftly by Accuracy International so the commercially produced bracket was never manufactured beyond the initial two trial pieces and it's not the Special Forces bracket that exists today, or so we thought.

Further research involving numerous people from the SAS (Special Air Service) and Royal Marines who were connected with both the L42 and L96 rifles during this period could not find anyone who could confirm the L42 was involved in any way with the first Gulf War. Some of them even laughed at such a suggestion, and not a single photograph could be located, nor could a credible personal account confirming its presence be recorded. I think the time of the conflict in conjunction with the timing of the L96 failure enabled the believers to indulge in the fantasy that the old war horse that may never quite have received the recognition it may have deserved finally went out with a bang, or to put it simply, it never happened.

However, as far back as the Iranian Embassy siege, Princes Gate, London, 1980, the SAS were not entirely satisfied with the sniping equipment available to them. During their now world famous storming of the Embassy which brought the six-day siege to an abrupt end, they did deploy the L42 with only one of their snipers releasing a shot which I am reliably informed did hit its target, but in the same period they were employing a lighter .22/250mm calibre Tikka Finlander

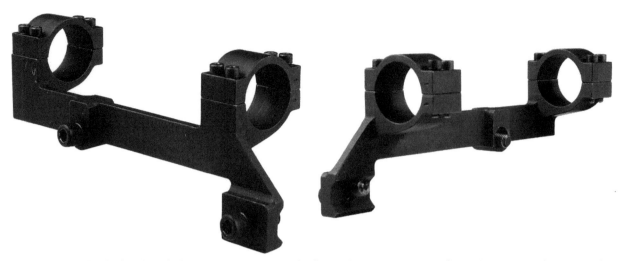

ABOVE: Pictured is the bracket which has become known as the SF bracket for mounting the Schmidt & Bender telescope on the L42A1 rifle. This bracket was introduced to the SF community by the SAS but after the army supplied it to them for their appraisal it would be the SBS who took it beyond the trial phase.

M55 bolt action rifle fitted with a Kahles ZF69 telescope that offered fixed six power magnification. The rifle was at the time just one of many exploratory uses of kit in conjunction with the regiment's own research and development, which, completely independent of ITDU, had been looking at viable options to improve the L42A1 sniper system.

The bracket that exists today and which is largely referred to as the SF bracket is an exquisite piece of engineering heavily reproduced from a handful of original examples still in existence. Machined from a single billet of steel, the surviving examples I have seen are all finished in the same green phosphate finish and, when held in the hand next to a reproduced example, the quality of the original bracket is apparent. In the course of my research, and in an effort to glean some unequivocal facts which relate to the SF bracket, I spoke with several former members of the Special Air Service who served in the period of the L42 rifle, and this led to me speaking with one individual who was a fountain of captivating knowledge. The conversation meandered over

a broad range of subjects including the Iranian Embassy siege and how he was a team member on the roof. The police who had taken up vantage points on surrounding buildings with their Enfield Enforcers clearly had a lack of information, which was in all likelihood an intentional information blackout due to what was about to happen. He told how one of the police officers got a fleeting glimpse of him and presuming he was a bad guy took a shot, and recalled how at the time he was completely unaware he had been fired at but was told later of the event.

Another individual I spoke with was heavily connected with sniping in the regiment and remembered the bracket well. He told me it was not produced by the SAS and how he came into contact with the bracket in an exploratory capacity after the army brought it to the SAS. He recalled the bracket was trialled by the regiment at the request of ITDU initially with both Zeiss and Schmidt & Bender telescopes, the Zeiss being dropped due to the reticle being too "busy". As the trial developed the SAS found both the black 10 and 12 x 42mm Schmidt &

Bender telescopes worked superbly in conjunction with the L42A1 rifle, and the SAS would go on to later adopt these Schmidt & Bender telescopes and use them with their Accuracy International PM Rifle. He also told me how it was unlikely I would find an example finished in Suncorite black paint which I found striking, as indeed I have not. The lack of a final paint finish and the handful of examples available would suggest the bracket was for trials development use only; furthermore his account does certainly suggest the SF bracket could actually be the commercially produced bracket mentioned in the 1988 14 Maintenance Advisory Group report.

The bracket functioned in the exact same way as the No. 32 scope's own bracket but seated a 26mm scope tube and mounted to the rifle in the same way via two Allen key cap head screws so the traditional thumb wheels didn't foul the harnessing associated with their parachute operations, some of which involved the weapon being carried on the person, not strapped to a drop bag. It's also

LEFT: A typical Donnington receipt label found on the end of the L42 transit chest. The rifle serial number can be seen printed bottom left of the bar code. When a bar code reader is used, the bar code is also the rifle serial number.

worth mentioning at this point that the SBS who worked closely with the SAS did, after encountering the bracket, copy it for their own trials and fitted theirs with the traditional thumb screws as found on the No. 32 bracket. As with the SAS trialled brackets just a few are still around today, however I have encountered two brackets reportedly from the SBS that were given a final black paint finish and some thirty years later do appear to have had a service life. The statements from former members of the SAS seem clear cut: they did not invent the bracket and furthermore they did not use it, but the circumstances around the SBS use of the bracket appear different. These brackets today look to bear the wear of service use; in addition to this their allocation of L42 rifles does not tally with the Unit Identification Number list of rifles they returned to Donnington central stores before the impending delivery of their L96A1 rifles. This may suggest they retained several L42A1 rifles which they improved with the use of the SF bracket and L13A1 telescope.

The beginning of the end came for L42 in the mid-eighties when it began to give way to the L96A1 sniper rifle in earnest around 1986. A regiment at a time packed their L42 rifles in the transit chests with full CES and returned them to Donnington central store where on arrival the contents were checked and a pre-prepared label was applied to the end of the chest. The label is bar coded; the bar code when read is the rifle's serial number which is also printed bottom left of the bar code and served to identify the rifle individually amongst the hundreds that were shelved together. These labels are the only real evidence that the chest is the original that has always housed the rifle it is numbered to, as even with the scribbling often found within a chest referencing the equipment contained within, the Donnington receipt label acts as concrete provenance particularly when large sums of money are at risk between collectors today.

The rifles sat in stores as war reserve for several years before being declared obsolete in the early part of 1992 after which an estimated

ABOVE: As with the No. 4 T the L42 was sold out of service with an astonishingly low price tag compared to today's prices. This advert placed by Navy Arms in 1994 offers three grades of rifle for a prospective buyer to choose from each priced accordingly.

1,000 rifles began the disposal process. The slow procession of paperwork relating to the disposal of a thousand sniper rifles which must have been flowing back and forth, albeit very slowly, ceased in 1994 when the rifles were finally made available to civilian companies for purchase, and initially the entire collection of L42 rifles were to be sold out of the UK due to a piece of U.N. imposed legislation relating to the international sale of arms. The sale from the Disposals Unit at Donnington was implemented in three batches mostly of rifles housed in a transit chest with L1A1 scope and scope tin. All other CES items were removed and were not available for sale with the rifles as much of it passed straight to the L96 and although user manuals, IWS brackets and lens brush bottles were as obsolete as the rifles they were never officially released for sale to the public. However I suspect many examples have been "liberated" and are once again housed with an L42. The U.N. legislation was indeed observed with the first batch being sold to a U.S. company called Navy Arms, the C.E.O. of which, the late Val. J. Forgett, is on record as stating his company purchased 637 units in that single deal which was made up of L42s, L39s and Inglis No. 2 pistols with the price paid averaging out at roughly $100 per item. However it is unfortunately now a mystery as to the breakdown of items that made up the order although it's reasonable to assume the bulk of the consignment would have been made up of L42 rifles. When Navy Arms came to sell the L42 rifles in the U.S. they graded them as Dealer Grade, Collector Grade and Select Grade pricing them $595, $795 and $895 respectively.

A further two batches of rifles were still available similarly to those purchased by Navy Arms: rifle, scope, scope tin mostly housed in a chest. It would appear that once Donnington received the rifles from the units that used them they were shelved in warehouse conditions and handled minimally and then before being moved out of Donnington the relevant items were removed from the chest as many rifles were sold in their original chests with matching scopes and scope tins. Tony Hallam of the UK disposals company Charnwood Ordnance Ltd did in fact bid for all the L42 rifles that were available but was immediately discounted due to the U.N. legislation, however Tony was to be successful later. With two smaller batches of L42 rifles remaining, one of 157 rifles and the other of 209 rifles, Charnwood Ordnance Ltd bid again and was successful in the purchase of these 366 rifles. However, the U.N. legislation still had to be observed, therefore the sale came with the strict condition that all the rifles had to be exported. Charnwood Ordnance Ltd had a close relationship with the Canadian company Collector's Source who agreed to purchase all of the rifles after which they would return sixty rifles back to the UK to Charnwood Ordnance who sold them mainly within the UK with some into Europe. Navy Arms and the Canadian company Collector's Source were the principal companies who further distributed across North America as well as several smaller companies such as Brian Dick's BDL Ltd in South Carolina who has handled over 100 L42 rifles to date.

Those who have done the maths here using the figures quoted will realise the numbers that made up the batches total 1,003 rifles from the estimated 1,020 rifles that were potentially being disposed of. The end figure is unfortunately an estimate but there is clearly a discrepancy which I would suggest lies in a number of rifles supplied by the army to reference collections all over the world.

As with the 4T the rifles were cheap and considered important by few so a number fell foul of the garage DIY smith, and I'm sure a number of L42 rifles have probably been lost forever. More commonly

ABOVE: Brian Dick of BDL in South Carolina pictured in his workshop with one of the many L42A1 sniper rifles that have passed through his hands. Brian is pre-eminent in the USA when it comes to trusting someone with an L42 that may require work.

rifles returning from the U.S. are often missing their transit chest, reportedly due to the Canadian company who purchased roughly half of the rifles imported by Navy Arms but did not want to pay the shipping on the heavy chests so approximately 300 transit chests were scrapped. On occasions rifles are re-imported from the U.S. minus the telescope and its carry case. Miraculously some are after many years of separation brought back together. I know of one L42 rifle which G.E. Fulton & Son of Bisley reunited. Fulton's had for some years an L1A1 scope in its No. 8 carry tin, the tin numbered to the scope, and which also carried the all-important serial number of the rifle. The rifle it belonged to appeared out of the blue on a U.S. gun auction site. Fulton's purchased the rifle and brought both rifle and scope back together after their separation of some years. It boggles the mind how a 4T or L42 should come to be separated from its scope in the first place.

When they were first disposed of in the mid-nineties one could travel to Charnwood Ordnance Ltd, Leicester, choose a rifle from the dozens available and purchase it for around £600. Today at the point of writing an L42 in its transit chest with scope, scope tin, cleaning kit and Scout Regiment Telescope will cost you a cool £11,000, and I am sure collectors long into the future will wish he, or she, could buy one even at that price. I recall, several years ago when prices were around £5,000, Robert Taylor, the proprietor of G.E. Fulton & Son, forecasting the price of an L42 hitting £20,000 within a decade. At the time I scoffed but if prices continue to rise at their present pace he will be proved correct with a couple of years to spare.

Chapter 5
Accuracy International

Just a few years after RSAF Enfield's conversion of the L42 and its entering into service as the British Army's front line sniper rifle, the L42's ultimate replacement which was still twenty years away was already, on paper, in principle, sitting in a drawer in Worthing, Sussex. The incredible story of the birth of Accuracy International begins back in the early seventies with Dave Walls and Dave Caig and oddly enough a pair of Colt army revolvers.

Dave Walls had an interest in pistols and having seen images of a Colt Army 1860 and an 1873 Single Action Army wondered if he could create a perfect replica of each. The two Daves, who were both engineers by trade as well as work colleagues, and also belonged to the same shooting club, set about searching for printed images of the two revolvers in an effort to scale some measurements. Bear in mind this was at a time before the internet, so they could not just go online and Google images as we are so used to doing today; it was painstaking research through shooting magazines and books and the images found were often grainy and black and white. With scale drawings of the revolvers prepared, it would be some time later before pictures of the small parts from within the pistols would become available for their manufacture drawings to be completed.

After some time, and a lot of patience in the preparation of the drawings, work on the revolvers began using the milling machines and lathes at their place of work. With a revolver of each design completed to perfection the two Daves were eager for a professional opinion on their creations. They took the revolvers to a classic firearms auction house where an expert on Colt pistols subjected each revolver to a lengthy examination. He concluded them to be outstanding examples but one detail confused him. One of the revolvers they built had a notch on the right side but not on the left. The expert couldn't work it out and it was also a surprise to the two Daves. Dave Walls enquired what the notch was for and it was explained that some of this model of revolver had an optional shoulder stock which required a notch on each side for mounting. It was there on the right side of their gun but not on the left. After the expert had deliberated for some time the two Daves put him out of his misery and explained they had made them in their workshop at home.

Dave Walls realised afterwards that the images examined and used for scale were in fact two different revolvers; one obviously had the shoulder stock attachment option and the other didn't. At the time they had no clue as to what the notch was for, and with it being on what appeared to be one side only in a set of images that portrayed the study pistol as being the same gun, they rested on the opinion that it was a cosmetic feature. Before they parted company with the Colt expert he said, "If you built these pistols from a photograph, you should be in the business of making guns."

Both Dave Walls and Dave Caig were competitive shooters and had represented their countries, England and Scotland respectively, in various international tournaments and made it their responsibility to maintain the club's rifles. Fellow club members often turned to the two Daves for repair work to their own rifles or for fine tuning prior to a competition. Payment was always asked and the currency was always beer. Their reputation for superlative work coupled with their own shooting success travelled far and wide and requests for precision rifle smithing were overwhelming. It was at this point, and with the need to earn some money, that they started a business named C&W Products and operated from Dave Walls' shed at his home in Worthing. It would be through C&W Products that their first steps towards making history would be put on paper, although at the time they could never have predicted where they were actually heading.

Whilst attending a barbecue at a mutual friend's house they met Malcolm Cooper who was making a name for himself in the UK competitive shooting community. Cooper also owned a small gun shop in Portsmouth called Accuracy International Shooting Sports Ltd and was interested in what the two Daves were doing with C&W Products. Eventually the two Colt pistols became the subject of their discussions and Cooper was eager to see them, so much so that Dave Walls returned home to fetch them. Cooper was utterly impressed and said, "You have the potential to design and build your own rifle." The two Daves replied, "But we have already done that." The work C&W Products was doing was I think by now best described as world class and Malcolm Cooper started to pass all rifle smithing work Accuracy International Shooting Sports attracted to C&W Products. With the Daves' ideas for a rifle on paper, Cooper was set to compete in the 1978 World Championships

PREVIOUS PAGE: Pictured in the early nineties are (left to right standing) Malcolm Cooper, Dave Walls, Dave Caig and Martin Kay kneeling and holding an early Arctic Warfare rifle.

ABOVE: Pictured is a PM Rifle that predates the L96A1 variant. Note the swirl flash eliminator. This example was used by Durham Police.

in Seoul, Korea and asked Dave Walls to build him a rifle to compete with. The two Daves set about realising their design and built the rifle Cooper won silver with in Seoul. The success of the Caig, Walls and Cooper partnership was cemented by the forming of a new company, Accuracy International Ltd, in 1978.

Accuracy International continued to design and perform work on match rifles including those of Malcolm Cooper to earn a meagre living, as by 1981 they had only built three rifles but the process had helped evolve ideas as to how a competition match rifle should look and perform. Cooper continued to elevate his name and reputation, becoming World Champion and twice Olympic gold medallist, and saw his position in the company as being the face and using his influence to promote AI around the world. He put it to the two Daves: "Do you want fame or fortune?" Fortune was needed and it was agreed Cooper should front the company allowing the two Daves to concentrate on the design and build side of the business.

In 1982 the Falklands conflict put British forces on a far flung battlefield. The short but violent conflict would turn out to be the catalyst that would initiate change in fortunes of the three. The conflict laid bare the shortcomings in British equipment across the board from

boots to sniper rifles which led to the search for the L42A1 rifle's replacement. Cooper learned of the MoD's intentions to start the process to replace the L42 and met with the MoD without the knowledge of his two business partners. His success and reputation made it hard for the MoD to ignore and AI was invited to submit a trial example of their AI 7.62mm target rifle to the tender process. Cooper delivered the news to the two Daves, which was at first met with trepidation. While they were both unsure they decided it would actually be a good learning process and the feedback from the trial would be useful to improve their product, but they did not think for a minute they would win. Both Dave Walls and Dave Caig went to the drawing board and began to sketch the design of the new rifle. Their creation would

prove to be revolutionary, bringing together the ideas they had forged over the previous decade into one rifle they would christen PM (Precision Marksman) Rifle, the first British sniper rifle to be designed from the off as a sniper rifle.

It would not be until Dave Walls actually stood at his lathe at home in his workshop ready to cut the receiver of the new rifle that the unique, now world famous six sided shape would be created. The rifle on the drawing board had a conventional rounded receiver but he realised he had no round bar in the required size, however he did have a piece of rectangular bar which, with additional processes on the lathe, could have been rounded. However for simplicity he chose to leave the action body in a six sided profile. The rifles previously designed were purely for target

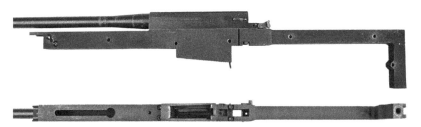

If we get under the skin of the L96A1 rifle we can see the chassis and how the flat bottomed receiver is attached to it. Note the weld in the chassis immediately behind the receiver. This had a tendency to break if the butt received a heavy blow.

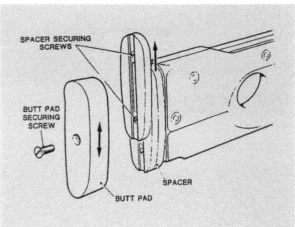

ABOVE: The butt formed by the two stock sides coming together has an integrally moulded cheek rest and thumbhole. Note the sling attachment point and butt spike. The accompanying diagram shows how the length of pull is adjusted by adding or removing the plastic butt spacers.

work and the incorporation of a magazine was a new first for Dave Walls, so he adopted the Springfield magazine to overcome the issue. This oversight led to the now world famous flat sided action body and also facilitated the ten shot double row magazine. The rifle created was what we know today as the L96, nicknamed The Green Meanie by British snipers who would use it. The rifle was built around a precision machined aluminium block, or chassis, on top of which a flat bottomed receiver was bonded and mechanically fixed via four screws. A fully floating match barrel was screwed to the receiver; the trigger mechanism also inserted into its

housing and was secured with the use of two screws.

An integral bipod was mounted in the forward end of the block and could be rapidly deployed, or removed if desired. The now world famous look was completed with the use of two green polymer skins, or stock sides, which formed an ergonomic stock around the aluminium chassis providing the sniper with a moulded thumb hole and grip reminiscent of the earlier target rifles designed by the two Daves, although it is possible to use the rifle should one need to without them attached. The stock sides were attached with the use of eight screws that passed through the

block, not to it so as not to interfere with the harmonics of the weapon. The butt had an adjustable monopod and rubber recoil pad behind which plastic spacers could be inserted to adjust for length of pull.

The Schmidt & Bender 6 x 42mm scope was selected and produced in an all-green finish to match the rifle. Designated L13A1, it has a fixed x6 magnification and is equipped with a post and wire reticle reminiscent of the reticle type used historically in British sniper optics. Its elevation and windage drums are adjusted in MOA (minutes of angle), the elevation drum adjusting to forty-two MOA, enabling the rifle's reach to extend to 1,000 yards. The rifle was also

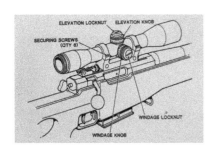
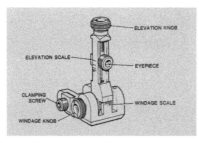
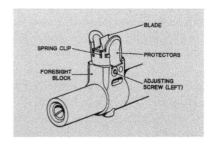

ABOVE: Tutorial diagrams making reference to the features of both the L13A1 telescope and the reserve battle sights of the L96A1 rifle.

supplied with back up battle sights, the rear of which also used the same dovetail rail as the main scope and was secured to the rail with a single screw. The forward battle sight, the design of which was initially taken from the General Purpose Machine Gun, also simply slid onto the barrel, the diameter of which was reduced much like the L42 barrel and was secured, again with a single screw.

With time to spare the PM Rifle was marketed to the British Special Forces who immediately saw the potential of a rifle that from the very beginning on the drawing board had been designed as a sniper rifle to do specifically the work that would be asked of it. In 1984 the SBS (Special Boat Service) ordered eight rifles which were delivered to the SBS, Dorset, UK the following year, 1985. In that same year the SAS (Special Air Service) ordered thirty-two PM Rifles. Given the number it would appear they replaced their entire stock of L42A1 sniper rifles in one fell swoop – no doubt due to their relief at finally having something that met their unique operational requirements as for some time they had not been happy with the equipment available to them and were sampling a number of different ideas to better their capability from their own budget.

ABOVE & FOLLOWING PAGES: An early Accuracy International sales brochure promoting the PM Rifle. Note the fully suppressed version. The brochure uses the versatility of field maintenance and its ability to accept various optics as strong selling features.

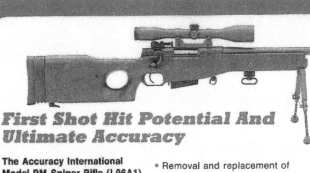

**PM Infantry (L96A1) with PM6×42
Telescopic Sight, Iron Sights
and Bipod**

First Shot Hit Potential And Ultimate Accuracy

The Accuracy International Model PM Sniper Rifle (L96A1) was selected for service by the British Army after extensive trials, evaluation and endurance firings. It is manufactured to quality standard AQAP 1 and developed by a team of experienced design engineers starting on a blank sheet of paper, whose brief consisted of these two basic requirements:

- to put the first shot on target in any environmental conditions, and

- to achieve and maintain ultimate accuracy.

The UK special forces needed one single weapon capable of coping with all their various tasks envisaged for anti-terrorist and covert operations to replace the collection of weapons in use at the time.

The UK infantry needed a rifle to replace the L42 Lee Enfield which had served for several decades.

With the design and production of the PM Sniper Rifle as a system sniping and counter sniping have entered into a new era. The rifle offers the following features, fulfilling its design parameters completely.

• First shot accuracy in any environment likely for UK forces, including arctic, jungle, desert and envisaged european scenarios.

• The accuracy of the system is effective at greater ranges than conventional sniper rifles, and so stretches counter-sniping.

• The stock is ambidextrous.

• Removal and replacement of sights should not affect zero.

• Rifle, sight and ammunition can be matched.

• Calibres are readily inter-changeable, ie. .308 win to .243 win.

• Conversion to moderated rifle is quick and easy.

• Simplicity of use, support and maintenance ensures an extremely cost effective service life.

• The complete rifle system is robust and reliable

• There are several options based on the PM system including infantry, counter terr-orist in high power and sup-pressed, and long-range.

• Derivatives for specialised use include models for arctic war-fare, folding (for inconspicuous carriage), and a dedicated magnum.

• The sights are steel tubed, robust and extremely efficient with 92% light transmission. Available in various powers, they incorporate either 'minute-of-angle' or 'mil rad' click grad-uations, as well as range graduations.

• The PM scope sight reticles are optically centred.

• The sight seals and o-rings are resistant to oil, water and ageing, ensuring high pro-tection and long life.

• Mounts and bracketry are available to fit a variety of night vision and telescopic sights.

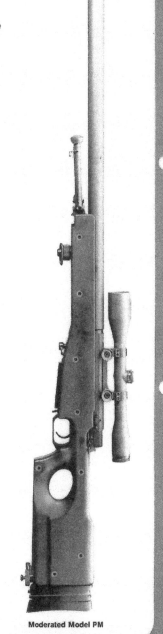

Moderated Model PM

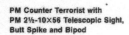

PM Counter Terrorist with
PM 2½-10×56 Telescopic Sight,
Butt Spike and Bipod

Basic Construction And Components

CONCEPT
Designed to be effective, simple and safe, the PM sniping rifle system incorporates several innovative components and design features.

SIMPLICITY
The rifle construction is so simple the user can maintain the rifle in all but the most major repairs. The bolt and its main components can be stripped by and the whole rifle can be stripped with the use of 3 allen keys and 1 screwdriver in 5 minutes.

SPEED
Barrels are stainless steel which helps prevent corrosion and erosion, and barrel changes can be completed within approximately 5 minutes without stripping the rifle.

EFFICIENCY
For observation where long periods of aiming are necessary, a retractable spike may be fitted to the butt which enables the user to set his rifle on the target without fatigue.

ADAPTABILITY
A quick-detachable, fold-away fore-end bipod which can be fitted or removed with one hand, allows the rifle to be rested in any type of terrain.

CONTINGENCY
Iron sights are available as back-up to scope sights

RELOADING
Magazines are quick-release, double-row box type, holding 10 rounds and removeable from the bottom of the rifle.

PRACTICALITY
Scuff resistant, olive green drab, matt finish plastic stock sides come in two halves and do not form a structural part of the rifle.

The PM chassis system and the use of modern materials eliminate the point of impact movement experienced with conventional wooden stocked rifles when used in varying humidities and temperatures. The PM system maintains its zero throughout because the stock does not form a structural part of the system.

The overall configuration of the rifle with its ambidextrous stock was designed to allow easy adjustment for different user's body shape, and, together with the mass of the rifle, enables the user to hold, fire, and watch the fall of shot whilst recycling the bolt, facilitating a quick follow up shot if necessary.

ACCESSORIES
A selection of accessories include a soft padded carrying case in d.p.m. with accessory pockets, carrying harness and handles; an aluminium transit case with plastizote furniture; cleaning equipment; cleaning rod guide; slings; action dust over in d.p.m.; and matched ammunition given guaranteed performance.

INNOVATION
The trigger is adjustable and may be removed without dismantling the complete rifle.

DAY VISION AND NIGHT VISION
Mounts And Bracketry

Mounts are available to fit various types of day and night sight to all the versions of the Model PM Sniper Rifle.

PM Counter-terrorist Model fitted with the Osprey OE 8050 Individual Weapon sight.

PM Infantry Model (L96A1) fitted with Simrad Optronics KN250 night sight.

PM Counter Terrorist Model fitted with Pilkington Kite sight.

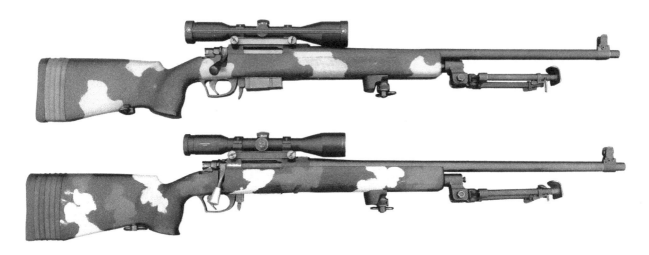

ABOVE: Two Parker-Hale M85 rifles displayed together. One in a jungle and the other in an urban camouflage stock. In total P-H offered six different camouflage patterns of the McMillan manufactured composite stock. Both rifles are also fitted with Kahles ZF84 telescopes.

The feedback from the SF units helped AI enormously; the rifle was hastily modified where necessary and fine-tuned before the trial example was submitted. In the same year the sales to the SF units were completed. The futuristic all-green PM Rifle sat in the company of other prestigious names submitted to the trial such as the SIG Sauer SSG 2000, Parker-Hale M85, HK PSG-1 and the Remington Model 700. Once the trial was underway all were quickly discounted with the exception of the Parker-Hale M85 which put up stiff competition. Designed by Eddy Taff of Parker-Hale, the M85 was worked on tirelessly in order for it to be ready for the MoD trial where it provided exceptional accuracy, matching the PM Rifle's eighty-five percent first round hit probability at a man-sized target between 600 and 900 metres, and being capable of harassing fire out to 1,100 metres, but after much deliberation from within the Land Warfare Centre, Warminster the P-H M85 was also discounted. The PM Rifle now stood alone, the trial over, but before the MoD would finally adopt the weapon the process moved to Canada where the Army Eight assisted SASC (Small Arms School Corps) in performing a detailed live fire performance

ABOVE: Two rare images captured during the performance comparison stage of the PM Rifle's trial to replace the L42A1 rifle. The provider of the images who is also featured in the pictures told of how these images were recorded after the PM Rifle had despatched all of the competition in the trial, and was all but formally adopted by the MoD. The scene captured in the first image shows both L42 and PM rifles on the range during a direct comparison. Starting at 100 yards they both fired a five round group every 100 yards back to 600. The groups were measured and sizes recorded by SASC. The owner of the images reports the PM Rifle came into a class of its own after 400 yards.

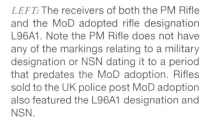

LEFT: The receivers of both the PM Rifle and the MoD adopted rifle designation L96A1. Note the PM Rifle does not have any of the markings relating to a military designation or NSN dating it to a period that predates the MoD adoption. Rifles sold to the UK police post MoD adoption also featured the L96A1 designation and NSN.

comparison of the PM and the L42 rifles.

The PM Rifle's accuracy coupled with a robust design and ease of maintenance also offered complete interchangeability of all parts; everything except the barrel could be replaced with just three Allen keys and an 85mm long screwdriver which became part of the rifle's CES equipment.

The complete package offered by the PM Rifle saw it across the line and to the utter astonishment of Accuracy International their rifle was selected to replace the L42A1. The decision was quietly announced and on 11th March 1985 the MoD awarded AI with a contract to supply 1,112 rifles plus spare parts. The production of the rifles was contracted out to a company specified by the MoD,

Pylon Industries Ltd, Dartford, Kent which was in fact more accustomed to building missiles than small arms. Regular batches of completed rifles started to return to Portsmouth where both Dave Walls and Dave Caig commissioned them after a test firing and full function test at Bisley, Surrey and then later at the Tunnel range, Devizes, Wiltshire.

The Accuracy International function test procedure was as follows.

1. Check serial numbers match (bolt and receiver).
2. Weapon safety check (as per normal safety precaution).
3. Locking ring check using tool.
4. Visual barrel inspection.
5. Fit sight.
6. Collimate to specific ammunition.

7. Test fire to test function and accuracy:
   - Fire sighters.
   - Fire two five round groups, both groups to score in the accepted range.

If the standard function test revealed a problem then points 1–4 were repeated. If accuracy was the issue the rifle was also subjected to a thorough clean before point 7 was carried out again.

If the rifle failed again it was rejected and subject to further investigation by the engineering team.

Rifles that passed the function test procedure had their test group sizes recorded before points 1–4 were carried out again before being thoroughly cleaned.

Once they were happy with their performance, the rifles were packed

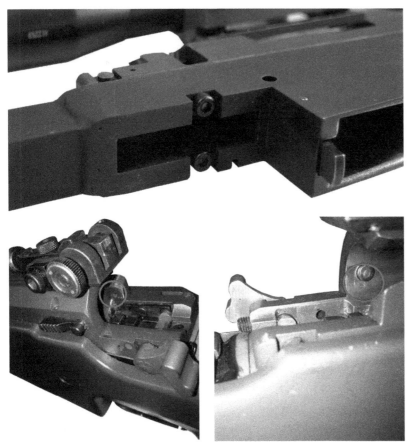

LEFT: The issue relating directly to the "C" suffix of the rifle serial number is illustrated in this group of images. The chassis image shows the position of the two screws of which the holes were overbored into the bolt housing. The red circles in the accompanying images detail the positions where the holes required filling. Within the red circles the grey filling material can be seen.

into their new green aluminium transit cases and shipped to Donnington central stores, Telford where they were officially received by the MoD being issued with NSN 1005-99-967-3405 and designated L96A1, both of which are actually engraved on the left hand receiver wall. The new rifle began to reach units in 1986, replacing the L42 sniper rifle. Soon thereafter disaster struck: a failure that would result in serious injury to one of the users of the weapon. The rolling issue of the rifle was halted whilst the weapon's failure was investigated. It was found the firing pin was breaking just in front of the cocking piece on closing the bolt which caused a premature detonation, resulting in the bolt being forced rearward towards the user. Unbeknown to Dave Walls who was Pylon Industries' AI point

of contact, Pylon had moved away from the firing pins' manufacture steel specification. Unaware, or ignorant, of the energy and forces present when the firing pin is released, they produced firing pins in one percent carbon silver steel as opposed to the specified EN24 forty ton tensile steel. History now tells us the silver steel was disastrously inefficient.

Under the direct control of AI a complete recall of all issued rifles was initiated and whilst under this inspection it was also found Pylon had overbored the two rear fixing holes in the receiver. These were two of the four holes drilled to attach the flat bottomed receiver to the top of the aluminium chassis block after it had been bonded. The two rear holes had broken through into the bolt housing chamber and the

choices to correct this were limited to a concession to the specification which involved filling the holes with specialist metal filler or scrapping the receiver and cutting a new one. A concession was granted and the two holes were filled and it is noticeable today among the extremely limited number of rifles still in existence by two black, greyish spots just inside the bolt housing chamber. The serial number also received a letter "C" suffix denoting the concession.

The issues regarding the two holes and firing pin were quickly overcome and recalled rifles received speedy correction under the direct control of AI in order to get the rifle on issue again. A further safety precaution and one that is still present on all AI rifles today involved the shroud at the rear of the bolt. Previously the square aluminium

ABOVE: An L96 heavily shrouded in desert brown sniper tape whilst serving in Afghanistan is seen here with its serial number on display. Note the serial number has the "C" suffix.

shroud completely sealed the rear end of the bolt but a modification was made which simply entailed drilling a hole so an extended firing pin could be installed which allowed the firing pin to protrude at the rear when the rifle was cocked. This was visible to the firer and acted as a simple visual aid that would indicate that the rifle was cocked. This also gave a prominent, at a glance, indication showing which rifles had been updated and which ones needed to be done.

Furthermore, much against popular belief, it's a significant stretch of the imagination that the L96 was suspended for a year or more as a result of the failure and that the L42 had continued service in its absence, as the entire restriction of use from the initial failure on the range to normal use of the weapon resuming was just six weeks after Pylon Industries manufactured all of the new replacement firing pins whilst AI redesigned and modified the shroud.

The searching enquiry that followed the whole episode resulted in Pylon Industries losing the MoD L96A1 sniper rifle contract and it has been suggested it contributed

to their demise, but the situation offered the unforeseen opportunity for AI to take total control of the manufacturing and assembly process. The partners all agreed it was the right and proper course of action and their case was put to the MoD who agreed without opposition. Two new CNC machines were purchased and as luck would have it Brett Walls, Dave's son who was following in his dad's engineering footsteps, had completed a CNC programming course. Brett's

help setting up the new machines was timely and going forward he helped train his dad to program and run the CNC processes needed to manufacture all the parts for assembly with very little contracting out, and AI delivered in total 1,247 L96A1 rifles to the MoD, with the last rifle delivered in 1992.

The two Daves now provided AI's military clients with after sales service and technical support whilst Malcolm Cooper continued to market AI around the world through his record breaking competition shooting. During this period the Swedish armed forces approached AI to design a rifle specifically to meet their cold climate requirements, and cited several features they wished to be included, a three stage safety mechanism being one, which would also be a deal breaker – no three stage safety mechanism, no order. So the challenge was set. It took months of head scratching to achieve a design that would deliver the three stage safety mechanism and once this issue was overcome it paved the way to a concept rifle. The development moved into the cold climate testing of the prototype which took place at the U.S. CRTC (United States Cold Regions Test

ABOVE: The modified bolt shroud can be seen here. This rifle is cocked and the rear of the firing pin can be seen protruding from the shroud whilst the rifle is ready to fire.

LEFT: The ice breaking grooves which can be found on the AW bolt. A feature born out of the extensive AW cold weather development programme.

Center), Fort Greeley, Alaska. CRTC provided harsh to extreme real world conditions, testing the prototype weapon under punishing conditions out of which some small design changes were brought about. The thumbhole, bolt, magazine and trigger guard were all enlarged so a sniper wearing cold weather gloves could better use the equipment. It was also at CRTC that a bolt freeze issue was discovered, resulting in a revised design of the bolt leading to grooves being cut in the bolt body just in front of the handle where the bolt body is shrouded by the bolt chamber when in the closed position. To give less surface area of the bolt in the action body and to allow the bolt rotation to break away any ice that may have built up in this area when opening the bolt, the handle was strengthened by being cast as part of the bolt body instead of being attached after the bolt body was manufactured, as was the case with the L96.

An additional feature was incorporated in the chamber which involved a shallow ring being cut so as to give any snow and ice on the ammunition an escape as it may have been dislodged as the ammunition was pushed into the chamber. The shallow cut prevented compacting between the chamber and bolt face, but this feature was later dropped from the specification. All the lessons learnt during the L96 era were used to better design the new rifle. Many of the features that made the L96 still existed in the now newly christened AW (Arctic Warfare) rifle. The hugely successful chassis system remained the core of the new system which still supported the flat bottomed receiver that was bonded and screwed to it. Many of the parts that were so successful on the L96 had their design tweaked, such as the stock sides which were greatly improved and produced from a more durable polymer. They were not as fragile as the L96 stock sides when not attached to the rifle; in fact all parts were manufactured from either corrosion resistant materials or were given a tough protective finish prior to assembly, and furthermore all parts were designed to be interchangeable with another AW of the same calibre.

MODEL 'AW' 7.62 SNIPER RIFLE SYSTEM

Sweden's order with Accuracy International for their new sniper rifle system coincides with the company's launch of their much modified and improved 2nd generation 7.62 system. The PSG 90, as it is designated in Sweden, was chosen after 6 years of evaluation.

The PM/L96 system was launched with purchases by the British Ministry of Defence in 1984/5 and since its introduction has been procured by 19 other countries, mostly for elite and counter-terrorist forces. Accuracy International has been working on its successor from this time. The new rifle supersedes the PM/L96 series which will only be available to special order. Spares, of course, will continue to be supplied.

The AW rifle maintains the basic features of the PM/L96 rifle. The action is still the three forward lug bolt system but is slicker and easier to use than its predecessor, making covert use easier.

Every part, process and finish has undergone revaluation with the intention of making it stronger, simpler and better able to function in climatic extremes, yet easier to train on and use. Endurance tests on four rifles have gone beyond 10,000 rounds without noticeable wear (except barrel), part failure, misfeed or malfunction. More importantly, the tests were carried out without maintenance.

ABOVE & FOLLOWING PAGES: An Accuracy International sales brochure from the later Arctic Warfare rifle period circa mid-nineties prior to the folding stock development. Again, note the fully suppressed model. With the L96 under their belts the brochure boasts of improved L96 technology and reliability listing the numerous innovative features.

Technical Specification

Weight without bipod	6.1Kg (13.4lbs)
Length	1180mm with 30mm of butt spacers
Magazine type & capacity	Double row, 9 or 10 shot
Calibre	7.62 NATO
Barrel Specification	650mm length, optional twist rate, fitted with muzzle brake and foresight mount.
Ammunition types	NATO standard, match and special saboted.
Action Type	Forward lug(3) bolt action, anti-freeze, anti-dirt.
Trigger	Two-stage adjustable 1.6Kg – 2.0Kg, anti-freeze, anti-dirt.
Stock	Chassis with structural filled nylon furniture, adjustable for length using butt spacers 10, 20 and 30mm wide. Rubber butt pad.
Bedding	None.
Bipod	Quick detachable, foldable modified QD Parker Hale lightweight LM6 type.
Iron Sights	Optional, pre-zeroed detached until required, ranges 2-600m.
Optical Sights	Hensoldt 10x40, .2 mil rad clicks (.8MOA) 2cm @ 100m wind and elevation and range marks to 1000m (1100 yds), 92% light transmission, 'Betalight' illuminated mil dot reticle for night shooting, objective bell fitted with extending hood, eyepiece diopter setting plus or minus 2. Weight .515Kg (1.13lbs). Eye relief 70mm (2.75"). Field of view 2.4 degrees (42m at 1000m). Power, 10X..
Scope Mount	One-piece, low profile.

Extras Available

* Blank firing magazines (plastic or metal blank types taken), 9-rounds capacity.
* Sling for carrying and shooting
* Action dust cover
* Stainless cleaning rod, breakdown for pocket carriage
* Iron sights in protective bag
* Cleaning kit
* Multi-purpose tool
* Soft carrying case for rifle and all accessories
* Transit case to take all the above plus extra magazines, ammunition, etc.

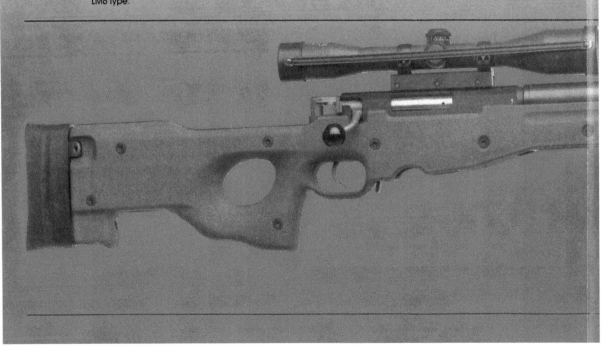

Main Features of the 'AW' Rifle

The rifle has a special anti-icing bolt mechanism allowing reliable use down to –40 degrees C, even in sudden temperature changes causing frozen condensation.

The rifle is fitted with a Hensoldt 10x42 day/night sight with .2 milrad click drums and ranges to 1000m.

The barrel is stainless steel and internally configured for the new precision saboted sniper round currently under development.

The guns are guaranteed to shoot inside 20mm at 100m with match grade sniper ammunition.

Pre-zeroed iron sights are available to be fitted with a standard tool in an emergency and together with dust covers, tools and cleaning kit are contained in a rain proof aluminium transit case.

The sling doubles for carrying and shooting from any of the 5 sling points.

The rifle comes with a modified Q.D. Parker Hale bipod.

All parts of the new system are protected against any likely corrosive agent.

A 3-way safety is fitted to the right hand side of the shroud.

It is fitted with a muzzle brake which facilitates spotting the fall of shot and quick follow up shots.

Reduced recoil from the design of the muzzle brake simplifies training and aids control.

The specialist types, 'Counter-Terrorist', 'Infantry' and 'Covert' will still be available based on the new system.

The rifle is in series production.

The rifle is in service with the Swedish Army and special forces and in production for the Belgian Armed Forces.

Safety Features

Safety Catch	3-way "safe" (bolt locked), "safe" (bolt unlocked), and "fire". The safety catch withdraws the firing pin and locks the bolt in the closed position ensuring safety during drops. Safety is fitted to the right hand side of the bolt shroud and is designed as an anti-freeze, anti-dirt mechanism.
Action	Gas protection is offered by minimum action cuts and tight tolerances. Ports are away from the user's face.
Bolt	Gas protection is by shroud deflection. The firing pin cannot protrude until the bolt is fully closed.
Proof	All rifles are subjected to British special 30% over proof using oiled rounds.
Carrying and Shooting Points	There are five carrying points, two each side and one under the forward end.
Corrosion Protection	All parts and surfaces are protected against the hardest environmental conditions, arctic or tropical.
Performance	Better than 20mm grouping at 100m.

Reliability

Test firings (not in machine rests) carried out with standard NATO ammunition show endurance of weapons without maintenance is in excess of 10,000 rounds using the same barrel, without malfunction, misfeed, part breakage or loss of basic zero.

Points of User Interest

All actions and manipulations carried out during the use of the AW model are easier than the PM/L96 series.

The lessened recoil and directional characteristics of the muzzle brake, amended sight and upgraded stock holding gives enhanced use of the rifle in the hands of all levels of skill, with marked improvement by less experienced snipers.

Robustness

All aspects of the AW as a whole or individual parts have been up-rated where robustness is concerned, when compared with the first generation rifles.

Portability

5 sling points and their position in the rifle gives optional carrying possibilities, whether normal or by harness (hands off, say for skiing).

Interchangeability

The AW rifle parts are designed and manufactured to permit total interchangeability as with the L96. This includes bolts and barrels and the maintenance of correct head space.

Maintenance

User and 2nd line only is as for the L96.

Major inspections would normally be expected at barrel changes. Barrel changes are based on 1st shot hit and accuracy capability and can be expected between 6000-12,000 rounds. Barrel life is long or short depending on damage caused by careless or over cleaning.

Minor overhaul and checking of the barrel and locking ring should be expected at approximately 12,000 rounds.

Major overhaul of the rifle system should be undertaken at approximately 20,000 rounds.

Accuracy

Dedicated by first shot accuracy:
At delivery   Less than 20mm at 100m
At 5000 rounds
                            Less than 20mm at 100m
At 10,000   Less than 30mm at 100m

The above is using match Grade Sniper Ammunition. Special barrel selection and batching will give 10mm at 100m. A basic change of zero in the rifle system is subject only to wear in the barrel.

Quality

The AW rifle and its variants are designed and produced by Accuracy International who are approved to the top NATO quality level AQAP 1. Every effort has been made to minimise wear, maximise strength, reliability and consistency, to make the rifle easy to use – therefore the user effective quickly, and to make the system as simple as possible for maintenance and cleaning by user and armourer.

Budgeting

Initial cost in comparison with conventional systems should be weighed against a reduction in maintenance, maintenance cycles, maintenance skills, spare parts and user training time. The ease of use and fast training time also reduce ammunition expenditure and resulting cost. However, the system should be used with the best possible ammunition if optimum and reliable accuracy is required.

Spares packages need only be based on breakage or damage due to accident or misuse.

The usable life of the system is extremely long for a weapon of this type.

Transit case to take all the above plus extra magazines, ammunition etc.

ABOVE: Dave Caig's folding stock would become a standard feature of later AW rifles.

In 1991 Sweden purchased 1,100 .308 calibre AW rifles soon after which the British MoD followed suit and adopted the much improved .308 AW rifle designating it L118A1, and later an A2 specification rifle followed featuring a folding stock designed by Dave Caig in 1998.

All AW rifles that followed the military contracts were built with a modification to the chassis joint behind the receiver that would make L118A1 and A2 rifles unique in their designation. The rifles produced after the military contracts had the joint pinned and bonded rather than welded. The bonding method was far more accurate as when the aluminium weld cooled the length of one chassis could vary as much as 2mm to another. The modified method of achieving the joint was further justified as the welded joint was vulnerable to breaking if the butt of the weapon took a heavy blow such as being dropped vertically; the L96A1 rifle suffered a similar issue. The AW served alongside the L96A1 rifle mainly within Special Forces units until it completely superseded it in a .338 calibre L115 model in the early 2000s, however officially the L96 withdrawal from service was a staged affair after 2008 as some

units saw the rifle removed from them quite early whilst others were still using it long into the decade, finally giving it up as late as 2012. I would suggest key operational requirements during the Iraq and Afghanistan conflicts extended its service life significantly.

The extensive development work put into the AW programme paid huge dividends later as it enabled AI to be innovative with that particular platform and with the close cooperation of the Finnish ammunition manufacturer Lapua, AI further developed the AW rifle producing the .338 Lapua Magnum variant in 1995, making them the first company to mass produce a .338 Lapua Magnum rifle. The following year, 1996, saw the British MoD adopt the .338 Lapua Magnum and designate it L115A1 which was further enhanced later with an A2 variant and almost a decade later again with an A3 variant.

In 1998 the AW platform was configured to the .300 Win Mag and was supplied to the German armed forces. The German-supplied .300 Win Mag rifle would be the first to incorporate Dave Caig's folding stock which today makes the AW range of rifles unique. The

innovations kept coming and in 2000 AI launched the bolt action AW50. Launched initially as an anti-material weapon, the .50 BMG (Browning Machine Gun) calibre rifle was immediately adopted by the British MoD. Around the same point in time AI also unveiled the AICS (Accuracy International Chassis System) specifically for the Remington Model 700 receiver. The AICS was developed almost as a byproduct of the AW programme and allowed the Remington 700 shooter to upgrade. The chassis system provided the AI ergonomic stock and functionality benefits as well as allowing the Model 700 receiver to become part of the AI full length self-aligning and self-bedding aluminium block, providing much improved performance. AW technology also assisted when AI were approached by U.S. law enforcement agencies who had specific requests; those requests were met with the AE rifle in 2002.

By the end of the nineties AI was a great British success story who were attracting the attention of investors and in 1999 ninety percent of AI was sold to an investment group. The sale brought with it a considerable debt which was costed, however predicted sales and new innovative products were not realised and the task of keeping the company afloat quickly became a struggle compounded by how the company's operations had shifted to keep pace with the previous year's meteoric AW growth phase. Raw material costs had risen and the practice of outsourcing had grown, inflicting crippling production costs on the struggling company. The depression deepened with the death of Malcolm Cooper in June 2001 and in 2004 there were attempts to sell the failing organisation, all of which failed. AI's options ran out and in 2005 they were declared bankrupt.

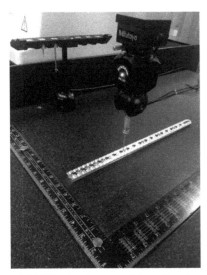 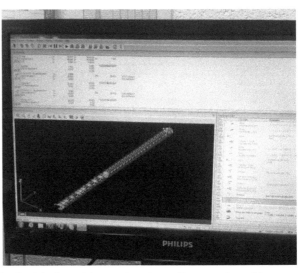

ABOVE: Today Accuracy International employ the latest precision engineering software and machinery.

As the news was being announced Dave Walls was indicating to the administrators he was interested in buying part of the company, and at the same time Tom Irwin, a dual UK/U.S. citizen who was an independent contractor based in the U.S., was visiting AI and immediately added his interest also. Within twenty-four hours Dave Caig and Paul Bagshaw, the financial director, joined the rescue party. Tom Irwin immediately set about contacting local banks. The four would be shareholders. Walls, Irwin, Caig and Bagshaw put together a new business plan in just twelve days and hired an accountancy firm to verify the numbers before entering their bid. All of AI's employees were made redundant on 18th February 2005 and the four prospective shareholders had to defend their offer through a short bidding war at which they would fend off all rival bids to emerge the victors. Tom spent ten weeks visiting AI's customers to reassure them, signing the documents that would transfer the company to their ownership on 29th April and they rebooted the company on 3rd May.

The new company started with just seven employees and four owners. With AI now completely stripped back, it gave them the opportunity to analyse everything they previously did in the manufacture process. As much as possible was brought back in house as they had done after the Pylon Industries lesson with the L96 and the subcontractors, agents and distributors they needed to function all being made preferred shareholders, giving them a vested interest in the new company's success. The machine shop was gutted and new CNC machinery, programs and fixtures were purchased so all parts could be manufactured in house to the most efficient methods possible. In conjunction with this Tom Irwin studied how William Edwards Deming revolutionised the Japanese

ABOVE: A component or even a rifle starts its journey as a design. AI uses the latest design software to create every component part. *(© MoDCrown copyright)*

ABOVE: Tom Irwin and Dave Walls in the board room at AI's Portsmouth facility. Dave holds UA 86 A0044 and reacquaints himself after thirty years since he function tested it and despatched it to Donnington central stores.

auto industry with a view to implementing rate-based workflow.

He studied successful companies such as Motorola and GE who implemented a similar output management system called Six Sigma. The new rate-based workflow system implemented better organised space; each employee no longer had to travel to retrieve the parts that were being fitted at a bench and needless waste was eliminated. The new manufacturing process now operates by production meeting a predetermined weekly output target of rifles, bolts, triggers and spares regardless of contracts. In contrast to the previous model of manufacture the company's delivery success rate rocketed to 99.75%. The last decade has seen AI grow year on year, the development of new exciting products continues,

and the standards to which they are produced continues to evolve through the embracing of new technologies such as rapid prototyping 3-D printing and high speed cameras.

Their quality control procedures are unforgiving, demanding the highest standards in precision. The availability of the AW to the public has long been ceased, however the continued use of the .338 Lapua AWSM (Arctic Warfare Super Magnum) by the British Army has continued its limited manufacture. The SSIP (Sniper System Improvement Programme) provided AI with an MoD contract for 582 systems in 2007 with the delivery of the weapon in 2008 and today that very rifle, designated L115A3, is stepping into the future as the British Army continues to upgrade and keep

pace with the most cutting edge systems available. The L115A3 will soon enter an upgrade programme that will involve its component parts being refurbished and mounted on the new AX ("A" denoting Accuracy International and "X" denoting the x ring on a standard target) chassis providing the British sniper with L115A4, the most innovative in stock ergonomics and rifle functionality available.

Chapter 6
The Green Meanie

The first victim of the L96A1 sniper rifle was Parker-Hale and its M85 submission to the MoD trials in 1985. The P-H M85 presented the greatest competition of all the submissions to the PM Rifle during the trial, at every level displaying excellent accuracy between 600 and 900 metres. History tells us it was a tough decision as it was very much liked by certain quarters of the Land Warfare Centre, Warminster. In the end it would come down to all aspects from accuracy to its usability by the sniper in the field and the logistical elements that would have to support it keeping it front line and serviceable.

The Accuracy International approach had the M85 beat by firstly building a chassis based rifle, groundbreaking at the time in comparison to the M85 which was a continuation of nineteenth century technology. The provision of four very basic tools as part of the L96 kit fit its collection of bolt on parts; no specialist skill was needed to change defective parts which meant if the unit armourer was not available the sniper could do it himself. Reducing the weapon to five major components, chassis, barrel, receiver, trigger and scope made for an unprecedented level of versatility. The knock-on effect was an unserviceable weapon that may have had a basic fault spent minimal time being unserviceable, reducing

the need to pack a rifle up in its chest with its complete CES and send it to a command workshop for repair by a skilled armourer as was the case with the L42, a practice which would have continued with the M85 had it been adopted.

Fans of the M85 will still fiercely debate today as to why the M85 should have had its place in British sniping history which in some ways it does, however the M85 did not die after the MoD trial; in fact around 800 examples were produced by Parker-Hale assembled by Eddy Taff, Parker-Hale's principal armourer, and Bill Smallwood. Limited numbers of the M85 did in fact see service with the British Army as it is confirmed the SAS purchased several as well as the Parachute Regiment, particularly the second battalion who had several in their armoury. In addition to these examples there are other accounts from snipers of other regiments who confirm at least one example was available to them such as snipers from the first battalion, the Royal Green Jackets, who were also familiarised with the weapon. The vast majority of the 800 examples produced were supplied to organisations such as UK police constabularies as the Enfield Enforcer's replacement as well as the Falkland Islands defence force and several foreign armed forces elsewhere around the world. I once purchased a Schmidt & Bender 12 x 42 telescope set up in a M85 mount which was marked with an M85 serial number 00245F (F which features in all M85 serial numbers reportedly stands for FIELD). When I investigated I discovered the following information:

- 00245F – Hand built and assembled 4th March 1988 by Bill Smallwood
- Parker-Hale factory fitted Schmidt & Bender 12x42mm sight

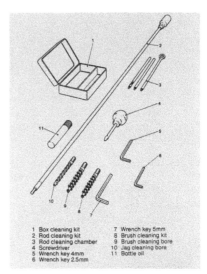

1. Box cleaning kit
2. Rod cleaning kit
3. Rod cleaning chamber
4. Screwdriver
5. Wrench key 4mm
6. Wrench key 2.5mm
7. Wrench key 5mm
8. Brush cleaning kit
9. Brush cleaning bore
10. Jag cleaning bore
11. Bottle oil

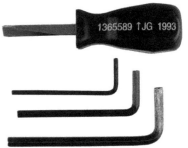

ABOVE: Pictured are the very basic tools which are also illustrated in the accompanying line drawing which lists the cleaning and maintenance equipment belonging to the rifle's CES. These simple tools are all that is required to strip the rifle back to chassis, receiver and barrel.

- Trigger adjusted for single pull 2¼ lbs
- 17.7mm group of 10 rounds at 100 yards
- Fitted with NATO green furniture
- Issued to the Sri Lankan Royal Air Force

If the trepidation Dave Walls and Dave Caig felt when Malcolm Cooper first suggested they submit a rifle to the MoD trial had steered them in another direction the Parker-Hale M85 would have undoubtedly become the British Army's new sniper system in 1986.

PREVIOUS PAGE: A would-be Royal Marine sniper going through his cadre in the early nineties. He stands up as his stalk has just ended due to a trained spotter having found his position. Mastering concealment and the use of ground is essential for any student to pass his cadre and critical if he is to survive on the battlefield.

Rifle 7.62mm Parker-Hale M85

Technical Specification	
Calibre	7.62mm
Magazine Capacity	10 Rounds Double Stack
Overall Rifle Length	1150mm
Barrel	Stainless Steel 27.5 inch
Twist Rate	4 Groove 1:12 R/H
Weight	6.24kg
Scope Mounted	Overbore
Iron Sights	Yes
Manufactured By	Parker Hale
Qty Manufactured	800 approx

ABOVE & RIGHT: The Parker-Hale M85 solidly built and equalling the L96's accuracy but beaten by innovation. Note the telescope is the same Schmidt & Bender 6 x 42mm as the L13A1 which also has the same post and wire reticle. This example 00347F was built on 23rd May 1989 by Bill Smallwood. It achieved a ten round test group which measured 16.6mm.

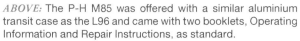

ABOVE: The P-H M85 was offered with a similar aluminium transit case as the L96 and came with two booklets, Operating Information and Repair Instructions, as standard.

ABOVE: Old adversaries pictured here together. The acute difference between the two rifles' designs is clear to see when placed side by side.

Rifle 7.62mm L96A1/L13A1 Telescope

With the British Army's adoption of the PM Rifle, designating it L96A1, NSN B1/1005-99-967-3405, it entered service in 1986. Its original title has long since been forgotten, some even thinking the PM Rifle was a different rifle altogether in some way. I spoke with a former member of the SAS who was convinced the PM Rifle was an accurised version of the L96, but of course it is not. It just predates the weapon designated L96A1, which holds a cult-like status today. It's incredible to think a rifle which is looked back upon with such adoration nearly never happened with its mechanical failure in the beginning.

A former Sergeant Major of the SAS told me about a call he received reporting a near miss one of their guys had on the range when a bolt blew back at him and he avoided injury by the narrowest of margins. Before he could pick up the phone and report the near miss up the chain of command he himself received a call instructing a blanket ban on the use of the weapon as a Royal Marine elsewhere on the same day had been seriously injured in a similar incident. However, the dark cloud that shrouded the L96 in its infancy did clear to a bright future for the new concept of a chassis based rifle which introduced for the first time to the British Army not only a purpose built sniper weapon but also a weapon that considered ergonomics for the user. The end result was a very accurate weapon that was comfortable to shoot, translating into a much higher pass rate of the sniper badge test.

Warminster sniper wing, however, were quite slow to change the test to be more challenging to the new weapon; even as late as the early nineties regular as well as territorial sniper students were still going through the old course that had existed for the L42 since 1973. It taught deadly fire out to 600 metres and harassing fire out to 800 metres, whereas anyone with any experience of the L96 will know the rifle can comfortably deliver deadly fire out to 800 metres all day long. However, change was coming and was heralded in 1991 as the six week course become a two week course for the territorial battalions as for them their sniping capability was reduced to sharpshooter.

The all-green L13A1 Schmidt & Bender scope provided fixed six power magnification as opposed to the three power of the L1A1 No. 32 scope which, coupled with the all-weather accuracy of the L96, greatly improved its reach. The new doctrine allowed for this and *Pamphlet No. 4* was amended; from the mid-nineties all snipers were taught deadly fire out to 900 metres and harassing fire out to 1,100 metres. This was the only officially recognised change to the course laid down by *Pamphlet No. 4*, however the plethora of spotting scopes which were appearing at unit level was like a revolution as snipers from one unit to another were sporting all manner of telescopes purchased through unit funds. The modern spotting scopes were providing huge increases in magnification compared with the twenty power provided by the Scout Regiment Telescope which brought about change to the Observation Stand training within units. The knock-on effect was one unit training its sniper differently to another; these changes were not officially sanctioned and the term "Creeping Sniper Excellence" was commonly used when referring to these practices.

ABOVE: The fixed six power magnification of the L13A1 telescope is seen here as this Figure 14 Hun's Head target is viewed at 300 yards.

In the late nineties, when the L96 received its mid-life upgrade by receiving the new Schmidt & Bender 3-12 x 50mm telescopes, the course received further amendments. The now standard and more powerful L17A1 telescope came with stepped

ABOVE: Markers in the butts indicate to a firer where his shot has fallen on this Figure 11 target during a marksmanship test.

ABOVE: The L17A1 telescope bracket of this L96 rifle has been marked with the rifle's serial number. Note the bracket number's position so it can be quickly cross referenced with the rifle. This was not standard practice and is another example of "Creeping Sniper Excellence". Some units did it, others did not.

ranging stadia lines as well as the Mildot reticle which aided the sniper immensely as now he could measure the target with the reticle, allowing him to use the mils measurement as an indication of range which consequently altered the judging distance section of the course. The L96 introduction also brought with it a relaxation in the rigid numbering system of key components of the previous decades where the 4T and L42 possessed their own parts and scope that made that rifle perform. The chassis system ended all that;

the L96 was pretty much made up of parts that were universal by design.

When speaking with Dave Walls I asked why scopes and brackets were never mated to a weapon by numbering by Accuracy International. His face said more than any words he could speak as he initially looked at me with a genuinely perplexed look on his face as he tried to compute my question. His explanation started with a question: "Why?"

He went on to explain that the precision engineering behind the

manufacturing of all parts had eliminated the need to bespoke finish anything for an individual rifle and almost all parts were interchangeable between rifles. Further to his explanation, AI were first and foremost a civilian company; none of the founding members came from a military background and therefore had not been infected by the incessant desire to put a number on everything. The L96 featured here is serial number 0044, literally the forty-fourth rifle AI built and its L13A1 telescope is serial number 0081. Dave described how during assembly in those early days he and Dave Caig would set the rifles up before function testing and although the telescope with serial number 0044 was probably somewhere in the pile it just didn't matter to them to match the two; it had no purpose so it was not done.

On examining an L96 rifle you will find the bolt shroud often carries the rifle's own serial number on the right hand side for easy cross referencing to the rifle's own serial number. The practice, which was done by AI, mates the bolt to the rifle for obvious reasons, however years of service meant a worn out shroud was replaced sometimes

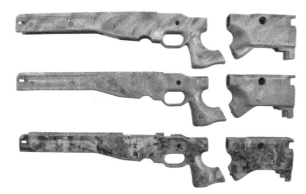

RIGHT: A sniper in Afghanistan applies the finishing touches to the spray paint camouflage of his rifle. Note there is no camouflage material attached to the barrel; a best practice ruling halted this tradition for many. Note the three sets of stock sides (*ABOVE*), each of which have been camouflage painted by individual snipers. The styles illustrate how personal the camouflaging process can be.

ABOVE: A sniper in Afghanistan armed with an upgraded L96 sniper rifle. Note the sniper tape camouflaging the weapon extends to the barrel. Creeping Sniper Excellence? The situation can be confusing with one unit operating very different practices to another. Note the sling fitted to this sniper's rifle is a narrow web Seyntex L8A1 sling. (© MoDCrown copyright)

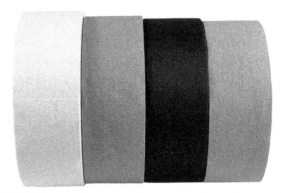

ABOVE: The practice of wrapping a sniper rifle in sniper tape is largely viewed as having started with the L96A1 rifle, however snipers armed with the L42 in the eighties were indulging in this practice long before the introduction of the L96.

several times and subsequently the replacements never received the serial number engraving. But look further and you will not find, other than its own official serial number, any number referencing marks tying a component part specifically to any given rifle. However in later years that followed its arrival CWS (Common Weapon Sight) and L17A1 scope mounts could be found marked to a rifle; this was a sporadic practice done at unit level and was hit and miss across the army. I can only surmise it was done to keep detachable items such as the scope together with its rifle if camouflaged by the sniper, for example, telescopes and weapons matched in colour tones and pattern as the camouflage was applied by hand and unique to each sniper who created it.

The most common system was to number the rifles one to eight and write a corresponding number on each scope case – a flawed system if the cases were swapped though. Or maybe the numbering of such brackets was down to a finicky sniper platoon sergeant with a sergeant major's eye for detail. The practice of camouflaging the weapon dates back to the Great War and has continued ever since. Wrapping hessian around a rifle which has woodwork going almost to the muzzle was never detrimental to the performance of the rifle until the L42 rifle entered the sniping scene and brought with it the exposed heavy barrel which presented a straight, black, shiny profile to any potential enemy, a feature that has remained and is common to all sniper rifles today.

Snipers of the L42 era dealt with the problem by wrapping the barrel in hessian and then later with the introduction of sniper tape they taped the barrel, eliminating shine, and then added scrim to break up its straight profile. With this came a robust debate as to whether adding all this material directly to the barrel interfered with its harmonics when fired and ultimately moved the bullet's point of impact. Some argued the practice had no effect and if it did the effect was so minimal it was negligible, on the other hand there were many who argued it was disruptive to the performance of the weapon. But the practice continued and bridged across to the L96. However, in the mid-2000s during the Afghan conflict some units banned the practice amongst their snipers, allowing only paint as an acceptable level of camouflage to be applied to the barrel. This appears though to be a unit decision as the conflict was heavily photographically documented and there are many examples of snipers who have their weapons completely shrouded in sniper tape.

An argument from another perspective, though, did add weight to the debate. It came from unit QMSs who did not like the practice of applying sniper tape as it made it very difficult for REME armourers to externally inspect the barrels.

Unlike the L42 which saw active service almost straight away in Dhofar, the L96 would not be "blooded" until four years after its adoption in the Gulf War in 1991 where it would be tested in conditions that had broken the first of the No. 4 Mk1 T rifles some fifty years earlier. The Kuwaiti desert offered blistering heat and fine powdery sand that seemed to penetrate everything, a real test for the new system. The barrel fitted to the L96 was match grade stainless steel, twenty-five and a half inches long with four grooves and a one in fourteen inch right hand twist rate. The barrels were manufactured

Rifle 7.62mm L96A1/L13A1 Telescope
NSN, B1/1005-99-967-3405

Technical Specification	
Calibre	7.62mm
Magazine Capacity	11 Rounds
Overall Rifle Length	46.26in with butt spacers
Barrel Length	25.5in
Twist Rate	4 Groove, RH 1 in 14 Twist
Combat Weight	14lb
Iron Sights	Yes
Approval Date	11th March 1985
Manufactured By	Accuracy International
Scope Mounted	Overbore
1985 Contract Qty	1112

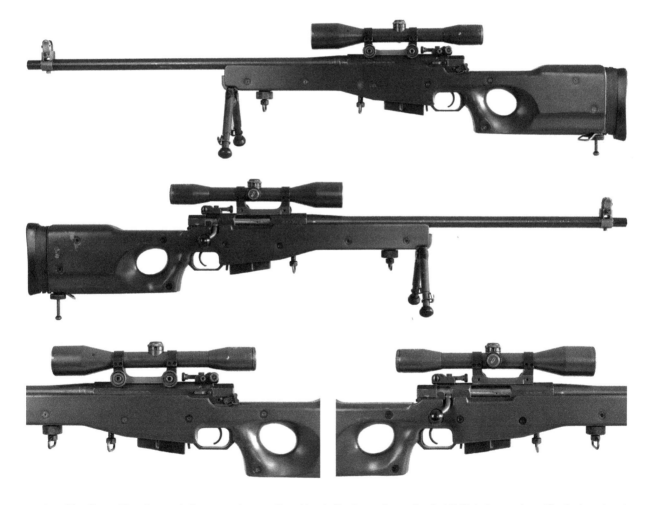

ABOVE: The Green Meanie, revolutionary and groundbreaking in its day as it was the first British Army sniper rifle designed and built to specifically be a sniper rifle. Note the colour tone of the L13A1 telescope closely matches that of the rifle. Only the earliest scopes matched this closely to the rifle as when the contract got underway the scopes became more of a bronze green.

by several companies at different stages. Border Barrels, Madco and Lothar Walther were all involved, however Border Barrels were the most prolific, guaranteeing 10,000 rounds with just one MOA shift of MPI (Mean Point of Impact) with wear. The barrel and receiver body were finished in the same grass green painted finish, and the stock sides were produced in a resin to match.

ABOVE: A sniper inspects the bore of the heavily camouflaged barrel of his L96. Note the improvised cheek rest.

Telescope, Schmidt & Bender L13A1 and Backup Sights

The 6 x 42mm Schmidt & Bender telescope, NSN V5/1240-99-967-4564, of which the excellence was cited in the 1988 14 Maintenance Advisory Group report, performed superlatively. The scope lenses were protected by bikini style lens caps, NSN B1/1005-99-770-1094. The caps linked to each other by double rubber straps and had clear plastic lenses unique to Schmidt & Bender which if the sniper wished allowed them to remain in place fitted to the scope whilst the sniper rifle was in use, however the sand and grit when in the desert made light work of the lenses, scratching them so much that the benefit of the clear lenses was quickly lost.

The scope came equipped with BDC (bullet drop compensation) with the elevation drum wearing two sets of numbers: a yellow set around the base of the drum indicating MOA adjustment, and a white second set of numbers sitting above the MOA adjustment numbers indicating a quick reference to distance, allowing the sniper to quickly engage targets

at a predetermined range, i.e. a sniper in a pre-prepared position who has prepared a range card or panoramic referencing all prominent features and their distances can rapidly engage a target that appears on or near any of the marked features. So, if the enemy appears half right near the lone tree marked on the range card or panoramic as being 300 metres away, the sniper can quickly turn the elevation drum to the white number three and engage.

The scope is held within a double ringed single piece mount with two large thumb wheels on the left side, almost a nod to the appearance of the L42, which when loosened allows the scope to be mounted/dismounted. Mounting of the scope involved the mount sliding onto a dovetail base running along the top of the receiver. The underside of the scope mount has a stud protruding from the forward end which locates in a recess in the dovetail base, ensuring the scope sits in the same position every time, eye relief being

ABOVE: The markings on the elevation drum of this L13A1 telescope are clearly visible in this image. Note the yellow MOA graduations around the bottom of the drum and the BDC reference numbers in white around the top.

ABOVE: The underside of the L13A1 scope bracket is illustrated in this image next to the top of the rifle's receiver. Note the locating stud on the underside of the bracket and the hole in the receiver that accepts it.

ABOVE & LEFT: The reserve iron sights, or, battle sights of the L96 are effective out to 700 metres. The graticule readings on the rear sight can be difficult to see, particularly the elevation scale on the left side of the sight. Note the plastic protective muzzle cover.

set by the position of the scope in the rings. The whole scope ensemble was specifically designed to be removable and had available to it a carry case to house the scope when dismounted. Manufactured in Cordura-like material, the case was produced in DPM and SF (Special Forces) black and was equipped with a full length zip, shoulder strap and ALICE (All-purpose Lightweight Individual Carrying Equipment) clips for flexible attachment to other kit; however the issue of these cases appears to have been extremely limited, and probably a one-time issue in the late 1980s. Many were utilised for other purposes and as normal wear and tear took their toll they were not replaced. They do not appear in the equipment schedule and surviving examples do not appear to carry a NSN marking, making this particular case thin on the ground today.

The backup sights which are deployed in the event of the L13A1 scope becoming damaged, rendering it unreliable or completely unserviceable, are on the L96 in the form of a collapsible rear sight leaf and adjustable foresight. The rear sight can be adjusted for both windage and elevation with each click value being one MOA in both. When the sight is deployed from its forward folded position it stands vertical with a knob for adjustment sitting directly on top. The knob when operated will control the setting of the elevation scale and eyepiece against the engraved range setting on the side of the leaf which is graduated from 200 to 700 metres in 100 metre graduations. The base of the rear sight has a control knob on the left which allows the sniper to correct ten MOA either side of zero. The rear sight unit attaches to the rifle by clamping onto the continuous dovetail that runs along the top of the receiver.

The foresight, which was reminiscent of the GPMG (General Purpose Machine Gun) foresight, operates loosely on the same principle as the No. 4 foresight arrangement in that the foresight blade sits on a platform that dovetails and slides laterally on a block band fixed to the rifle barrel, and is retained by a screw on each side. The foresight blade is retained by a sprung clip and the complete assembly raises the foresight blade to correspond with the rear sight on top of the receiver. The blade is threaded and can be adjusted for elevation by screwing in or out. The lateral adjustment is achieved by adjusting each of the aforementioned screws on either side of the foresight block.

Schmidt & Bender L13A1 Telescope
NSN V5/1240-99-967-4564

Technical Specification	
Manufacturer	Schmidt & Bender
Length	13in
Weight in the mount	1.17lb
Objective Lens DIA	42mm
Field of View	7m at 100m
Magnification	X 6
Reticle	Post & Wire
Elevation Graduations	100–1000 Yds (1–42 MOA)
Bullet Drop Compensation	Yes
Focus Capability	Yes
Parallax Adjustment	No
Sunshade	No
Lateral Adjustment	16-0-16 MOA
Mount Type	Single

LEFT: Typical Schmidt & Bender markings to the eye piece of the L13A1 telescope. Note the PM designation rarely referenced regarding this scope. Also note the "West Germany" mark, a reminder of Germany's modern historic past.

This L13A1 telescope has a much higher serial number to that of the scope pictured on the rifle; note the colour is much darker. Note the lenses, the anti-scratch and anti-reflection coating can be seen. The lens coatings also enhance the light being transmitted and fine tune it, cancelling distortion and improving colour and clarity.

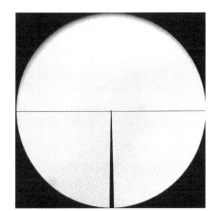

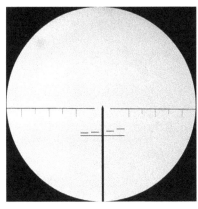

ABOVE: Pictured are the two reticles found in the L13A1 scope. The reticle at the top is the standard post and wire reticle commonly found in British L13A1 telescopes; underneath is the less common post and wire reticle featuring ranging graticules used by SF units. *(Right © MoDCrown copyright)*

TOP: The L13A1 scope is illustrated in its soft carry case. The case featured is SF black although it was issued in DPM camouflage in greater numbers.

ABOVE: A sniper pair pictured during a stalk. The best route is never the easiest route.

As mentioned earlier, zero set-up of a No. 32 scope was generally unique to the rifle on which it was zeroed and when fitted to another rifle there almost certainly would be a shift displayed in the group's point of impact on target. To overcome the general issue of shift in zero and to realise scope interchangeability between rifles would previously have involved very expensive custom rifle smithing, a bespoke solution to the problem. AI applied precision engineering techniques to the manufacture of all the parts that formed the revolutionary new rifle; precision engineering on a mass scale enabled repeatability within a very tight tolerance resulting in one rifle after another leaving the assembly line and performing to the same high standard time after time. A zeroed telescope could be removed and swapped between several rifles which when fired would be less than one MOA out of zero from one rifle to another at 100 metres. Invariably the rifle would in fact shoot as accurately as the rifle the scope was originally zeroed to.

I have a personal experience of collecting an ex Bedfordshire police L96A1 rifle which was still wearing its police barrel with the swirl flash eliminator. I already had in my possession an early L13A1 scope which unbeknown to me was set up in its mount. I dropped it in a bag and travelled to the Bisley National Shooting Centre where G.E. Fulton & Son had a military barrel for the rifle waiting for me. The rifle was re-barrelled on arrival after which I

ABOVE: Pictured in more recent times this surviving example of a military L96A1 rifle is putting in a rare appearance on the range.

ABOVE: The L96A1 rifle pictured in the guise of its midlife upgrade. The battle sights are now gone and it carries the more powerful L17A1 telescope albeit without the SIMRAD top hat bracket. Also note a very new feature to the rifle, the STICS side rail.

visited the zero range, and mounted the scope on the rifle for the first time, thinking I would have to do a bit of a zero session as the rifle, barrel and scope had never so much as met each other before. To my astonishment the rifle shot a five round group spot on; I did not have to adjust a single millimetre. I then went straight to a 600 yard firing point on Century range and enjoyed a morning's shooting. The rifle is still in my possession and has never required any adjustment since that day.

When the .308/7.62mm calibre AW entered service it did so in a much smaller capacity to that of the L96, highlighting some of the shortcomings of the now slightly aged rifle which was at this point notching up around fifteen years of service. The L42 by comparison had at this point in its service been condemned with the decision to replace it already having long been made.

If a sign was needed to reaffirm how ahead of its time the L96 was, instead of replacement the L96 received several changes to modernise it and make it compatible

with the suite of optical devices now available which would in turn make it comparable to the AW of the same calibre and extend its service life by a further decade. The L96 had proven from the off it was capable of 1,000 metre accuracy although the all-green L13A1 scope with its fixed six power magnification was not capable of making such engagements routine so the 6 x 42mm scope was removed and in its place the rifle received the same L17A1 scope that entered service on the L118A1 Arctic Warfare rifle, and in doing so it also lost its battle sights, mainly as the rear sight would have fouled the L17 when fitted. The L17A1 was a black 3-12 x 50mm Schmidt & Bender telescope with an enhanced ranging reticle designated P4 by Schmidt & Bender. It also paved the way, enabling the rifle to take advantage of the SIMRAD night sight as well as the STIC (Sniper Thermal Image Capability) sight.

Whilst the L96 was still in operation with specialist units as well as SF units there was, for these

ABOVE: The L17A1 scope gave the L96 access to Sniper Thermal Imaging Capability therefore a new bipod mounting block was designed to also carry the side rail necessary for STIC to attach to the weapon.

units, a requirement for the weapon to become fully compatible with STIC therefore the alloy bipod block housed in the front of the fore-end was redesigned and replaced with a dual role component which now carried the bipod as well as a detachable picatinny side rail for the STIC device to mount on the weapon in the intended fashion.

Complete Equipment Schedule

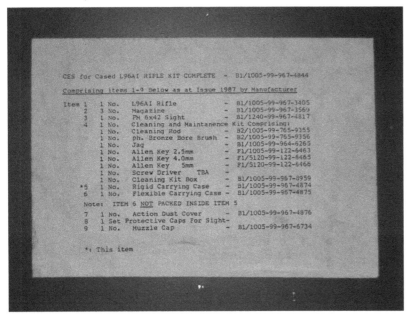

```
CES for Cased L96A1 RIFLE KIT COMPLETE  -  B1/1005-99-967-4844

Comprising items 1-9 Below as at Issue 1987 by Manufacturer

Item 1    1 No.   L96A1 Rifle            -  B1/1005-99-967-3405
     2    3 No.   Magazine               -  B1/1005-99-967-1569
     3    1 No.   PM 6x42 Sight          -  B1/1240-99-967-4817
     4    1 No.   Cleaning and Maintenance Kit Comprising:
          1 No.   Cleaning Rod           -  B2/1005-99-765-9355
          1 No.   ph. Bronze Bore Brush  -  B2/1005-99-765-9356
          1 No.   Jag                    -  B1/1005-99-964-6265
          1 No.   Allen Key 2.5mm        -  F1/1005-99-122-6463
          1 No.   Allen Key 4.0mm        -  F1/5120-99-122-6465
          1 No.   Allen Key  5mm         -  F1/5120-99-122-6466
          1 No.   Screw Driver    TBA
          1 No.   Cleaning Kit Box       -  B1/1005-99-967-8959
    *5    1 No.   Rigid Carrying Case    -  B1/1005-99-967-4874
     6    1 No.   Flexible Carrying Case -  B1/1005-99-967-4875

     Note:  ITEM 6 NOT PACKED INSIDE ITEM 5

     7    1 No.   Action Dust Cover      -  B1/1005-99-967-4876
     8    1 Set Protective Caps For Sight-
     9    1 No.   Muzzle Cap             -  B1/1005-99-967-6734


     *: This item
```

ABOVE: A 1987 CES label pasted to the inside of the L96A1 rifle's aluminium transit chest lid.

The rifle had with its CES equipment a nylon scope/action cover, NSN B1/1005-99-967-4876, which had a full length Velcro fastening and tight elasticated ends. The cover wrapped around the rifle and scope which when fastened along its length with the Velcro strip was sealed at the ends by the elastic "cuffs" protecting the action and scope from the desert dust and abrasive sand. The cover was not produced especially for the Gulf War, although the foresight of its creation was a stroke of genius when taking into consideration the environment in which the rifle would be ultimately tested in 1991 and would go on again to be predominantly used. The dry dusty desert environment would become

CENTRE & ABOVE: Both the early DPM and later plain green versions of the scope/action cover are illustrated. Note the accompanying image of the sniper using the heavily camouflaged L96. In the foreground one can see a DPM scope/action cover put to one side.

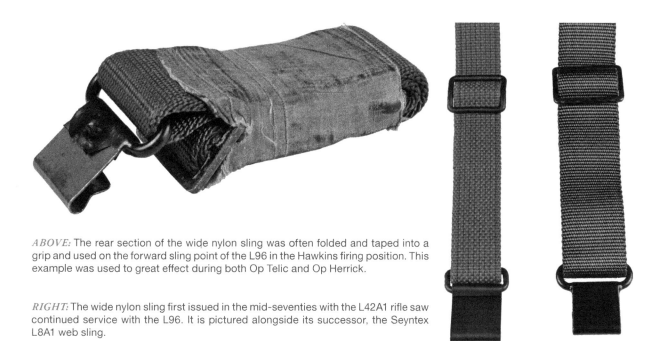

ABOVE: The rear section of the wide nylon sling was often folded and taped into a grip and used on the forward sling point of the L96 in the Hawkins firing position. This example was used to great effect during both Op Telic and Op Herrick.

RIGHT: The wide nylon sling first issued in the mid-seventies with the L42A1 rifle saw continued service with the L96. It is pictured alongside its successor, the Seyntex L8A1 web sling.

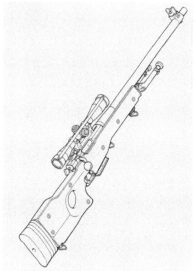

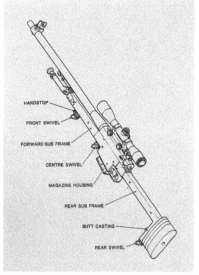

ABOVE & LEFT: The L96 rifle is pictured minus the stock sides and looks almost skeletal. The accompanying illustrative line drawings show the weapon complete and also minus the stock sides as per our photograph. The purpose of the educational drawings is to familiarise the user with the weapon in this state by making reference to the key features as even without the stock sides fitted the rifle can still be operated.

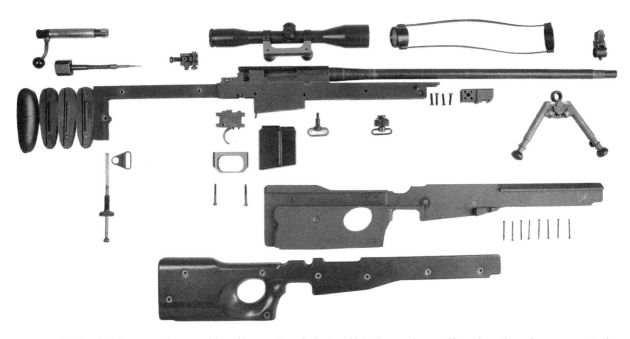

ABOVE: This level of disassembly was achieved in a matter of minutes. Note the receiver and barrel are the only components the CES tools cannot access.

the theme and the AI system could be described as a desert specialist as a large part of the AI range of rifles have forged their reputation in such an environment. The cover was, as it turns out, a standard piece of kit that belonged to the CES from the start. The first version was a lightweight DPM (Disruptive Pattern Material) nylon cover which was replaced later with a plain green and slightly larger variant of the same design, however the nylon material was heavier and capable of withstanding more robust treatment suggesting the first variant worked as a concept but needed beefing up a bit.

The rifle came issued with a comprehensive collection of ancillaries which made up the CES and continued to expand. In addition to the 1987 contents list from within the chest the 1990 CES booklet also contains a chamber stick and sling, both of which passed straight from the L42 chest to that of the L96.

There was also the addition of a short cleaning rod, in fact a three piece rod taken straight from the GPMG (General Purpose Machine Gun) cleaning kit which in its three pieces was individually NSN coded, B1/1005-99-960-2027, B1/1005-99-960-2029, B1/1005-99-960-2030.

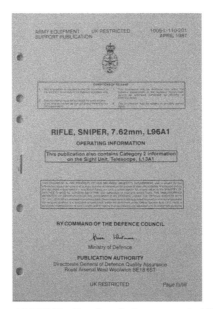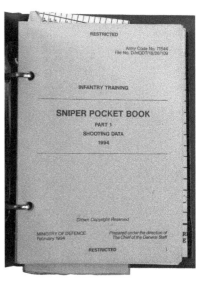

ABOVE: The literature that accompanied the CES booklet in the transit chest for the sniper's own reference was the Operating Information booklet for the weapon and his own personal Sniper Pocket Book formatted the same as that issued to the L42 sniper.

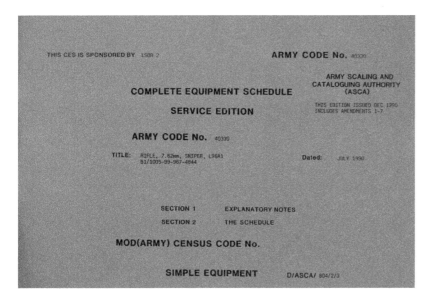

The rod was ideally suited to the cleaning of the chamber and the bolt housing chamber, an extent of cleaning uncatered for with the L42 which was another influence of Accuracy International. Their competition shooting approach to not only the design of the rifle but to its care and maintenance as well was another positive step forward in this new age of British military sniping. The modern sniper was in fact given an unprecedented level of mechanical access to his weapon. Previously the L42 sniper could remove the bolt, attach, and detach the scope and sling and that was it – anything further required an armourer. The L96 sniper in comparison was issued three Allen keys, sizes 2.5mm, 4mm and 5mm which were accompanied by an 85mm long screwdriver with a 6.3mm flat head, NSN F1/5120-99-136-5589.

These simple tools were all that was needed to remove the component parts with the exception of the barrel and enabled the sniper to apply a higher standard of care and maintenance to his weapon. The role of sniping within the British Army was rapidly becoming a technical and in-depth element of the infantry unit which previously was a handful of skilled individuals; the tools of their trade were basic and limited. The British sniper was now in charge of a precision weapon that was constantly morphing with new

LEFT & ABOVE: This 1990 dated CES booklet for the L96A1 sniper rifle is an edition that is inclusive of seven amendments added to the first edition that would have originally entered service with the rifle. Furthermore, this CES booklet has stapled to it amendment number eight dated 1992 which brings the CWS bracket into the rifle's equipment schedule.

technically advanced equipment being made available to it.

Literature for the sniper's own use which was contained within the chest followed suit to that of the L42 and included *Rifle, Sniper, 7.62mm, L96A1 Operating Information* booklet, the sniper's own Sniper Pocket Book, plus a copy of the CES booklet. The pocket book remained in its original format of two parts, shooting record information and sniper's aide memoire.

Transport of the rifle was in the green aluminium L7A1 transit chest, NSN B1/1005-99-967-4874, which housed the rifle and its associated equipment. The CES item the transit chest did not house, however, was the soft carry case made of a DPM Cordura type material. Bag, Rifle, 7.62mm, Sniper, L1A1, NSN B1/1005-99-967-4875, in comparison to the soft case the L42 was issued, was luxury. The outer panels were padded and as well as a full length zip for

ease of access there was plenty of storage space in the form of external pockets and compartments. The rifle in the case could be carried via carry handles, slung via the shoulder strap or worn like a pack as it also came with two back pack style shoulder straps. However, the teeth of the zip of this rifle bag did after a certain amount of wear have a tendency to separate after closure allowing the rifle to fall out when carried muzzle up via the shoulder strap.

ABOVE: The soft case supplied with the L96 rifle was in terms of padding and storage light years ahead of the basic canvas bags previously supplied with the L42. The one drawback with this case was the nylon zip which had a tendency to burst open, allowing the rifle to fall out unexpectedly.

BELOW & LEFT: The L96A1 sniper rifle laid out with all of its associated equipment. Note the shooting sticks which were handmade from broom handles; like the rifle they were camouflaged by the sniper. The rifle is also illustrated packed in its aluminium transit chest with full CES.

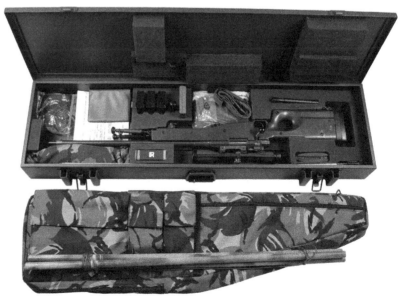

Observation and Spotting Equipment

When the L96 entered service the Swift Telemaster 841 Telescope was already in service with other elements of the army such as intelligence units in Northern Ireland hence its NSN V5/6650-99-527-7191 which was not allocated on its selection as sniper equipment but much earlier, when it was adopted for OP work. At this early stage in the L96's service the sniper cadre was still training snipers under the original 1973 course format with Scout Regiment Telescopes but the optics and accuracy of the new weapon made it clear to the snipers using it that in real world conditions the distances would be much further and therefore the spotter required a spotting scope that could offer him the power to observe targets with clarity and detail out to 1,000 metres.

The Swift scope, being already in service, was adopted by some and

ABOVE: Snipers are pictured here on the range practising shooting off sticks. The homemade sticks were also useful as a steady platform off which to use the spotting scope. Note the practice of donning full ghillie suit for range work was still essential and standard practice.

it joined an extensive list of models of telescope – Barnar, Kowa, Greenkat and Opticron to mention just a few – which were being used by a whole host of units in favour of the Scout Regiment Telescope.

ABOVE: Royal Marine sniper students attending a sniper cadre in 1994. They are on the Observation Stand looking for small items of kit secreted in the landscape before them. More interesting is the spotting scope they are using. The Scout Regiment Telescope, or Antique Brass as they called it, is still going strong. Note the steel trip flare pickets being utilised as supports for observing. This practice was commonplace right across the sniper community within the armed forces and remained well into the M49 scopes service also.

ABOVE: Already in service within the army, the Swift telescope was wholly inadequate in the sniper role.

Today one can ask ten different former snipers what spotting scope they used and one will get almost ten different answers, although the Scout Regiment Telescope, or Antique Brass, as it was referred to by the new breed of young sniper, remained a common theme as it continued to provide sterling service within the sniper community long after the L42 was withdrawn. Quite incredible, a piece of equipment that was in constant military service for well over a century, a length of service that must qualify the three

ABOVE: The zoom and focus controls were the weak point in the Swift scope and acted as an entry point for dust and dirt. The tripod was robust yet reportedly unstable.

draw telescope for some sort of record as the longest serving single piece of British military equipment.

It is easy to understand why the Swift scope became popular with snipers; the variable magnification range was 15–60 power and it came equipped with a separate focus control; the 60mm objective lens provided excellent light gathering and image quality at all distances out to 1,000 metres but that's where the advantages end. The telescope came with a tripod that offered pan and tilt capability but was also reportedly unstable; the whole ensemble was housed in a small domestic-like suitcase lined with bright red felt which indicated its previous non-sniper existence and was not in keeping with the requirements of the sniper. The telescope, excellent with regard to its optics and housed in a robust body did, though, have its Achilles heel which turned out to be the magnification and focus controls. I suspect this had already been noted by the Land Warfare Centre, Warminster.

The spotting scope the MoD decided to adopt was a telescope that had no more power than the Scout Regiment Telescope it was replacing and therefore officially

adopted a fixed twenty power telescope in the form of the U.S. M49, a decision that came in time for its inclusion to the new 1990 *Pamphlet No. 4* but too late for the L96 sniper rifle's first real test. It is noted that the Swift scope did take part in the desert conflict, Desert Storm, in 1991 with units who chose to keep it. The desert confirmed what many already knew as it was defeated: its magnification and focus adjustment controls offered an entry point allowing the scope to slowly fill with fine sand and eventually rendering it useless. Its failure led the British Army to speed up its adoption of the American M49 spotting scope along with its M15 tripod, a battle-proven design that had served the U.S. well during the Vietnam War and was an evolutionary step up from the WW2 M48 spotting scope. It was liked immensely by the USMC who continued to use it well into the 2000s after their adoption of the Leupold spotting scope. However, it was viewed by many as inadequate and did nothing to settle the issue of "Creeping Sniper Excellence" as sniper units across the army continued to privately purchase telescopes that offered a much greater power of magnification.

ABOVE & RIGHT: The spotting scope the army eventually adopted was the U.S. M49 with its M15 tripod. The M49 spotting scope is featured in both the 1990 and the 1996 editions of Pamphlet No. 4.

The British version of the M49 manufactured by United Scientific Instruments Ltd was largely unchanged and kept the U.S. M49 designation, however it did receive an integral sunshade and received the NSN V5/6650-99-709-4323. Examples encountered today are often dated 1991, indicating its rapid introduction to service post-Gulf War, but in the following years the issuing of the M49 spotting scope became painfully slow. Some units appeared to never even receive it and many of those that did, did not receive the M15 tripod. Incidentally this was never really a problem as British snipers more often than not will improvise the support when spotting, furthermore when the Scout Regiment Telescope and M49 telescope was in service it was standard practice across the army,

Royal Marines and RAF regiment to improvise a spotting scope support from a trip flare picket. The M49 scope continued to be the principal spotting device for snipers as it appears again in the 1996 edition of *Pamphlet No. 4*, but even as late as 1999 snipers from one unit who

deployed to Kosovo as part of the NATO led KFOR did so without a spotting scope altogether, having to borrow equipment from a Canadian unit serving alongside them.

ABOVE: The British take on the M49 telescope was manufactured by the British company United Scientific Instruments Ltd, however the tripod looks to be U.S. manufactured with a U.S. data plate. Note both the scope and the tripod bear British broad arrow marks.

UNITED SCIENTIFIC

Telescope, Straight

M 49

NATO Stock No. V5/6650-99-709-4323

The compact and lightweight design combined with robust construction of the United Scientific's Telescopic Straight (M49) ensures this instrument's effectiveness for use either in observing artillery fire or as a sniper's tele- scope. In addition it provides an excellent gen- eral purpose observation instrument.

The Telescopic Straight is a 20 power, dry air sealed instrument having a field view of 38.5 Mils (2°12') with an exit pupil diameter of 0.018 inches. The image is erected by a porro prism system and incorporates an extendable tube beyond the objective lens thus providing either a sun or rain shield.

The Telescope Straight, currently in service with many Defence Forces, including the United States of America and the United Kingdom, is supplied with Tripod, Case Carrying, Case Telescope, Ocular and Objective covers.

ABOVE & NEXT PAGE: United Scientific Instruments Ltd produced this literature promoting the M49 spotting scope in the early nineties. Like Accuracy International they often distributed their sales literature at equipment exhibitions and arms fairs.

Telescope, Straight – M49

The following associated equipment is normally supplied with the Telescope M49.

Case, Telescope M164	V5/6650-99-700-5351
Tripod, Telescope M15	V5/6650-99-001-3003
Case, Carrying M42A1	V5/6650-00-310-2534

Technical Data

Magnification	x 20
Field of view	38.5 mils–(2° 12')
Limits of operation:	
Angle of sight	Limited rotation
Azimuth rotation	No limit
Height	88.7 mm. (3.5 in)

Length Fully Extended	417 mm (16.4 in)
Length Closed	367 mm (14.5 in)
Width	70 mm (2.75 in)
All up weight (with equipment)	1.816 kg (4 lb)
Environmental Conditions	Operation –5.5°C to +67°C
	Storage –28°C to +72°C

UNITED SCIENTIFIC INSTRUMENTS LTD.

REPRESENTED BY:
United Scientific Instruments Limited
Phoenix House, Unit 1 Dalehouse Lane
Industrial Estate, Cotton Drive, Kenilworth
CV8 2UE England Tel:44(0)1926863593
Fax:44(0)1926850615 email:office@usiltd.co.uk

ABOVE: The Avimo, or L12A1 binocular, is a robust and reliable instrument which saw service with snipers during Operation Herrick, Afghanistan. Like the reticle in the rifle's telescope the graticules in the binocular (below right) had also become a standard feature in British binoculars since WW1.

The binocular which was made available to the L96 sniper was invariably the Avimo 7 x 42mm binocular, or L12A1 to use the correct nomenclature, NSN 1240-99-965-6105. The rubber armoured L12A1 binoculars were overall excellent and provided superb image clarity and continued to use the graticule in the right hand lens as was first found in the Great War prismatic binoculars and the WW2 vintage binoculars that preceded them. The binocular was self-focussing but on the heavy side being around two and a half pounds and a little bulky. The quirky feature of the eye pieces sitting above the objective lenses points to the fact that they were never designed as sniper equipment, or infantry for that matter. The L12A1 binocular arrived with the British Army around 1979 and was mainly the reserve of the artillery and tank commanders whilst most elements of the infantry soldiered on with the WW2 vintage 6 x 30mm prismatic binocular.

The L96A1 sniper rifle was covered by several training pamphlets from its conception to its demise and these pamphlets would be amongst the last of the printed paper series

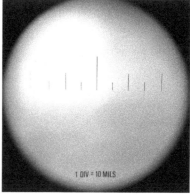

1 DIV = 10 MILS

ABOVE: A sniper team takes up a position on the roof of a newly captured compound in the Upper Sangin Valley, Afghanistan.

At Forward Operating Base (FOB) Inkerman, B Company 2 Para were the first troops to operate in the green zone for the entire summer season of 2008. Patrolling the local area was very intense, with patrols regularly coming under attack from enemy forces some of which were just 30 metres away.

The Operating Base and its men play a vital role stopping Taliban fighters moving within the Sangin valley and disrupting vital reconstruction projects in the area. *(© MoD Crown copyright)*

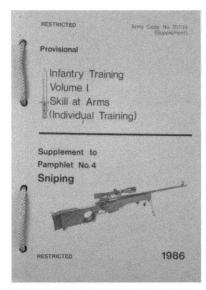
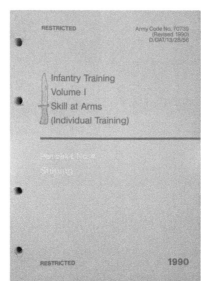
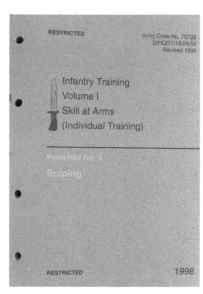

ABOVE: The training pamphlets that covered the life of the L96 are illustrated including the bridging supplement dated 1986 which covered the weapon specific information from Pamphlet No. 4, 1976 to Pamphlet No. 4, 1990.

made available to the instructor. The training pamphlet still exists but has with the modern digital age moved to the Battle Box format, whereby all training pamphlets are held digitally, being supplied to the user on a disc and printed by the user for his use. *Infantry Training Volume 1, Skill at Arms (Individual Training) Pamphlet No. 4, Sniping 1976* superseded *Infantry Training Volume 1, Infantry Platoon Weapons Pamphlet No. 10, Sniping 1951* and its 1973 dated L42 supplement and remained the official training literature for the L96 with a supplement pamphlet being issued, as was done in 1973 to cover the weapon specific information. *Infantry Training Volume 1, Skill at Arms (Individual Training) Supplement to Pamphlet No. 4, Sniping 1986* was circulated and accompanied the 1976 pamphlet until a specific pamphlet was written and issued in 1990. Interestingly the 1990 dated pamphlet has no guidance regarding the Swift

ABOVE: I wonder what the old chap and his wife make of these sniper students who are using Woodbury Common in Devon for their training. Perhaps his thoughts are: "They've gone soft these days. We didn't use knee pads in my day."

Telescope but instead features the M49 telescope, an illuminating point that gives some insight into equipment selection of that period.

A further edition of the training pamphlet was issued in 1996 which outwardly appeared to be the same but included several amendments.

Common Weapon Sight, L8A2, Cased

The beleaguered introduction of the SA80 assault weapon which was part of the British Army overhaul post the Falklands conflict included a new night vision device, the CWS (Common Weapon Sight) L8A2, NSN Z7/5855-99-495-6221. The Pilkington produced device was also known as the Kite Sight and was a huge leap forward in image intensifier technology, being considerably smaller and a fraction of the weight of the IWS it was replacing. The x4 magnification device was designed for short to medium range target engagement; for longer ranges the sight also had another variant known as the Maxi Kite but was large and cumbersome for sniper work and was best suited to the GPMG and surveillance work.

The CWS was marketed as having a detection range of a man at 526 metres under clear starlight and 3,269 metres under moonlight which was more likely optimistic sales jargon as the operating information booklet uses a more conservative estimate of a standing man being detected at 400 metres in starlight, although in very good ambient light conditions a sniper is expected to use a maximum operating distance of 600 metres. Again the sales marketing quoted a battery service life of 100 hours when realistically the average running time provided by the two 1.5v AA batteries was around forty hours. However the compact size, light weight and high resolution image made it a versatile piece of equipment well suited to the L96, its main drawback being it sat very high on the rifle, making cheek weld difficult and resulting ultimately in poor ergonomics overall.

As with the IWS the CWS came fitted with a heavy duty rubber lens cap marked "Do Not Remove in Daylight". The lens cap came with a small pinhole in its centre so the sight could be zeroed to a weapon in daylight conditions. The "tube" within the device is exceptionally vulnerable to bright light therefore the pinhole allowed just enough safe light to enter the device when switched on for daylight use. The zeroing of the CWS device to the L96 sniper rifle was carried out at 100 metres using the tip of the inverted vee as the point of aim. The MPI (Mean Point of Impact) of the zeroing group was adjusted to fall 106 millimetres above the point of aim at this distance so the recommended use of the reticle would correspond with the use of the L2A2 NATO 144 grain (9.33 grams) ammunition. The illuminated inverted vee reticle which had its own on/off switch on the device was also equipped with a dot within the vee. The recommended use of the reticle prescribed that the tip of the vee be used for engaging targets out to 400 metres and the dot within the vee be used to engage targets between 500 and 600 metres.

The CWS had also made available to it an urban filter, NSN Z7/5855-99-967-7429, which protected the sensitive internal components from potentially damaging street lighting

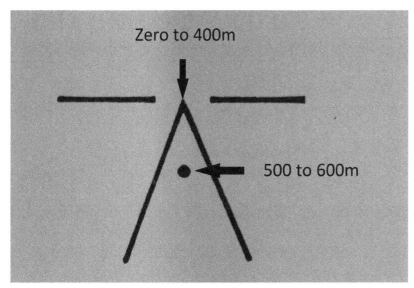

Zero to 400m

500 to 600m

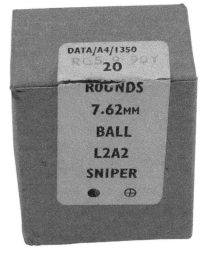

DATA/A4/1350
20
ROUNDS
7.62MM
BALL
L2A2
SNIPER

ABOVE: The illustrated reticle of the L8A2 CWS shows what points were utilised within it to achieve the fall of shot at a desired range. For the reticle to work as prescribed it was necessary for the sniper to use the issued L2A2 ball ammunition.

ABOVE: The L14A1 bracket for attaching the CWS to the L96 rifle. Note this bracket has been numbered to the rifle.

whilst being deployed to urban environments such as Northern Ireland.

The sight attached to the L96 via its own L14A1 CWS bracket, NSN B1-1005-99-252-1125. The underside of the device had a universal mount that slid onto a range of weapon brackets like the IWS and its universal bracket. Previously in order for the IWS to mount onto the L42 the universal bracket was removed so the IWS could mount directly onto the L5A1 bracket. The CWS ended this practice and instead used the L14A1 mount to attach itself to the L96, effectively using two separate mounts to get the sight onto the weapon. An opportunity was possibly missed to improve the usability of the night scope on the L96, had a replacement mount for the device been produced that would have made the L14A1 bracket redundant and being fixed directly to the underside of the CWS device would have directly utilised the L96's own dovetail on its receiver in the same way the day scope did.

Unlike the L96 sniper rifle the L42's L5A1 IWS bracket was part of its CES schedule from its very beginning; the L96 CWS bracket was not and did not join the official list of equipment until 1992 when an amendment was issued and attached to its CES booklet. The sight came in a tough compact transit case that contained a soft carry case, lens tissues and screwdriver for zeroing and as a complete ensemble was coded L14A2 and carried NSN Z7/5855-99-513-3322.

Common Weapon Sight, L8A2, NSN Z7/5855-99-495-6221

Technical Information	
Weaponsight (with Universal Mount):	
Height	110mm (4.33in)
Length	275mm (10.8in)
Width	106mm (4.1in)
Weight	1.1kg (2.4lb)
Optical Characteristics:	
Operational Range	400m in Starlight (for a man standing)
Magnification	4.01 ± 0.2
Focus Range	15m to infinity
Field of View	140mils
IIT (Type	3rd Generation
Distortion	4% at 70% field of View
Graticule	Inverted "V" with Cross (Bar and a Dot at 500m Range)
Graticule Boresight:	
Adjustment Range	15mils
Eye Relief	30mm
Eyepiece Settings	1 to +0.35 dioptres
Clear Aperture	64mm
Objective Type	Refractor

Power Requirements:

The weapon sight uses two AA size batteries that will give a 3v supply and service life of approximately 40 hours at 20 degrees Centigrade.

ABOVE & LEFT: The L14A2 cased ensemble. The CWS came cased with soft carry case, spare batteries, lens brush, Operating Information booklet and screwdriver for zeroing.

ABOVE: The CWS pictured attached to the rifle. Note the very high position it has on the weapon; being a Common Weapon Sight it was not specific to any one weapon which when used in conjunction with the L96 introduced cheek weld problems to the sniper.

ABOVE: When the L8A2 sight first appeared in the 1980s it was well received. With the IWS seeing nearly twenty years of service before it the light and compact CWS with its much improved definition was a joy to use.

LEFT: The brightness of the CWS reticle can be controlled or turned off completely if desired. Note the two small black spots to the left of the reticle in this image. These are referred to as "burns" and are damage to the scope's tube, usually by bright daylight or urban street lighting entering the device.

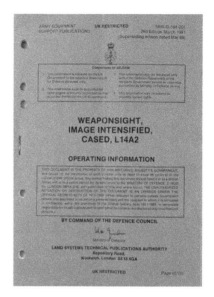

RIGHT: Operating Information booklet for the L14A2 cased ensemble.

The early 2000s saw the L96 "Green Fleet" upgraded and ready to take its part in Operation Telic, Iraq. The Royal Marines 40, 42 and 45 Commandos varied the organisation of their snipers who operated in traditional pairs that made up six and eight man teams. The Royal Marines deployed their snipers to Op Telic with four basic principles by which all of their sniper operations were run.

1. **Control.** This must be at the highest level to prevent conflict with other units.
2. **Protection.** The sniper team needs protection and backup available due to its willingness to compromise its position whilst on task.
3. **Endurance & Time.** Concealed movement and observation are tiring, lengthy tasks and time given to complete it must be realistic. Weather and terrain must be taken into account.
4. **Mobility.** Snipers need to be able to deploy quickly so they can take advantage of the confusion of an encounter with the enemy before they regroup or escape. When mobile it is possible to deploy into blocking positions well ahead of

friendly forces on the intended route of the enemy, or turn from defensive to aggressive and hunt down the most mobile of enemy. Mobility enables the sniper to achieve maximum disruption to the enemy around the battlefield.

The following passage is a synopsis of an operation carried out by 3 Commando Brigade's snipers using the above principles in the six and eight man team orbats.

Between Thursday 20th March and Saturday 22nd March 2003, company sniper pairs and the sniper team of 40 Commando were used by C Company and B Company in the initial helicopter assault on the oil facilities of Al Faw Peninsula before they could be destroyed by the Iraqi forces. These were the first non-Special Forces to enter Iraq. The sniper team was involved in calling in indirect fire and delivering long range precision sniper fire to help defend these facilities.

In the early hours of the 21st March snipers of 42 Commando and J Company landed north of the Al Faw Peninsula by helicopter to set up a blocking position. The snipers deployed forward of J Company to

act as an early warning screen. On Saturday 22nd March A Company, 40 Commando conducted assaults against defended buildings in Al Faw town where their company snipers were used to pick off well hidden/defended enemy. Between Sunday 23rd March and Saturday 29th March 2003, having completed the clearance of Al Faw, 40 Commando moved northwest clearing the southern bank of the Shatt al Arab waterway. Their sniper team was used to fix enemy positions and provide close position fire support to troops clearing the positions on the ground.

A Company snipers were grouped together and pushed forward to get eyes on and look for in-depth targets and if need be would push to the flank and cover the ground as the company moved up. On Tuesday 25th March 42 Commando relieved the USMC forces in Umm Qasr. Snipers bolstered an aggressive patrol routine across Umm Qasr, provoking a number of minor contacts with the enemy. On Wednesday 26th March, Challenger II main battle tanks were attached to 40 Commando to assist with maintaining the security of Al

Faw Peninsula together with the Brigade Reconnaissance Force. 40 Commando continued to maintain a blocking position preventing enemy forces moving south from Basra, thereby fixing the enemy.

On Thursday 27th March, the enemy launched their final armoured attack from Basra against 40 Commando positions. On this occasion the Challenger II MBTs destroyed all 14 enemy tanks. This minimised the threat from Basra, enabling 40 Commando to launch an assault on Abu al Khasib some ten kilometres southeast of Basra, code named Op James.

Between Sunday 30th March and Friday 4th April Op James and the clearance of date palms southwest of Basra took place. On 30th March the sniper team was used to engage a military camp with long range precision fire. Over a six hour period they managed to clear the camp of enemy thus enabling B Company to clear its area of operations more safely. Due to the close environment, A, B and C company snipers all patrolled with sniper weapons to take advantage of close opportune targets. 40 Commando took over 200 enemy prisoners including a number of Iraqi senior officers. Simultaneously 42 Commando continued to patrol Umm Qasr. The snipers were operating from positions where they could dominate large areas of ground.

On Tuesday 1st April while the campaign progressed in other directions 40 Commando secured their areas in the Abu al Khasib region. The company snipers operated from defensive positions dominating ground. The sniper team acted as a fourth reconnaissance team ditching their sniper role. Together with recce troop they dominated 40 Commando's western flank with aggressive patrolling resulting in two contacts with the enemy after which the enemy lost their will to operate in that area. In the days to come 40 Commando took control of their area of operation.

42 Commando began clearing smaller towns between Umm Qasr and Basra. Their snipers were used in support of K Company to clear the town of Umm Qyall and seize a water treatment plant in the middle of town. Their snipers were also used on roof tops in support of K Company who by this time had been reinforced by J Company. Together it took them three days to clear the town of Umm Qyall.

The Sniper's Garments

The issued sniper smock remained, the third variant from the L42 era bridging across to the L96 but to the relief of those who used it was replaced in 1990 as part of the Soldier 90 modernisation programme. The smock's specification remained exactly the same but was produced in the 1990 DPM pattern; the colour tones of the pattern were getting darker with every new variant which was becoming a problem for the wearer as when the garment was wet it looked even darker, a detail any trained observer would be looking for as "colour change" on the ground.

The early nineties also saw the introduction of a one-piece DPM camouflage coverall, NSN 8415-99-978-5013, which when initially introduced was utilised by SF and Close Observation Platoon members, however the benefits of this garment for the sniper were soon spotted which led to its extended circulation to many unit level snipers. The coveralls were heavily quilted and manufactured from Gore-Tex material making them ideal for sitting, or lying, exposed to the elements for long periods and were indeed used for "cutting in" where a sniper armed with a set of gardening secateurs will cut into a hedge or thick cover in order to create a concealed position. The coverall came with the standard sling hooks on the upper arms and an array of pockets situated all over the garment including two large stowage pockets on the back.

With the advent of conflict in the Middle East a desert camouflage sniper smock was produced in a lightweight material for comfort in the heat. The smock was manufactured to the standard specification but was not popular and its existence was short lived, as even with the lighter fabric the desert heat made its use very difficult. For daylight operations many snipers in this theatre customised a standard No. 5 desert combat dress camouflage shirt rather than be subjected to the suffocating heat inside a zipped up sniper smock. At night it was found that the desert camouflage in general had an undesirable appearance; its pale tones did not subdue in the dark but stood out, being described as having an appearance that glowed. Night fighting commonly took place between 400 and 600 metres therefore ghillie suits were never employed and desert camouflage garments were avoided, standard DPM shirts and smocks being strongly favoured in their place.

The head/shoulder net which first appeared post WW2 was still an issue item to snipers operating the L96, although dated examples do not seem to appear beyond 1991. The

ABOVE: The standard issue sniper smock was in the nineties still the same specification. Note the DPM pattern; the colours are darker in comparison to the earlier examples.

ABOVE: A new garment introduced in the nineties was this Gore-Tex quilted suit; complete with sling hooks and bristling with pockets it seemed to disappear with the L96.

ABOVE: The desert DPM camouflaged sniper smock, although constructed from a lightweight material, did not prove popular and saw little service.

ABOVE & RIGHT: Snipers were more inclined to customise a desert DPM shirt. This example was used in Iraq and Afghanistan. Note the improvised pockets at the rear as well as foam padding added to the forearm.

The L96 being put through its paces during pre-deployment training in Oman around 2008.

Sniper knee pads produced in the later, darker DPM pattern; these were the last of their kind.

The last of the DPM pattern to see service with the British Army included the desert DPM. All were superseded by MTP in 2011.

large knee pad was also continued with the new 1990 DPM camouflage pattern although its use was by this time beginning to fall to the wayside as commercial equipment was becoming increasingly available, offering a more technical solution to the protection of knees and elbows.

The following personal account was written by a member of the Parachute Regiment who served as a sniper in Helmand Province; his weapon was a L96A1 sniper rifle.

First Kills

As the patrol lead scout got to the junction, he paused there was that sixth sense sort of moment and he turned back to look at us all.

Immediately there was a massive bang that knocked me over and I was showered with debris. Getting back up, I felt nauseous and light headed. My first action was to check my trusty L96, it was still ready to go, right by my side and in one piece. I don't even think the zero had been affected at all. What a great reliable weapon, no wonder we snipers loved them so much.

Fortunately we had suffered no real casualties but visibility was poor due to the dust cloud on top of us all. Quickly checking each other we got ready for what we knew was coming next. I shouted "heads up" and then the whole fucking world erupted around us, the lads got

busy returning rounds but we were caught in the killing area of a Taliban ambush. We had no choice but to run forward into the fire and get into the ditch that offered some cover from fire. A Smoke grenade was thrown and we moved out of the kill zone.

Quickly attaching my bipod on the L96 I was fortunate to get into a pretty good firing position and settled down to search for the enemy. My spotter was on my right shoulder with his binos and x40 scope. He was cursing that he had not brought a more stable support for the spotting scope, using his daysack as a rest.

Slowly the dust cloud cleared and we could clearly identify three potential firing points and one person clearly firing at us over the top of some cover. Dealing with the immediate threat first I simply aimed central as the insurgent was no more than 125m away. In the background I could hear our patrol GPMGs putting down an immense wall of controlled fire. I almost felt sorry for anyone on the receiving end. Back to my target he was still firing away undeterred, I took a quick deep breath in and out, then the shot was away, striking him cleanly in the face. Quickly rechambering another round I watched for more movement. "Good kill, he is definitely down" I heard my spotter say.

Slowing down now, trying to get into my sniper bubble, my spotter indicated another target near the low wall to our front, range 300m. At first I could see nothing but after some direction from my spotter and a quick patient study of the wall using my x12 zoom I could see a loop hole. "Murder holes" we called these. The shooter was behind and I could see the outline of the muzzle. Calculating where he was most likely to be I used a Mildot hold for speed, adding no deflection, as there was no wind. I fired three deliberate rounds into the loop hole. The firing ceased in this area.

In the next second a large series of explosions bracketed the wall and surrounding compound. It was the mortar platoon giving us fire support. After an immaculate accurate "fire for effect" they switched to smoke and that gave us a chance to pull back to our original start point. What seemed like seconds had been a 20 minute firefight!

Later that night I was credited with two kills. I had no problems with what I had just done to two living people. They were trying to do the same to me.

I was surprised at how close the fighting had become, not the long range sniping we had practised and perfected before deploying. However that would come later. Tomorrow was another day in Helmand.

With the introduction of the L115A3 long range sniper system in 2008 and its general issue across the army, RAF Regiment and Royal Marines, the L96A1 sniper rifle steadily disappeared and was by 2012 wholly retired. The L96 remained in Donnington central stores for several years whilst debates took place as to what the final outcome for the rifle should be. There was talk of a refurbishment of the rifles and reissuing as a lighter shorter range sniper system and then there was an indication that they would be issued to the Afghan National Army as part of Britain's continuing support for the cash strapped army, particularly as the British withdrawal from Afghanistan

was scheduled for 2014. But it was not to be. Thirty years after the rifle's introduction it would see no more service in any capacity as around late 2014, early 2015 they were removed from stores and stripped of their L17A1 telescopes before each rifle was chopped into several pieces. The scrap remains of well over 1,000 L96A1 sniper rifles were loaded onto a tug boat and taken out to sea where at an undisclosed location they were thrown overboard into the North Sea. It would seem the MoD went to extraordinary lengths to ensure nothing from these incredible weapons remained which could be used in any way, shape or form later in a civilian capacity such as trophies or war memorabilia.

Thankfully there are a handful of complete and original examples still in existence which exited MoD ownership prior to the weapon's withdrawal and now reside in private as well as several reference collections across the country.

ABOVE: A British sniper having a sit down with Afghan villagers. Although the weapons of his trade are leaning against the wall he has adopted some local attire in an effort to help discussions flow more freely.

One U.S. collector writes how his passion for British sniper rifles began and how he became the owner of a former British Army L96A1 sniper rifle, one of the rarest of all the military snipers' rifles.

THE LONG AND WINDING ROAD (to a L96A1)
Nick the Greek

My fondness for the British began at a very young age, and was cultivated in many different ways. In elementary school I was a voracious reader, and was fascinated by WW1 and WW2 aviation. In particular I was in awe of the bravery shown by the men of the RAF during the Battle of Britain. My godfather flew a Hawker Hurricane as a member of the Greek contingent of the RAF. My older sister was in the fashion industry and lived in London for several years, marrying an Englishman from Bournemouth. I have many fond memories of Christmas Crackers... In high school, I joined my sister and brother in law for a trip to England in the late 70's. While they were "working" I struck off on my own to indulge myself at the British Museum in London. It was a personal treat to see a Super Marine Spitfire in the flesh, the only fighter aircraft matching my enthusiasm for the P51 Mustang. It must be because they share the Rolls-Royce Merlin engine... Later as an adult and wearing the uniform of my country, I was impressed by the UK troops. Our nation owes a debt of gratitude to the UK for establishing the foundational concepts two centuries ago, which have been refined into a brotherhood that has withstood the test of time.

As a pre-teen, my first job was to clean firearms in the "back room" of a small gun shop in Southern California. Our owners bought and sold used firearms, so we became a magnet for many veterans (or their widows) seeking to turn their bring backs into cash. I saw many interesting firearms over the years there, and often wished that "the guns could talk" to tell me their stories. I remember seeing many Luger and Walther pistols in mint condition, except for circular splotches of bare steel, devoid of blue. I learned that those splotches were made by blood's corrosive effects...

I can still vividly recall `seeing a long green wooden box on the floor of my boss' office, and me asking him "what is that?" to which he replied: a "British sniper rifle." He allowed me to open the lid, and inspect the contents. I was impressed with the simple modifications done to a service rifle, which turned it into a specialist's tool. Even at that very young and inexperienced age, I recognized the significance of a detachable magazine and cheek piece. This stood in stark contrast to the Springfield or Mauser sniper rifles of that era and conflict that I had handled previously.

As my interest in sniping grew, my appetite for information was poorly sated by the very few books on the topic. Peter Senich's "The German Sniper" was the first book on the topic that opened my eyes to the tools used. Ian Skennerton's book "The British Sniper" later piqued my interest in the Commonwealth tools of the trade. My military service allowed me to indulge my keen interest in applied long range marksmanship. I trained with the M21, M24, and M25 systems.

My first acquisition of a British sniper rifle occurred at a large gun show in Washington State. I was there to meet Charlton Heston and have him autograph his book for me. While I quickly walked the aisles, a long, low, green chest caught my

attention from the deepest corner of my eye – something surreal beckoned me to stop and turn back. I stopped, recalling the other green chest from my youth. I took a few steps back, and had to lean over the table in order to see the poorly displayed contents of that chest. In it, I saw what appeared to me as an Enfield, but with a medium weight, exposed barrel. Much to my surprise, it was an L42A1, and after a few seconds of thought, and a deep breath, a decision was made. I had to have it! It was this rifle that started my journey in collecting British sniping rifles. When I took it apart to inspect, clean and document every piece, I found SAND inside the action's bedding area. I have often wondered if this was the rifle shown in Ian's book, being cradled by the SAS trooper in the desert (who incidentally reminded me of Charlton Heston in the Ten Commandments...)

The L42A1 became the centre of my collecting efforts, and thanks to friends on both sides of the pond, the treasure hunt for the entire CES was successful. Peter Laidler's books on the rifles and scopes only deepened my respect for what the British Army and Holland & Holland had done to convert wartime No4s into serviceable sniper rifles in the 1940's. It was all the more remarkable to know what was done 30 years later in updating the No4Ts into a very capable system that extended the lifespan of the Lee Enfield past the century mark. Several No4Ts have passed through my hands, and I am honoured to maintain two, each in its own unique state (one very worn, with green

ABOVE: A very rare sighting on an American range. This former UK military L96A1 rifle is amongst just a handful that exist in the world let alone the USA.

paint splotches evident, and the other in "unissued" condition).

It was several years later while stationed in North Carolina that a co-worker, aware of my interests, approached me. Sometimes fate smiles on each of us in ways that we cannot fathom at the time. He stated: "I have a rifle that you may be interested in." As it turned out, his wife wanted a pool, and he needed to raise funds to finance her wishes. When I asked him what he had, he replied "a British sniper rifle." With that very cursory description, I said "sure, I'll take a look." Several days later, he opened up a soft case to show me a tan, spray-painted bolt gun with a very scarred plastic spacer functioning as a butt plate. I looked at the action, and could barely make out the inscription "Accuracy International." For the briefest of moments I honestly felt that my heart had stopped! I looked up at him, and said "I'll take it." He then muttered in embarrassment the words every collector dreads— "someone else is interested and you are next in line..." After several days of pensive waiting, he found me to deliver the news: "I know that you will appreciate this rifle more, so I want you to have it."

I could not wait to get home so that I could disassemble this rifle, strip off the tan spray paint, and learn all that I could from it. When

I assumed caretakership of this rifle, it consisted of the rifle, a single magazine, a mounted scope. It was devoid of a rubber butt pad, front sight, or any accessories. I stripped it down, and found one of the green stock panels cracked. The scope had significant dings and scratches on both the tube and front lens, but it was still very usable. Under borescope inspection, the stainless steel barrel was heavily pitted. Until that time, I did not know that a stainless steel barrel could pit so heavily. Talk about a lack of truth in advertising!

Having an AW on hand with the necessary barrel change kit, I was able to completely disassemble the L96A1. I found rust inside the action body and bolt surfaces.

Despite its apparent lack of care and appropriate maintenance (my "gut" told me that this rifle was in the possession of unskilled hands for many years), it had withstood the elements and time to remain a functional tool. The scope was a Schmidt and Bender variable and while abused, was still in very functional condition. The mount appeared to my eye as a "field-improvised" interim solution. The one-piece scope base had single screw rings, but the front top ring had a "two screw" adapter for the SIMRAD night vision device.

My previous experience with hunting for L42A1 CES was child's play in comparison with the daunting task before me. Thankfully, this newer and more difficult challenge

ABOVE: A heavily worn L17A1 telescope was recovered with the rifle complete with SIMRAD mount.

met its match and was bested by my even greater enthusiasm for this rifle! Many folks will fuss about ebay, but I actually found many items, and made contacts leading to more bits, and so on. The Milsurps website had an excellent thread on this rifle. It was on this thread that I learned of how special this rifle was.

Through the internet "grapevine" I heard that G. E. Fulton & Son had acquired a bulk of L96 spares. I quickly filled my wish list, knowing these items were made of "unobtanium..." Fulton's was wonderful to deal with, and even sourced an original SuB "green scope" for me. It has taken many years to assemble the complete CES, but I hope that you can appreciate the completeness from the full layout photo.

This rifle's original barrel was deeply pitted, but I wanted to shoot this rifle, and develop a load to explore its potential. Again, fate smiled broadly, and I was able to find a used take off barrel as a replacement. It went on the receiver

as expected and lined up perfectly. After careful load development I can only describe this rifle as a combat-hardened tack-driver. My current load consists of a Sierra 155 grain MatchKing Palma bullet, Lake City Long Range case (match-prepped), Federal 210 Match Primer, an appropriate charge of Vihtavuori N140 powder, with an overall length of 2.80 inches. Off the bench in 80 degrees F weather, this rifle put 10 shots into a 0.67 inch group at 100 yards. Average velocity was 2801 feet per second 10 feet from the muzzle. This combat veteran rifle could shoot!

By now you are probably wondering how this L96A1 made it to my side of the pond. I will share with you what I know: I purchased if from a co-worker about 10 years ago. He had acquired it in the mid-2000's from the widow of one of his Special Forces team-mates. She was married to a Special Forces Soldier who deployed to Iraq twice in the early 2000's during our Global War on Terror. He took this

rifle as a trophy during his first tour after killing the Iraqi insurgent who wielded it against Allied forces. Unfortunately, he was killed in combat on his second tour. It was at the wake celebrating his life that his widow dispersed his collection to his team-mates, his Brothers... This rifle has a 1986 date on the receiver. The barrel was proof marked in

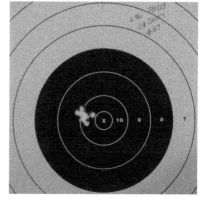

ABOVE: Even after all this rifle has been through it is still delivering a level of accuracy many other rifles would struggle to match.

London in 1987. Inspecting this rifle closely I have no doubt as to its MOD heritage. Its excessive wear, abuse and general state suggests to me that it was in Iraqi possession for quite some time. I surmise that it was an issued rifle taken to the Iraqi desert in the first Gulf War in 1990/1. Who carried it and how it was lost are the missing pieces to this puzzle. If only this rifle could talk...

Chapter 7
Arctic Warfare

Today Arctic Warfare encompasses a group of weapons rather than one. The AW series of sniper rifles was born from a designated programme to produce a sniper rifle for the Swedish armed forces who commissioned Accuracy International to develop a system specifically suited to their sub-zero winter environment. It was not a product that simply evolved from the L96; its build and features were dictated more by a punishing development programme, although the L96 did prove the concept of many of its parts. The AW platform would subsequently present to the world a range of weapons in different calibres with a continued innovative development of its features making each model increasingly user friendly and highly desirable to both the civilian shooter and military sniper.

The Swedish armed forces adopted the .308/7.62mm calibre Arctic Warfare rifle in 1991. The same rifle was also adopted in its full AW specification in the following years by the MoD, being designated L118A1, and although the weapon is approaching twenty years of age at the point of writing it is still largely shrouded by secrecy due to its inception being predominantly in British Special Forces, and precise details surrounding this particular weapon are still categorised as restricted information. The L118A1 rifle, also known as CTSR (Counter Terrorism Sniper Rifle), was introduced to British Special Forces in a fixed stock and with a much improved sighting system, the L17A1, which was a 3-12 x 50mm Schmidt & Bender day scope. It also introduced for the first time in nearly 100 years an alternative reticle to the post and wire. The P4 reticle ended what had become almost tradition in the British sniper optic.

In stark contrast to the environment the weapon was specifically commissioned to operate in, the British Army took the L118A1 to the Iraqi desert where it served alongside the L96A1 rifle which was later upgraded and given the same L17A1 scope making it a comparable weapon, in desert conditions only, it has to be said. The L118A1 was well received and continued pushing the boundaries of excellence already laid down by the L96 which paved the way allowing for a folding stock A2 variant to follow which preceded the covert rifle.

Rifle 7.62mm L118A1/A2/L17A1 Telescope

Although the L118A1 rifle was specific to Special Forces units and was not issued generally to the field army it is featured here as it bridges the leap from the L96A1 to the AW series of weapons which have become the workhorse within British military sniping. To not include the L118 rifle would be to leave a gap in continuity as it served as an important step towards the L115 series of weapons that would ultimately become the principal sniping weapon of the British Army in the form of the A3 model.

The British Army took receipt of a relatively smaller number of L118A1 rifles, NSN 1005-99-535-4279, in comparison to the contract number of L96A1 rifles originally ordered to replace the L42A1 across the armed forces. The L118 possessed certain features that made it an extreme cold weather specialist and was procured for Special Forces units such as the Special Air Service, Special Boat Service and Arctic and Mountain Warfare Cadre of the Royal Marines. The L118A1 had a fixed stock with an adjustable raised moulded cheek rest and a butt spike which actually had a large diameter foot that adjusted in ten millimetre increments plus fine adjustment. The L17A1 scope was held in a quick detachable mount which attached to the rifle via a picatinny rail running along the top of the receiver and had

battle sights in reserve that were retro fitted should they be required.

They were stored in their own small pouch after being zeroed to the weapon. The night vision device which the L118 used was SIMRAD which is a "piggy back" device that utilises the day scope and mounted to the weapon via a short "top hat" attachment on top of the front scope ring. The rifle came with multiple sling fixture points, up to six in the A1 fixed stock variant and seven in the folding stock A2 variant, in both forward and rearward positions with an additional attachment point provided on the hand stop as well as a stud that when fitted was positioned at the most rearward point of the underside of the fore-end in front of the magazine housing. The A2 also had a sling attachment point incorporated into the folding stock hinge assembly.

PREVIOUS PAGE: Pictured is a British sniper with his L115A3 rifle on board a Merlin helicopter en route to Camp Shawquat, Nad-e Ali. *(© MoDCrown copyright)*

The weapon was fed by a ten round capacity double stack magazine which was completely compatible with the L96, later becoming the standard issue magazine for the L96 in the latter years of its service.

This new radically different system also carried a new innovative accessory never before seen which came in the form of a small spirit level mounted to the rear of the picatinny rail behind the scope mount. The small spirit level was positioned so the sniper could, whilst in a fire position, see it and its purpose was to aid the sniper with long range shots indicating any camber in the rifle.

The weapon also came equipped with another new feature which completed the appearance making it look unique and like nothing that had gone before: this was in the form of a short picatinny accessory rail, predominantly carried on the right hand side of the fore-end to simply accommodate small accessories as well as control pressels. On the underside of the fore-end the rifle carried a hand stop which also doubled up as a second optional mount for the Parker-Hale type bipod. This bipod attachment provided considerable elevation and was directly related to the weapons role as CTSR, the purpose being for situations such as passenger jet hijack scenarios. The attachment allows the sniper to take shots on windows and doors of a parked aircraft from a prone tarmac position.

The barrel selected has a 1 in 12 rifling twist rate selected for the flexibility this twist rate offers which suited the role of the weapon; depending on the situation it could effectively use the 155 grain NATO Black Spot as well as 144 grain and 185 grain rounds. The barrel was completed with a single chamber muzzle brake that allowed a short tactical suppressor to be attached. A fully suppressed version of both the L118A1 and A2 rifles was also produced.

Rifle 7.62mm L118A1/A2/L17A1 Telescope
NSN 1005-99-535-4279

Technical Specification	
Calibre	7.62mm
Magazine Capacity	10 Rounds Double Stack
Overall Rifle Length	1200mm
Barrel	Stainless Steel Match grade 26 inch including Muzzle Brake
Twist Rate	4 Groove 1:12 R/H
Combat Weight	9kg
Scope Mounted	Overbore
Iron Sights	Yes
Approval Date	Classified
Manufactured By	Accuracy International
Contract Qty	48

BELOW: The folding stock revised the L118A1 designation to A2, and the example pictured is how the weapon may be found today, equipped with cosine indicator and STIC rail. This cold weather specialist also conquered the desert where it saw a considerable amount of service; note the small screw in the front of the picatinny rail which is an anchorage point for the mirage band. Still in the armoury of SF units, much of the information concerning the L118 rifle is still classified.

ABOVE: A scarce image of an early fully suppressed L118A1, or CTSR rifle, in original specification. The first variants included the short accessory side rail, predominantly on the right hand side. Note the sling attachment stud in front of the magazine housing, or Lower Swivel Sling Loop to use its official title.

LEFT: The L118 heralded the arrival of the bolt on accessory, and the spirit level was a new feature to be found on a British sniper rifle. This basic but robust spirit level was housed in a solid metal body indicating camber of the rifle which aided long range accuracy.

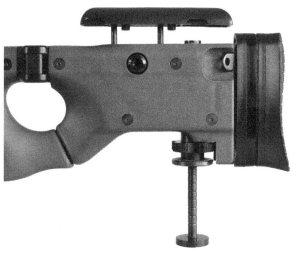

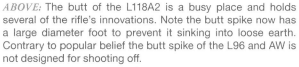

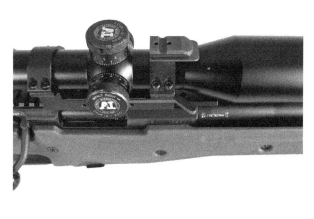

ABOVE: The butt of the L118A2 is a busy place and holds several of the rifle's innovations. Note the butt spike now has a large diameter foot to prevent it sinking into loose earth. Contrary to popular belief the butt spike of the L96 and AW is not designed for shooting off.

ABOVE: The top hat SIMRAD scope mount and lever of the L17A1 scope mount seen here from a slightly elevated angle. Unfortunately this first variant of the lever operated system did not itself lock and if accidentally caught would release the telescope. The mount is still in service today on the AX rifle with a lever that now locks when closed.

ABOVE: The L118 rifle's single chamber tactical muzzle brake is pictured with both the thread protector and brake cover fitted. The short tactical suppressor is illustrated fitted to the weapon. Note the suppressor completely covers the muzzle chamber of the brake. A seal is created with the use of a rubber "O" ring within the brake housing of the suppressor.

The growing family of AW rifles at this period also included the .338 calibre L115A1 rifle which was adopted by the MoD in 1996 and had very similar, but not the same features as the L118A1. The L115 barrel was longer, fluted and much heavier and it lacked the continuous picatinny rail on the receiver. This rifle was also very much the preserve of SF (Special Forces) units. It is also worth noting both of these rifles no longer utilised the L8A2 Common Weapon Sight for their night vision capability. The sight by this period had given way to the SIMRAD device which mounted to the day scope via the small "top hat" bracket on top of the front scope ring mentioned earlier and was largely issued to Special Forces only until 2008 prior to the SSIP. When Dave Caig designed the folding stock for the AW in 1998 both the L115 and L118 saw an A2 variant unveiled around 2000.

Telescope, Schmidt & Bender L17A1 and Backup Sights

The new scope was larger with a 34mm main tube and 50mm

ABOVE: The graduation scale of both the elevation and windage drums of the L17A1 telescope are illustrated. Note the elevation adjusts in 0.1 MRAD clicks; there is a click position in between each marked line. Also note the BDC range reference numbers above the MRAD scale.

objective lens greatly improving the light gathering ability and was a big improvement overall on the former L13A1 green 6 x 42mm fixed magnification scope. The L17 also sported a new reticle system featuring the U.S. mildot system under which in the bottom of the sight picture was a series of stadia lines for the purposes of quickly ranging a man at 400, 600, 800 and 1,000 metres by placing the bottom line on his belt and the top line on the top of his head or helmet, which roughly represented one metre; if the figure fit in between these two lines then he was in the prescribed range. The elevation and windage was now adjusted in the milliradian, or milrad system of adjustment which was a metric adjustment instead of the former imperial MOA system. The BDC system was also still present making the scope very versatile, offering the sniper several ways of quickly ranging and engaging his target without having to leave his firing position to use a device.

The L17 was equipped with variable magnification ranging from three powers to twelve as well as an adjustable eyepiece which like the L13's eyepiece fine-tuned eye relief and sharpened focus. The L17 also had a third drum or turret on the left side of the scope which allowed the sniper to adjust for the effects of parallax. Parallax is particularly noticeable when engaging at long range and is best described as an optical illusion. As an exercise to test for parallax the sniper can maintain

ABOVE: Reserve iron, or battle sights, were made available to the L118 rifle which are kept separate in their own pouch. Note the apertures of the rear sight are numbered 2–6. The numbers relate to distance in increments of 100 metres.

cheek weld with the rifle but move his head up and down, left and right to see if the reticle moves over the target. If it does then the parallax turret can be adjusted whilst still moving the head and one will see the reticle become stationary on the point of aim. The parallax turret can adjust the focal plane of the reticle to the same as that of the target image through marked graduations on the drum which on the L17 is marked fifty metres to infinity.

The scope was still mounted in a single piece mount however the thumb wheels that had become a characteristic of the British sniper rifle over the previous sixty years had now been made obsolete, being replaced with three cap head Allen screws when fitting to the standard dovetail on the receiver of the L96, L115A1 and A2. The receiver of the L118 and subsequently the L115A3 were fitted with a continuous picatinny rail and used a mount that accommodated the castellation

of the rail. The L118 mount was particularly unique as it operated by a small locking lever on the right hand side of the mount's body. Its design and conception was SF led and proved to be particularly useful during their parachute operations where the scope could be removed, stowed and once on the ground quickly reattached to the rifle. Again the whole scope ensemble was designed to be removable with a padded scope case being provided for its protection whilst being carried separately from the rifle. Whilst the L96 served alongside the new AW it received a similar upgrade, losing its battle sights effectively making them redundant, and was also fitted with the new L17A1 scope in the mount that suited the dovetail that ran along the top of its receiver.

The L118 backup sights were designed to be zeroed to the weapon and then removed and stored until required. The rear sight clamped onto the picatinny

rail rearward of the receiver that suited eye relief best. The compact unit was comprised of two parts, a base, and an upper block that is married to the base via a dovetailed connection which allows the upper block to move laterally for windage as the screw on each side of the base is adjusted. The upper block also carries an elevation disc which is equipped with six different sized apertures numbered from two to six, each representing a distance that corresponds with the number and is simply rotated to select the aperture for the target distance. The foresight is a single machined block that carries the foresight post, screw for attaching to the rifle and screw for adjusting the post in or out for MPI height. The underside of the foresight block is shaped perfectly to allow it to sit and mechanically fix to the top of the tactical muzzle brake.

Schmidt & Bender L17A1 Telescope
NSN B5/1240-99-911-6011

Technical Specification	
Manufacturer	Schmidt & Bender
Length	440mm
Weight in the mount	1.2kg
Objective Lens DIA	50mm
Field of View	11.1–3.4
Magnification	3-12 Variable
Reticle	Mildot with Ranging
Elevation Graduations	100 to 1000 (0-13 MRAD)
Bullet Drop Compensation	Yes
Lateral Adjustment	6-0-6 MRAD
Focus Capability	Yes
Parallax Adjustment	50m to infinity
Sunshade	Yes, plus Killflash
Mount Type	Single

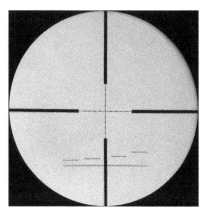

LEFT: The L17A1 eye piece with the original ribbed focus ring and 3-12 magnification ring displayed. Note the designation and NSN engraved below the Schmidt & Bender logo.

ABOVE: The L17A1 telescope is pictured in its own soft DPM camouflaged carry case. The scope is also illustrated with its sunshade and kill flash filter fitted.

ABOVE: The L17A1 telescope complete with sunshade and kill flash filter fitted to a L96A1 rifle. For the first time in nearly 100 years the reticle has moved away from the post and wire pattern. *(© MoDCrown copyright)*

LEFT & BELOW: The L118A2 laid out with all of its associated equipment, and again packed in its aluminium transit chest with complete CES. Note the rifle is packed in a short transit chest utilising its folded stock.

The CES equipment of the AW series of weapons mirrored that of the L96 for some years through the L118A1/A2 and L115A1/A2 rifles service with individual weapon specific items such as the action/ scope cover being changed. Like the 7.62mm calibre L118, the .338 calibre L115 also saw an upgrade whereby it received the same folding stock improvement which launched the new L115A2 variant. The .338 calibre weapon was now being extended in its issue to SFSG (Special Forces Support Group) units such as 1st battalion Parachute Regiment who were exclusively operating in direct support of the SAS and were therefore privy to a range of SF weapons and equipment to assist them in their support role.

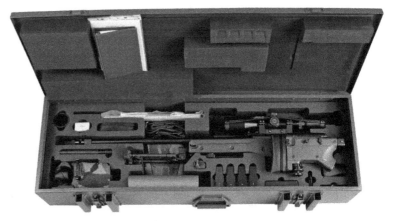

ABOVE & RIGHT: The .338 L115A1 rifle pictured here in black stock sides. The rifle is also pictured on a range shoot with British snipers during Operation Grapple in Bosnia in the early nineties. Note the spotter is using the Vector LRF.

The L115 was rapidly becoming the sniper's weapon of choice, seeing a considerable amount of action in Iraq and Afghanistan where it was liked enormously and was in these units being used extensively in favour of the 7.62mm calibre weapon. The round at the time was the 250 grain (16 gram)

Lapua .338 calibre bullet which has a considerable range as well as solid flight characteristics; it requires little windage adjustment in conditions that would easily push a 7.62mm bullet off its target therefore massively increasing the probability of a first round hit over an increased distance, delivering in most cases

an unsurvivable wound. The L115 was designed to engage targets at a conservative 1,100 metre distance but was often successfully pushed out to distances as great as 2,000 metres plus, on many occasions with a bullet flight time of roughly 1.5 and 3.5 seconds respectively. This advantage gave snipers a

ABOVE: The L17A1 telescope pictured with an improved focus ring. The original ribbed style ring became an entry point for dust and dirt.

ABOVE: The L96's scope/action cover evolved and went on to serve the L118 and L115A1 and A2 rifles.

devastating reach on the enemy who were increasingly learning how to operate against British forces outside of their small arms effective range.

In stark contrast to the army's attempts to field snipers in the North African deserts in WW2 where the equipment simply could not cope with the conditions and where all attempts to field snipers were eventually abandoned, today's snipers enjoy good hunting in such environmental conditions with a weapon and optics that have surpassed themselves. Having said that, the L17A1 telescope did develop a problem with its focus ring in the ocular housing. With wear the original ribbed style focus ring became an entry point, allowing the fine powdery dust to contaminate the internal compartments of the scope. A second generation focus ring was subsequently fitted and remedied the problem.

SIMRAD KN250 Image Intensifier

With the L17A1 telescope now picatinny rail mounted a new tool for the sniper to operate in the dark was made available, albeit to SF units only. The SIMRAD image intensifier unit or KN250 was manufactured by SIMRAD Optronics ASA of Norway. The device was a technological leap forward in terms of usability as well as performance as it attached, or piggy backed, on the day scope, enabling the sniper to continue using his day scope in the normal manner.

The all-weather KN250 image intensifier ended the need to remove the day scope and fit an entirely new sight unit to the weapon for night work. The previous device, the common weapon sight, was not specific to any single weapon it fitted to which brought about cheek weld as well as other ergonomic problems when mounted onto a sniper system.

The SIMRAD KN250 unit mounted via a small and short "top hat" style mount which sat on top of the front scope ring. Once slid onto the mount the unit locked with the use of a single small lever. The device then sat immediately in front of the day scope and by placing its own lens in front of the day scope's objective lens, via a prism the sniper used his day scope to look through a large 100 millimetre diameter light gathering lens that sat above the telescope. The KN250 offered just one power of magnification as the scope used its own variable power. There was no reticle as, again, the scope used its own, neither was there any requirement to sight the device in. The sniper simply needed to be aware that because the day scope was now viewing roughly 120 millimetres above where it would normally he needed to adjust his point of aim accordingly.

Power was supplied by two 1.5v standard AA batteries which provided roughly eighty hours of service, however the device was still vulnerable to natural or bright artificial light as was the case with previous devices. The device was used in Iraq where it enabled a lethal shot to be achieved at 1,000 metres, 400 metres beyond the normal 600 metre planning distance.

SIMRAD KN250 Image Intensifier

Technical Information	
Height	142mm
Length	187mm
Width	104mm
Weight	1kg

Optical Characteristics:	
Magnification	X 1
Focus Range	25m to infinity
Field of View	12 degrees
IIT (Type	3rd Generation
Graticule	Scope's Own Reticle

Power Requirements:

The weapon sight uses two AA size batteries that will give a 3v supply and service life of approximately 80 hours at 20 degrees Centigrade.

RIGHT: The SIMRAD KN250 pictured in its hard transit case, which with the device contained the soft carry case and spare batteries.

ABOVE: The device is pictured installed on the weapon via the top hat bracket. The KN250 is over half a kilogram lighter than the model that would follow and only required a small mounting bracket with a single locking lever.

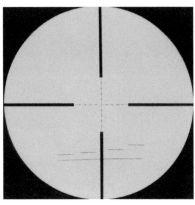

ABOVE & LEFT: Mainly the preserve of SF units, the KN250 model was phased out after the SSIP. Today the device is obsolete within the British Army. Also note there is no light omitting coupling sleeve on this model something which was rectified on the KN203D that followed.

ABOVE: A rare image of an early SIMRAD KN250 fitted to a L96 in the late eighties/early nineties.

The Battle for Musa Qala

BELOW & NEXT PAGE: The collection of six panoramic sketches are the original sketches prepared by the sniper pair of Easy Company. Each depicts the view, arcs of fire and distance to all significant features from the observation posts within the defended compound.

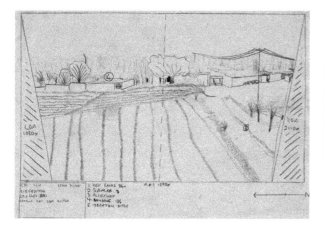

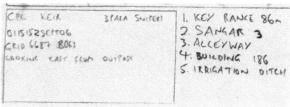

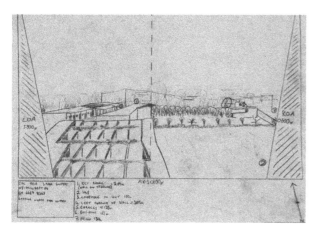

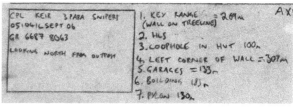

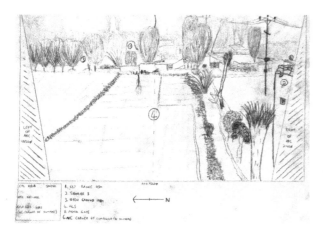

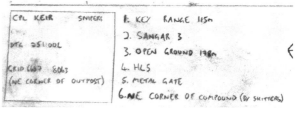

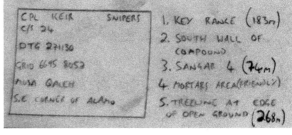

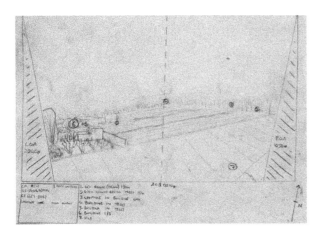
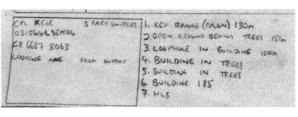

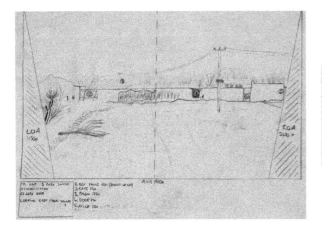

The use of range cards and panoramic illustrations assist the sniper immensely, particularly when bullets start to fly and adrenalin is pumping. Equipment needs to be robust and easy to use and a pre-prepared panoramic illustration of the ground before the sniper helps with quick target acquisition in the heat of battle; this was first used by British snipers in the trenches during the Great War. The group of panoramic views sketched by the sniper team illustrated here are originally prepared and used by one sniper pair; I also hasten to add the only sniper pair attached to a body of eighty-eight officers and men of the 3 Para Battle Group sent to operate at Musa Qala district centre in Helmand Provence, Afghanistan, 2006.

The group of eighty-eight men were call signed Easy Company and were a mixture of soldiers from both the Parachute Regiment and first battalion Royal Irish Regiment. The eighty-eight men of Easy Company were delivered to the town of Musa Qala in the northern reaches of Helmand Province by Chinook helicopters on 23rd August 2006 to relieve a Danish unit who had been struggling to bring stability and security to the remote area which was surrounded by barren empty desert.

The Danes occupied a compound area typical of the region; the collection of mud walled buildings with flat roofs was encircled by a relatively low compound wall constructed from mud, baked dry by the searing heat. The compound was taken over by Easy Company who, due to resource constraints, were only able to bring with them two heavy machine guns, a quad bike and a three man medical team.

After a short handover period they waved goodbye to a well-equipped Danish force who rolled out of Musa Qala into the desert in forty armoured personnel carriers, taking with them eight heavy machine guns and a twelve man medical team. Alarm bells began to ring and quite rightly so as the significant reduction of force did not go unnoticed by the Taliban; as soon as the dust created by the Danes' departure settled, they began their onslaught, confident of an easy defeat of British forces.

The Battle for Musa Qala erupted with the Taliban initially throwing all they had at the compound in a series of full frontal assaults attempting to scale the compound walls in order to overrun it. The fighting was savage and troops within the compound fixed bayonets fully expecting to do hand to hand combat with Taliban fighters who looked as though they would surely, in the end, overrun the compound. Initially the Taliban engagement was thought to be a test of the new resident force, however with no let-up from dawn until dusk and probing assaults through the night it quickly became apparent they intended to annihilate Easy Company, with confirmation coming from their interpreters who heard the Taliban "chatter" on their radios talk of how they would be drinking tea in the British compound HQ by dawn. As first light began to illuminate the town the Taliban assault began again as it had done

ABOVE: The snipers of Easy Company being transported on a Chinook helicopter in Afghanistan. Their weapons are .338 calibre L115A2 rifles with butts folded. Note the sniper nearest to the camera has his corrections written on sniper tape behind the receiver.

ABOVE: Both snipers of Easy Company are captured in this image "standing to" with the L115A2 rifle. On observing enemy movement and in anticipation of an assault they have donned helmets. In the picture they are operating as a conventional sniper pair, but note the spotter has his rifle near as invariably the attacks would become quite strong in which case each would "watch and shoot".

so previously and so did the British mortar team, springing into action with their mortar barrels almost vertical, indicating the close range at which they were dropping their bombs, just outside the compound wall in fact.

After days of being attacked constantly Easy Company were fatigued and had put a large dent in their ammunition. To make matters worse the RAF could not resupply due to the vulnerability of the Chinook helicopter of which had one been destroyed by the Taliban would have scored a huge victory in terms of support from the local populace who were simply hedging their bets as to which side to back. The realisation set in that they were on their own: no fresh ammunition, food, water, or help for that matter was coming. What they carried into Musa Qala was all they had and with the level and ferocity of the fighting many within the company doubted they would survive, and unfortunately after four days of fighting Easy Company suffered its first fatality. Lance Corporal Jon Hetherington, a signaller attached to the Parachute Regiment, died from a Taliban bullet which defeated his body armour.

After several days and a concerted effort on the part of the Taliban to breach the compound they could not sustain the deadly and punishing accuracy of the mortar team any longer and changed tactics, withdrawing into the town from where they resumed with their own mortars, rocket fire and sniping attacks, now from all sides of the British position. The change of tactics gave the two snipers from Easy Company the opportunity to do some work of their own. Defending the compound walls and preparing for hand to hand combat had given way to punishing bombardment of the compound. Observation points had been established at several

locations around the compound and varied from a simple flat roof that offered good commanding views to more defended positions built up with sandbags, one of which was named the Alamo. Sadly on 1st September this sentry position took a direct hit from a Taliban mortar and Easy Company suffered a further two fatalities, Royal Irish Ranger Anare Draiva and Lance Corporal Paul Muirhead who at the time were on sentry duty.

The illustrated panoramic sketches are from the various sentry positions and with a change of tactic on the part of the Taliban it became the snipers' responsibility to remain out in exposed positions observing enemy activity as well as eliminating any Taliban fighter who made the mistake of taking up an exposed position. The two snipers, both armed with a .338 calibre AWSM L115A2 rifle, often worked as a conventional sniper team of shooter and spotter utilising the panoramic sketches for speedy

target acquisition, however when fighting became intense they often each manned a rifle dealing with insurgents manning mortar barrels, individuals carrying rockets and fighters carrying out sniping attacks. They were also largely responsible for closing down any momentum that built for a fresh assault on the compound, knocking down fighters as they took up positions in the streets, buildings and irrigation ditches that flanked their position.

Their role was crucial to delivering an immediate response to the Taliban's hostile activities as well as intelligence gathering so the company commander Major Adam Jowett had a good overall picture of developments. After three weeks of daily intense fighting the besieged British force was running low on everything from ammunition to batteries and for most the outcome was looking extremely grim with individuals reserving one round of ammunition for themselves rather than being taken prisoner by the

ABOVE: Standing to at first light within the compound, ready to repel the enemy again. The sniper pair was in high demand therefore one sniper covers one set of arcs with a rifleman whilst the other does the same elsewhere in the compound.

ABOVE: The sniper pair board the cattle truck laid on by the Taliban before first light, then (RIght) as the sun is rising the convoy of cattle trucks and pickups wind their way into the desert from Musa Qala. No one was quite sure it was not a trap of some sort.

Taliban. Just as things seemed as though they could not get any worse, on 11th September the snipers as well as men in the OP positions reported the arrival of Taliban reinforcements, swelling their ranks to an estimated 500 men. It now seemed the end assault was very close and although Easy Company still had plenty of fight in them they lacked the ammunition to continue to resist. Riflemen were down to their last magazines of ammunition, the mortar team were in possession of a few mortar bombs, machine gunners were already using their last belts of ammunition and the snipers were down to twenty or so rounds between them.

Even so the men prepared for a ferocious final fight which incredibly never came. The elders of the town, having seen their homes all but destroyed from the fighting, persuaded the fighters to call a ceasefire, and the fighters, having suffered horrendous losses, and with no idea that the British were almost out of all supplies, agreed. 13th September saw Major Jowett leave the compound not fully convinced it was not a trap and meet with the Taliban in the centre of town where amongst a crowd of

people they thrashed out a deal. The company commander played his cards close to his chest although he had only one real choice to save the lives of all his men, so, after some hours of negotiation putting on a bold front so as not to indicate in any way to the Taliban they were almost a spent force, he agreed to relinquish the compound in trade for safe passage out into the desert.

Easy Company occupied the compound for a further month until the Taliban could arrange their transport which materialised

on 14th October in the form of a convoy of cattle trucks. No one in Easy Company was convinced this was not a trap of some sort and as they drove out of Musa Qala the Taliban picketed the route out of the town. The convoy drove out into the desert where they rendezvoused with two Chinook helicopters which confirmed for all that the fifty-six day ordeal was over.

Today the snipers' pencil-drawn panoramic illustrations are a tangible and lasting link to this fascinating episode that has since been likened

ABOVE: Their destination, a grid reference in the desert where they were picked up by two Chinook helicopters.

LEFT: A .338 Super Magnum calibre L115A2 rifle pictured in Afghanistan at night through a night viewing device. Note the sniper is operating in complete darkness; his weapon is fitted with both a suppressor and SIMRAD KN203D night sight. A deadly combination which helped conceal the direction from which the shot would come out of the darkness. *(© MoDCrown copyright)*

to a modern day Rorke's Drift when British soldiers held off 3,000 Zulu in 1879. The Battle for Musa Qala lasted fifty-six days in a remote part of Helmand Province and is today told by members of Easy Company who have since left the army.

By the mid-2000s the United Kingdom's armed forces had seen their busiest period since World War 2 and it was not about to get any easier with things in Afghanistan just warming up. The hugely successful .338 Lapua calibre rifle which had previously been the preserve of SF units was now under consideration of expansion through the field army under the SSIP (Sniper System Improvement Programme) which looked to upgrade the army's sniper rifle, day scope, night vision, and spotting scope as well as the introduction of new tools to the chest such as the Kestrel pocket wind meter and Vectronix pocket laser range finder, replacing the older and much larger Leica Vector. Accuracy International was the obvious candidate to supply the new weapon and did indeed win the contract in 2007 but not before they had to fend off stiff competition from Prairie Gun Works of Canada with their .338 calibre Timber Wolf rifle.

Around the same time, 2007, the stubborn and persistent problem of poor individual marksmanship was again, some forty years after it initiated change to marksmanship training, showing signs of disrupting the army's operational effectiveness, leading to some searching questions being asked of the army by SO1 Operational Shooting of HQ Infantry. The kill tally in Afghanistan was, when measured against the resources being expended, low, so in 2007 the army set up Project Odysseus specifically to look at operational marksmanship in Afghanistan. The findings of the project were published and were predictably negative; putting the failings of pre-deployment training in the spotlight, it exposed sniper training courses which across the army had a fifty percent failure rate as well as a statistic that mirrored that of the U.S. army in Vietnam. The British Army was expending an enormous amount of small arms ammunition annually which when divided against the number of Taliban kills equated to an average of 11,000 rounds of ammunition for each kill.

To combat the problem the former Northern Ireland Training Centre in

Lydd, Kent was re-designated Army Marksmanship Training Centre. The centre previously prepared soldiers for deployment to Northern Ireland but with hostilities in the province significantly less and the army largely withdrawn the centre, which houses a fantastic array of live fire range facilities, became the epicentre of Afghanistan pre-deployment training. Soldiers attending the centre went through an intense programme of live fire training under the watchful eye of Defence Operational Shooting Staff who coached individuals on all aspects covering shoot to kill, individual marksmanship and the zeroing of their own weapon. Staff from the centre also deployed to Afghanistan and patrolled with units to maximise training. With an extremely poor pass rate of the sniper course the Marksmanship Training Centre also became involved with the training of snipers across the army which coincided with the launch of the new L115A3 sniper system in 2008 by which time the pass rate had been improved to eighty-eight percent.

The snipers who would operate the new long range rifle are selected in their own unit through their unit's own Sniper Selection Course, and those that pass are then eligible to attend the arduous Basic Sniper Course, Part 1 run by Sniper Division, Support Weapons School at the Infantry Battle School (IBS), Brecon, Wales. The course runs for several weeks and covers marksmanship which used to be a graduated system when the L96A1 rifle was in service; students would have to have passed a marksmanship module using the L96 before they could graduate on to the .338 calibre L115A3 rifle. Successful candidates return to their own unit for Part 2, which covers field craft, which at the point of writing is under review.

There are currently three separate sniper training courses running within UK armed forces. The Royal Marines run their course at Commando Training Centre, Lympstone, the army run their course at Sniper Division, Infantry Battle School, Brecon and the Household Division Parachute Regiment Combined Course is run at Pirbright, the latter having been established since the mid-nineties. All are designed to be the toughest course an infantryman can attempt.

Rifle .338 Lapua AWSM L115A3/L24A1 Telescope

In 2007 the SSIP was in full swing and was affirmed with an order awarded to Accuracy International Ltd for an initial 582 .338 Lapua Arctic Warfare Super Magnum rifles to be supplied in 2008 with flat dark earth stock sides and in a composite transit case. The new rifle now superseded all that had gone before it; the L96 now almost completely withdrawn from service and with its demise making the .308/7.62mm calibre sniper rifle redundant as by 2012 all L96A1 sniper rifles had been retired and were returned to stores, and the .338 calibre weapon was now the primary sniper system in the British Army.

ABOVE: A sniper armed with a suppressed .338 Super Magnum calibre L115A3 rifle during a live field fire exercise. He has his rifle mounted on sticks, and note he has the kill flash attached to the L24A1 scope and has the STICS rail attached also. *(© MoDCrown copyright)*

Rifle .338 Lapua AWSM L115A3/L24A1 Telescope
NSN 1005-99-372-3045

Technical Specification	
Calibre	338
Magazine Capacity	5 Rounds Single Stack
Overall Rifle Length	1230mm
Barrel	Stainless Steel Match Grade 27 inch with Muzzle Brake
Twist Rate	1 in 11
Combat Weight	6.9kg
Iron Sights	Yes
Approval Date	October 2007
Manufactured By	Accuracy International
Scope Mounted	Overbore
Contract Qty	582

ABOVE: A sniper taking aim through the L24A1 on his L115A3 rifle. He appears to be standing on a combat ladder with his rifle resting on a Hesco gabion basket. (© MoDCrown copyright)

ABOVE: The L115A3 rifle is the culmination in the evolution of the .338 calibre Arctic Warfare rifle and certainly fulfilled all expectations most had of it over the last decade. Although currently still in service it will in the near future give way to the L115A4 which is based on the Accuracy International AX generation of rifles.

268/2007   14 November 2007

Deadly Precision: Snipers get new longer range rifles

Snipers in the Army, Royal Marines and RAF Regiment are to get a new rifle that will give them lethal precision at even greater distances under a £4M contract announced today.

The British firm Accuracy International Ltd will supply 580 rifles with day telescopic sights for snipers across the services, which will fire a larger calibre bullet than the existing weapon.

The new rifle is being supplied as part of a broader Sniper System Improvement (SSI) programme to give UK snipers more power, precision and stealth than ever before. All-weather new advanced day and night sights will mean snipers can operate round the clock in difficult conditions, and laser technology will allow distant targets to be accurately located.

Baroness Taylor, Minister for Defence Equipment and Support said:

"We are committed to providing our troops on the front line with the equipment they need.

"Military snipers provide vital capability on operations, defeating the enemy and protecting our troops on the ground. In response to feedback from operations we are investing in new sniper equipment. The first contract is for the new longer range rifle and day sight, and we expect to start taking deliveries of this kit early next year."

Training units will familiarise themselves with the weapon and how it works with other parts of the sniper system. The rifle is due to be ready for operational use next spring.

LEFT: With the government's commitment to the SSIP, Defence Media began the fanfare creating an air of positivity as they announced the planned supply of new sniper equipment to soldiers who operated within an area of the armed forces that to this day is still frowned upon in some quarters. The purpose of the press release was probably multi layered as at the time the MoD was being heavily criticised for the poor equipment, and indeed lack of equipment troops were being asked to operate with. Any big expenditure on equipment was at the time worth shouting about but it's doubtful had the army entered the conflict in better shape this equipment would have even been mentioned. *(© MoDCrown copyright)*

255/2008   12 NOVEMBER 2008

ON TARGET – FINAL SNIPER RIFLE IS DELIVERED TO TROOPS

Snipers fulfil a vital and enduring role on the battlefield, in terms of intelligence gathering, target identification and eliminating high value targets.

Unveiled earlier this year the L115A3 rifle, part of the Sniper System Improvement Programme (SSIP) is a larger calibre weapon and provides state of the art telescopic day and night, all-weather sights, increasing a sniper's effective range considerably; thereby beating enemy forces capability.

Group Captain Paul Ridge, the DE&S Light Weapons, Photography and Batteries Integrated Project Team Leader said:

"I am delighted to accept the delivery of the last weapon of this order from Accuracy International whose co-operation and performance has been outstanding.

"The new weapon system has already been used on operations and is proving to be an outstanding system. Having just returned from Afghanistan, where I had the opportunity to discuss the weapon system with snipers – it is clear that this battle-winning equipment has already proven to be a reliable and extremely accurate system that is giving our forces a real edge"

The first batch of SSIP systems was deployed to Afghanistan with members of 16 Air Assault Brigade in May this year with subsequent deliveries being made to training units across the UK.

Tom Irwin, Managing Director of Accuracy International said,

"Accuracy International has supplied sniper rifles to the British forces since the eighties. We accepted the challenge to provide a new .338 calibre rifle and were selected by the MoD, after testing and trials and against international competition. The SSIP contract is extremely significant to us and we have exerted all of our effort to complete this programme on time. We are proud to supply the best .338 sniper rifle in the world to our forces."

ABOVE & RIGHT: A close-up of the double chamber muzzle brake with both the thread protector and brake cover fitted. The accompanying image illustrates the rifle with the tactical short suppressor fitted, completely shrouding the chamber section of the brake.

In addition to the new AWSM, NSN 1005-99-372-3045 sniper system, around forty Special Forces A1 and A2 predecessor rifles were completely refurbished to A3 specification and as was previously done with the L96 each new rifle was completely function tested, this time by Frank Fletcher of Accuracy International before being dispatched to Donnington central stores.

The L115A3 came with a heavy twenty-seven inch long fluted barrel with a 1 in 11 rifling twist rate fitted with a tactical double chamber muzzle brake that allows the tactical short suppressor, NSN 1005-99-867-8548, to slide over and screw onto it. Unlike the .308 calibre brake which is a push fit secured with a single screw to the barrel, the muzzle energy passing through the .338 brake requires it to be attached to the rifle in a somewhat more robust manner. Therefore it first screws onto the muzzle and then like the .308 brake is tightened on the barrel by a single screw. The fluting to the .338 calibre barrel was intended to assist cooling and primarily to remove some of the weight from this substantial piece of metal. The fluted design is however very much a military feature found

only on the military specification rifle owing to the two issues that dictated it being concerns held only within the military due to operational conditions.

The fluted design does, though, carry some controversy as Accuracy International do not offer this barrel to any other customers, instead offering a conventional round profiled barrel. Doubts as to the performance of the fluted design first crept in during Accuracy International's own research and development of their .50 calibre programme where the fluted barrel presented accuracy continuity issues and was with this uncertainty discontinued. However the fluted barrel does live on in the L115A3 specification laid down by the MoD who continue to use it specifically in conjunction with originally the 250 grain bullet which has since become the 252 grain Swiss-P Ball, L4A1 round manufactured by RUAG to what is widely now known as the "AI length" as opposed to the longer European CIP (Permanent International Commission) for the Proof of Small Arms – commonly abbreviated as CIP standard .338 calibre cartridge length. The L115A3 is therefore a 252 grain rifle due to the barrel and magazine fitment

being tailored to this ammunition. When used in the L115A3 rifle the 252 grain round travels at 850 metres per second, reaching transonic speed at 1,350 metres and dropping to subsonic speed at around 1,450 metres. The tailored nature of the L115A3 rifle presented a problem to SF units who favoured the 300 grain weighted bullet.

The 300 grain bullet is longer, therefore the cartridge overall length does not fit the L115A3 magazine. It also performs optimally with a 1 in 9 twist rate barrel. To overcome this SF units have since 2014 employed the AIAX rifle designated L115A4 which accommodated the use of the

ABOVE: The RUAG manufactured Swiss-P 252 grain .338 calibre round designated L4A1.

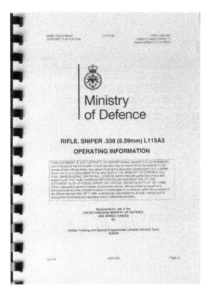 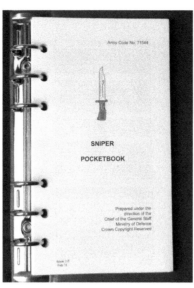

ABOVE: The sniper had the Pocketbook as well as the rifle's Operating Information booklet for his own reference which were generally kept with the rifle in its transit chest.

.338 Lap Mag 300 grain cartridge. The SF preference for the 300 grain round lies in its external ballistic characteristics. The bullet travels at 820 metres per second reaching transonic speed at 1,460 metres and dropping to subsonic speed at 1,560 metres, providing around 100 metres' extra supersonic flight over the 252 grain round, allowing the 300 grain bullet to defeat mediums and armour at increased distances.

The L115A3 weapon was launched as a long range sniper weapon with a bit of a fanfare on the part of the MoD who boasted of the edge it would bring to British snipers day and night and in all weather conditions. The weapon had some distinct changes to its specification and of course was no longer the preserve of Special Forces; the .338 calibre weapon now became the staple of the British sniper right across the field army and as such *Pamphlet No. 4* was amended entirely to be inclusive of the new weapon, scope, Leupold Mk4 tactical spotting scope, Kestrel weather meter and the pocket

laser range finder. The practice of providing the sniper with an Operating Information pamphlet for the weapon and Sniper Handbook was continued.

The A3 is essentially the same platform as the A1 and A2 models fed by a single stack five round magazine but received further enhancement as part of the SSI

programme. The Parker-Hale style bipod which was fitted to the A1 and the Parker-Hale spigot attachment that allowed the L96 type bipod to attach to the A2 is now gone, exchanged for the American Harris bipod which makes available to the sniper a much lower shooting position, although the robustness of this bipod has been called into question many times on this large calibre weapon with legs actually snapping on occasions. It is also interesting that the resin stock sides were manufactured to one specification which was to fit an unmodified .308/7.62mm AW and in order to fit a military specification rifle and/or .338 calibre rifle the stock sides required a hand cut modification. The butt sides had to be cut to accommodate the new larger butt spike and if fitting to a .338 calibre rifle the magazine opening needed to be cut to accommodate the larger magazine housing.

The top of the receiver is fitted with a continuous picatinny rail which has mounted the new Schmidt & Bender 5-25 x 56 PM MkII telescope designed specifically for large calibre weapons and long range precision. The scope sits in a

ABOVE: The butt of the L115A3 is indistinguishable from that of other folding stock variants such as the L118A2 and L115A2.

ABOVE: The Cosine Indicator was a new addition to a British sniper rifle under the SSIP.

scope mount that also has an integral SIMRAD mount incorporated in its design, a further enhancement as a direct result of the SSIP. Just forward of the telescope a new device called a Cosine Indicator, NSN 1005-99-134-8146, is mounted to the picatinny rail and sits on the left side. The small device was particularly useful in the Afghanistan terrain as its use was to indicate to the sniper the angle of shot whether shooting up or down hill; the normal corrections for the distance are reduced in levels of severity which depend on how acute the angle is.

The same device is available in both cosine as well as degrees; the latter which is used widely by U.S. forces requires a conversion chart, however the British version tends to be cosine which allows the telescope's correction for the bullet's

drop to be calculated with a simple mathematical formula which works by aiming the rifle at the target and taking the closest cosine reading. This figure is then multiplied by the line of sight distance measurement and the result of this calculation is the distance figure of which the scope should actually be set for i.e.

.707 cosine reading on target. The laser range finder reading to target is 500m.

500 x .707 = 353.5

The scope is set for a 350m shot.

Also to be noted is the stark lack of CES items carrying any designation or NSN code markings although they are all issued with NSN codes which are listed in a CES

booklet; the rifle itself however is one of the few items that is marked, and carries its own L115A3 designation.

For the first time in some decades the sniper's weapon and equipment had undergone complete modernisation and to accompany the new rifle a range of new equipment was also made available. The spotting scope was upgraded to the American Leupold tactical Mk4 spotting scope which is a 12-40 x 60mm variable zoom device which is also accompanied by a 3000 pocket weather meter. The Kestrel 3000 is invariably a spotter's tool which is used in conjunction with the spotting scope and enables the spotter to accurately measure climatic conditions as it occurs so the information used to calculate the corrections to be dialled into the telescope by the sniper is accurate to the second.

This is vital when considering the role the L115A3 rifle was originally employed for by the British Army: it was specifically a long range rifle therefore the climatic conditions such as air temperature and humidity, which are always at play, are characteristics that have a direct impact on a bullet's trajectory, particularly when operating at long range. Understanding the device

LEFT & ABOVE: The Kestrel 3000 weather meter was also part of the suite of new equipment introduced to the sniper through the SSIP. Note this spotter holds the Kestrel next to the Leupold spotting scope for easy reading with minimal movement. *(FIG Left © MoDCrown copyright)*

ABOVE: A sniper in Afghanistan using the PLRF-15c predecessor, the Vectronix Vector LRF. Note the sniper's knee pads which are of the commercially manufactured type that replaced the foam knee pad that stitched to the trouser.

and its operation is another skill the modern sniper must undertake and master, and is indeed covered by a forty minute lesson on the cadre. Much like a marching compass you have to trust the information it provides when your senses are sometimes trying to tell you something different.

Laser range finders have become an important tool to the sniper in recent times with the Leica Vector putting in limited appearances in the nineties, mainly amongst Special Forces units and then more so as an Urgent Operational Requirement during the Iraq (Op Telic) and Afghanistan (Op Herrick) wars.

However the SSIP changed that as with the introduction of the long range rifle the suit of equipment that accompanied it to ensure the sniper's first round hit included the issue of the Vectronix Pocket Laser Range Finder 15 Compass, or PLRF-15c. This device is truly a modern wonder and has certainly expanded the capability of the modern sniper due to the electronic gadgetry being in fact a number of devices that provide the sniper with accurate information which simply was not available to a sniper twenty years ago. This makes shots possible today which a sniper of yesteryear would never have even contemplated.

The PLRF-15c is powered by two 3v Lithium batteries and is a six power monocular with a field of view of 106 mils (milliradian), is waterproof and weighs 670g. Unlike the more powerful range finders used by units such as the artillery which use a laser that is harmful to eyesight and which have to be treated like weapons, used only on live fire ranges with an audible warning when the laser is fired, the PLRF-15c laser is a class 1 eye safe laser capable of measuring distances from five metres to 3,000 metres with an accuracy of plus and minus two metres.

The reticle in the device is both engraved and electronic with an illuminated aiming mark which can be activated at the sniper's discretion. The reticle is made up of a sequence of horizontal lines which from its centre has a sequence of lines going vertical; both sets of lines are spaced at ten mils with a five mils dot in between and extend to fifty mils in both deflection and elevation.

The device is capable of providing a basic measurement of distance from the device to target, and is capable of providing a compass bearing as well as measuring inclination with accuracy of plus and minus three mils. If required the device can perform all three tasks in one reading with a display choice of yards, metres, feet, degrees or mils, furthermore the distance between two objects can be measured as well as the distance to multiple objects making the device indispensable when plotting the route of a stalk, or coordinating several snipers to fire simultaneously at multiple targets.

The future is undoubtedly moving in the direction of electronic devices of which the functions are designed to remove the human element, which in all fairness is where the risk of failure lies, but the electronic "device", whatever it may currently be, and indeed whatever it may become in the future, does and will keep expanding the operational abilities of the sniper. The evolution of weapons and optics over the last century has thus far propelled the sniper's reach on the battlefield to unprecedented distances in all terrains. A sniper thirty years ago armed with the L42 obviously shot up and down hill but was never trained to shoot at extreme acute inclinations and the sniper of that period was not equipped with any tools that would measure the angle for such a shot to be executed. That kind of training would not be on the horizon until late in the years of the L96, and even then the tools, training and practice was sporadic

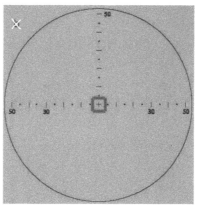

ABOVE & RIGHT: The Vectronix Pocket Laser Range Finder 15 Compass pictured with its carry case and reticle. The device was of a size that could be carried easily in a grab bag or smock pocket which made it far less cumbersome than the Vector model.

with most British snipers getting a taste of acute angle shooting when visiting the U.S. where the training and facilities were commonplace.

Today the British sniper has several tools available, Mildot Master, weapon mounted Cosine Indicator and PLRF-15c to ensure a first round hit on a target that may be located at the end of a sharp incline. The downside of the electronic device taking over each of the separate calculations that need to be made to pull off that one shot is the

skills will be lost, and indeed we are beginning to see that erosion of the core skills as although the current generation is still taught the skills of judging distance and wind strength they are naturally reaching for a device relying heavily on gadgetry to give them the information. But it's all part of the evolutionary process, and in terms of military sniping there can be no place for sentimentality as dominating the battlefield partly lies in the hands of this vital infantry asset, which will ultimately leave the

old school methods on the civilian range where enthusiasts will keep the skills alive.

The desert plains of Afghanistan offered searing heat and a bone dry earth often covered with powdery dust that found its way into everything but the landscape was often ideally suited to the sniper, day or night. The vast open space that would surround the occupied high ground, or which lay beyond a F.O.B. (Forward Operating Base), which would often be a small

ABOVE: The images depict two sniper pairs. One pair in Afghanistan with the spotter using the PLRF-15c handheld suggesting the target is of medium range. The second image illustrates a sniper pair set up for maximum long range with the PLRF-15c mounted on a tripod. The tripod allows the reticle's target marker to be precisely placed on a distant object enabling the range to be calculated by the device without any handshake. Note the rifle also has its butt spike deployed for observation purposes. *(FIG Left © MoDCrown copyright)*

village compound, gave snipers big arcs of fire and long distances to reach out to and the successes being achieved against the Taliban continued to mount. The success, however, did not go unchallenged; the Taliban made a concerted effort to examine foot patrols to identify any patrol members who may have been carrying a "Long Gun" and would go all-out to eliminate anyone they thought was a sniper. Snipers from both the Rifles and Parachute Regiment have told how the threat became significant enough to warrant patrolling without a sniper rifle and the weapon would often be brought out to them by vehicle or helicopter once they reached their destination, and many folded the butt and cradled the weapon to make it appear like an SA80 assault rifle.

ABOVE: The Afghan plains stretch out far and wide which suited the L115A2 and A3 rifles' long range capability perfectly.

ABOVE: A sniper taking part in a live field fire exercise in Canada. The Canadian prairies offer the far reaching landscape needed to truly test a sniper and his L115A3 rifle. Note the privately purchased spirit level on the picatinny rail under the scope. *(© MoDCrown copyright)*

Telescope, Schmidt & Bender L24A1

The overhaul and modernisation SSIP programme also delivered a new telescope designed specifically for use on large calibre weapons capable of precision accuracy. The L24A1 scope, NSN 1240-99-455-1353, has a variable 5-25 magnification power range with an increase sized objective lens of 56mm to assist with long range shooting, but as with the L17A1 the scope tube has remained 34mm in diameter and sports windage and parallax adjustment drums, however the PM MkII also has an illuminated reticle feature. The centre cross in the reticle is the only part of the reticle to be lit up and is controlled by a separate smaller drum which acts as the battery housing and control for eleven brightness settings.

The new scope also has a unique facility which offers the sniper further corrections for bullet drop outside of the normal range of what one would be expected to use.

Branded Dual Turn by Schmidt & Bender, the elevation drum rotates only twice; each complete rotation contains fourteen milliradian adjustments, with the bottom white set of numbers referring to the first rotation and the yellow upper set referring to the second rotation. On top of the drum there is a set of blacked out windows that circle the drum. When the sniper enters the second rotation these windows turn yellow as a visual aid to the sniper to show he is using potentially the last of the corrections available to him. In addition to this the BDC system seen on the British Army's previous two sniper telescopes has been dropped from the PM MkII as a shift in technology has moved the subject of bullet delivery from the "point and shoot" to ballistic charts.

As previously explained, the BDC system worked in conjunction with the telescope being calibrated to work in conjunction with specific

ammunition and so long as the sniper made a reasonable estimation of distance he would hit his man-sized target. This worked out to 1,000 metres but the increased calibre came hand in hand with increased distance which would make for a very busy elevation drum. Instead, the British Army has now adopted the system of ASATS (Advanced Small Arms Targeting System) which, although it was first adopted around 2005 for use with the A1 and A2 variants, was not issued to the field army until 2008 with the L115A3 rifle under the Sniper System Improvement Programme.

The system allows the sniper to select a range of ballistic charts that suit his individual weapon best.

Once the sniper has measured the muzzle velocity of his individual L115A3 rifle on the range with the use of a chronograph, and in conjunction with the prescribed 252 grain ammunition, he can then use the ASATS software which allows him to select from a list of muzzle velocity figures the MV figure that matches his rifle best. The selected figure is essentially a file that contains ballistic charts that will match his weapon in temperate, Arctic and desert zones. The charts provide the necessary "come ups" out to 2,000 metres as well as wind drift and cosine figures, although these figures are representative and "real world" testing on the range is always necessary to record the actual adjustment data.

The scope is mounted via a single mount which has forty-five MOA built into it and clamps onto the picatinny rail with three cap head Allen screws. The mount itself looks quite futuristic with an elaborate SIMRAD mount that bolts on to the mount without interfering with either of the scope rings so can be viewed

ABOVE: A close-up of the elevation drum of the L24A1 scope. The elevation drum has just two rotations. The first rotation is denoted by the bottom set of numbers scaling MRAD adjustment in 0.1 click graduations. The upper yellow set of numbers denotes MRAD adjustments in the second rotation. Note the windows around the top of the drum which turn yellow when the second rotation has begun.

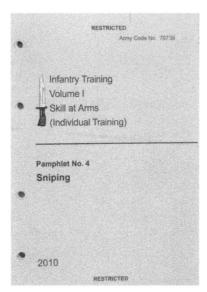
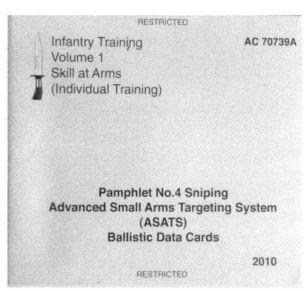

ABOVE: The literature relating to the L115A3 in terms of training student snipers was Pamphlet No. 4, 2010 which replaced the Long Range Rifle Instructors Guide dated 2000. The ASATS software is also heavily featured in the pamphlet and is indeed itself titled Pamphlet No. 4 Sniping, 2010.

as an optional accessory, NSN 1005-99-961-4275. A kill flash filter, NSN 1240-12-373-8857, is available to the scope; note the German "12" in the NSN as opposed to the regular British "99" odd bearing in mind the scope itself is also German manufactured and carries an NSN identifying it as British in origin. In addition to the honeycomb style kill flash filter which is standard issue to the L115A3, the British Army is also using an alternative take on the idea of shielding the objective lens from light that can reflect or glint off the objective lens when exposed to the target. The alternative piece of kit is called the Sniper Hider, NSN 1240-99-392-1276, and is a screw on lens extension tube much like a sunshade, however it does not contain a filter like the traditional kill flash attachment but has within it a lens cover, or shield. On the external side of the tube there is a thumb wheel which controls the lens shield which the sniper uses to open and close it to a degree that offers a usable sight picture in the light conditions on the occasion. When fully closed the shield also acts as a weather proof lens cover. The Sniper Hider is currently in service with SF and SFSG units on both their L24A1 scopes as well as their L17A1 telescopes on the L129A1 Sniper

ABOVE: The standard issue honeycomb kill flash filter is pictured with the newest device in objective lens concealment, the Sniper Hider. Note the lens shield disc is partially open. In daylight conditions this level of lens obscurity still offers a perfectly normal sight picture.

ABOVE: Sniper pairs heavily camouflaged whilst taking part in a live fire exercise on the Otterburn training area. *(© MoDCrown copyright)*

Support Weapon. Its success in an operational capacity has already ensured its inclusion in the CES of the L115A4 rifle.

Backup battle sights were, during the rifle's trials, deemed unnecessary going forward under the SSIP revision of equipment, therefore breaking away from decades of a British sniper rifle being equipped with emergency iron sights, the decision was made to drop them from the L115A3 Complete Equipment Schedule. The weapon did indeed enter service in 2008 without any kind of reserve sight and has since clocked up many hours of combat service in Afghanistan without any situation occurring that would call into question the decision to exclude them on this particular weapon system. The decision was based on logistical and tactical reasoning; firstly the modern British Army employs a complex yet effective supply chain to its forces wherever they may be operating in the world. Should the sniper's rifle scope become unserviceable the G4 supply chain can have a replacement scope in the unit armourer's hand within hours of its request. Tactically, should the rifle scope become damaged during an engagement the sniper pair cannot simply withdraw from, then the spotter's L129 SSW (Sniper Support Weapon) provides a heavy rate of fire out to 800 metres, furthermore the L17A1 scope can be removed from the SSW and fitted straight onto the L115A3 leaving the SSW to operate on its own battle sights. It was also felt that as the L115A3 system was launched exclusively as a long range sniper rifle the backup sight for the AW system would be inadequate due to the effective range being 600 metres.

Schmidt & Bender 5-25 x 56mm PM MkII, L24A1 Telescope
NSN 1240-99-455-1353

Technical Specification	
Manufacturer	Schmidt & Bender
Length	417mm
Weight in the mount	1.4kg
Objective Lens DIA	56mm
Field of View	5.3–1.5m
Magnification	5-25 Variable
Reticle	Mildot with Ranging
Range Graduations	14 MRAD per Turn
Bullet Drop Compensation	No
Lateral Adjustment	6-0-6 MRAD
Focus Capability	Yes
Parallax Adjustment	Yes
Illuminated Reticle	Yes
Sunshade	Yes, plus Killflash
Mount Type	Single

The L24A1 telescope pictured in its mount with integral SIMRAD mount, and kill flash filter fitted. The scope with just two rotations of the elevation drum and large objective lens is a specialist long range precision scope for large calibre weapons.

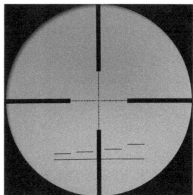

LEFT & ABOVE: The sniper's view through the scope remains the P4 mildot crosshair with ranging stadia lines in the bottom of the sight picture first introduced with the L17A1 scope. This reticle is now the standard pattern in both the British sniper telescope and spotting scope. *(FIG Left © MoDCrown copyright)*

ABOVE: A sniper attempting to rapidly engage the enemy but impeded by his body armour as he tries to get into a comfortable fire position.

Complete Equipment Schedule

The rifle complete with its original 2008 CES equipment is separated into two categories: the first, Rifle L115A3 System Complete, which covers the weapon and all of its immediate equipment is NSN coded 1005-99-888-9310 as an ensemble packed in a composite Explorer case, NSN 8145-99-705-3036, manufactured in dark earth the same as the stock sides of the weapon, as is the foam interior which differs to the civilian version of the same case. The second, Kit User Maintenance 338 L115A3, covers the extensive range of cleaning tools which as a complete set is NSN coded 1005-99-382-4637.

The Complete Equipment Schedule also includes the U.S. Mildot Master, NSN 1220-01-493-9977, devised to work in conjunction with the U.S.M.C mildot reticle

which is present in both the PM MkII scope as well as the spotting scope, enabling both sniper and spotter to have the same view of their target. The Mildot Master was in 2008 by no means new and had been in service with U.S. forces for some time as well as being an already well-established tool in the civilian shooting community some years before the British Army adopted it. The slide rule calculator is a sleeve that contains the slide rule within it and offers both MOA and Mils calculations for the user and assists in the calculation of the distance to target by converting a mildot measurement of the target taken with the use of the scope's own mildot reticle.

The rule offers a fixed list of MOA or Mils measurements against a second column that lists both imperial and metric measurements, giving the sniper the choice of which he would prefer to work in and of course which suits his equipment best. The key to success and some would say the downside to using the Mildot Master is that having some knowledge of the size of your target is crucial as the device works by operating the slide rule and matching the target size to your mildot measurement. Lining these two pieces of information up provides the distance to target, so obviously if your measurement is not accurate or indeed your estimation

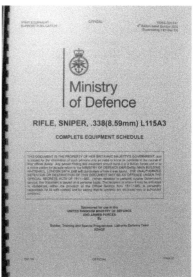

ABOVE: This Complete Equipment Schedule booklet of the L115A3 is accompanied with a further booklet which catalogues the CES items pictorially.

LEFT: The Mildot Master pictured with its manual. The close-up shows the sliding rule with the mils measurement and target size which equates to a distance.

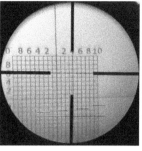

ABOVE: The Hawke Shot Saver collimator had the potential to be an effective check zero device but was largely viewed as unreliable. The Hawke Shot Saver failed due to poor engineering in the joining together of the optical unit and the bracket. The accompanying image does indeed show the graph in the optical unit viewed through the telescope is out of alignment vertically with the crosshair in the telescope.

of target size is wrong then the range will not be correct and can be wildly out, but, used as an aid and in conjunction with the other ranging tools at hand, it is a superb tool.

In addition to the first part of the CES, in 2008 the L115A3 had its own collimator, NSN 1240-99-865-6288, to roughly zero the weapon prior to final adjustment during a range live fire session. The collimator was the Hawke Sport Optics Shot Saver model which attached to the muzzle brake of the weapon via a specially manufactured bracket, NSN 1240-99-443-0239, which utilised the same single screw hole in the top of the muzzle brake which the front battle sight would have used had backup sights been adopted with the weapon. The collimator was not liked by snipers and was not successful in keeping its place in the schedule.

The device quickly became redundant as the snipers who used it lost confidence in its reliability. It would appear the fitting of the optical unit to the spigot of the mounting bracket was not a precision fit, resulting in a different reading every time the device was fitted to the rifle. Instead, many snipers privately purchased a civilian device which came in the form of an ammunition cartridge specific to the calibre of the weapon. When chambered the device delivers a continuous light beam on the target which is then used as a physical datum to shift the MPI. A sniper platoon commander of the 4th Battalion The Rifles conducted trials within the unit and found that when used with the SA80 assault rifle the device significantly reduced the quantity of ammunition expended during a range zero session. On average it took thirty-five to fifty rounds of ammunition to zero the SA80, depending on the ability of the rifleman, however when the laser firing cartridge was used it reduced this quantity of ammunition to just nine rounds to complete the zeroing of the SA80 rifle. After the trial the sniper platoon commander wrote a paper on the device and submitted it, recommending the army conduct further trials with a view to making it a standard issue item. His recommendations were immediately rejected on the basis that a live round of ammunition could be mistaken for the device.

The L115A3 rifle is well catered for in terms of carrying systems. For safe transport during international shipping and storage in field stores the rigid composite case provides protection from high impacts as well as being completely waterproof. With the introduction of the AW range of weapons the British Army adopted a DPM drag bag some ten years earlier that provides excellent protection to the weapon whilst in the hands of the sniper. The drag bag offers a full length zip for easy access, internal retaining straps as well as a continuous stud fastening foul weather flap that seals the zip. The panels of the bag give the enclosed weapon a great deal of protection from the outside world in terms of weather but are also padded with dense foam shielding the weapon and optics from knocks. There is excellent storage space for extra ammunition and space for the spotting scope plus a protective hood that slips over the nose of the bag; this aids the bag when actually being dragged along the ground through foliage and thick cover.

The bag also has conventional carry handles plus backpack straps. By 2011 the British Army had adopted the new MTP camouflage and the conflict in Afghanistan was showing no sign of easing which brought about the speedy replacement of not only the uniform clothing items but units deploying also started to receive PLCE (Personal Load Carrying Equipment) items produced in the new MTP camouflage pattern, or at the very least flat dark earth such as the L115A3 transit case

ABOVE: The carrying system introduced with the AW rifle carried on from where the L96 rifle bag left off. The bag became a drag bag and was beefed up somewhat to cope with the length and weight of the AW series of weapons. The external storage was improved enabling it to carry items such as the Leupold spotting scope and tripod.

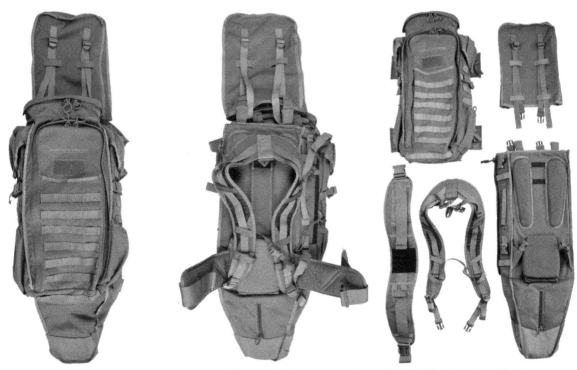

ABOVE: Although the DPM drag bag is still in service albeit to a limited degree, the conflict in Afghanistan brought about a new carrying system for the L115A3. The Eberlestock system allows the weapon to be carried like a backpack with stock folded and is extremely ergonomic.

LEFT & BELOW: The L115A3 rifle laid out with all its associated equipment. Note the rifle is fitted with a muzzle cap. The rifle is also illustrated packed in its composite transit chest with all CES items, plus the Eberlestock carrying system, packed, and Leupold spotting scope also packed in its carry case.

and stock sides. The targeting by the Taliban of individuals carrying a "Long Gun" was met by the same age-old response seen one hundred years earlier in the trenches where need was the mother of invention which gave rise to an entirely new weapon carrying system that took advantage of the rifle's folding stock.

The Eberlestock Phantom Sniper pack enables the rifle to be carried with the butt stock folded and resembles just another backpack to the untrained eye. The system breaks down into key component parts which when fully assembled offers a versatile and ergonomic load carrying system with stowage space for spotting scope and ammunition. The Eberlestock system is currently used only for deployment or major field exercises, while the DPM drag bag is still in service and carries the weapon to range.

Observation and Spotting Equipment

The Leupold Mk4 tactical spotting scope, designated L1A1 and NSN coded B5/1240-99-146-7493 by the British, has regardless of the L1A1 designation no modifications for British service as did the M49 which in British hands received a sunshade; the Leupold spotting scope however came straight from the manufacturer supplied in the same specification as that issued to U.S. troops. With a 12-40 variable power zoom and huge 60mm objective lens it first appeared with British snipers in 2008 and was first supplied to the British Army by Riflecraft Ltd who was awarded a contract by the MoD in May 2008 for the supply of 629 kits.

This initial Leupold equipment was hugely successful and highly regarded by British snipers, and has therefore continued in its service with an upgrade of its tripod to the Cullman tripod. Although the practice of using a customised trip flare picket for support is still very much commonplace, the Leupold L1A1 remains today as the primary spotting scope with British snipers. The means by which the spotting scope was carried by the sniper is varied and seems to largely have been either in a soft case with shoulder strap and ALICE clips with rigid foam interior, or most commonly by simply stuffing the spotter and tripod in a backpack. As with the rifle scope the L1A1

Leupold came equipped with the P4 mildot reticle and has in its CES a honeycombed kill flash filter and soft carry case with shoulder strap.

The slow withdrawal from service of the L12A1 Avimo binocular has seen the vacuum filled with a mixed bunch of replacements which have come and gone, none quite satisfying the needs of the modern British soldier including the Pyser SGI Francis Barker 8x42 binocular. The current model, which has been in service since 2014, and which appears to meet most if not all requirements, is the German manufactured Steiner 8x30 binocular. The all-green Steiner binocular has a unique ergonomic shape making it easy

ABOVE: A spotter heavily camouflaged with his Leupold spotting scope resting on a set of sticks. *(© MoDCrown copyright)*

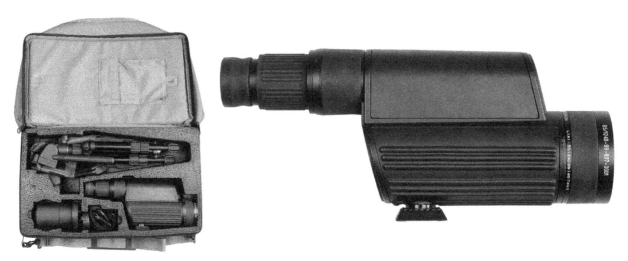

ABOVE: The L1A1 Leupold spotting scope and associated equipment in its soft carry case. The case was of limited issue during Operation Herrick, Afghanistan. The close-up of the telescope shows the British L1A1 designation and NSN on the objective lens rings.

ABOVE & RIGHT: The L1A1 Mk4 tactical Leupold spotting scope illustrated on its Cullman tripod with kill flash filter fitted. Note the reticle is exactly the same as that found in the L24A1 telescope so both sniper and spotter have the same view of the target.

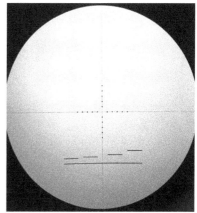

ABOVE: A sniper pair can be seen on this compound roof in Afghanistan. The spotter is using the L1A1 spotting scope. The sniper is behind the L129A1 SSW. The barrel of the L115A3 is also visible.

and comfortable to hold when observing for long periods. It's a robust instrument protected by a tough exterior and is equipped with typically superior German lenses. Its entry to service was not before it completed a rigorous evaluation process by ITDU, Warminster. On its approval the MoD placed an order for 15,000 pairs which serve today as the standard issue binocular in the British Army.

 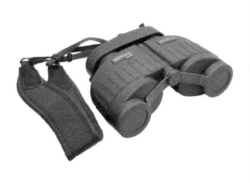 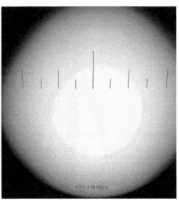

ABOVE: The all green Steiner 8x30mm binocular is illustrated. Note the ergonomic shape, lens caps and the ever present ranging reticle in the right hand lens.

SIMRAD KN 203D Image Intensifier

The 2008 issue of the L115A3 under the SSIP made available a SIMRAD image intensifier device to sniper units across the army who would no longer use the Common Weapon Sight image intensifier that had so many ergonomic problems when used in conjunction with the L96. The KN 203D, NSN 5855-99-897-2757, although it carries the same third generation image intensifier tube, has some slight incumbencies to the KN 250: it is slightly heavier, has a slightly smaller field of view and requires desiccation and the overall dimensions are larger, however, it is a huge improvement on the CWS that went before it.

SIMRAD KN 203D Image Intensifier
NSN 5855-99-897-2757

Technical Information	
Height	192mm
Length	220mm
Width	127mm
Weight	1.55kg

Optical Characteristics:	
Magnification	X 1
Focus Range	25m to infinity
Field of View	10 degrees
IIT (Type)	3rd Generation
Graticule	Scope's Own Reticle

Power Requirements:

The weapon sight uses two AA size batteries that will give a 3v supply and service life of approximately 80 hours at 20 degrees Centigrade.

ABOVE: The KN203D is pictured attached to the L115A3 rifle via the scope mount's integral SIMRAD mount. Note the device attaches with the use of two locking levers and is also equipped with a light omitting coupling sleeve on the objective lens of the telescope.

LEFT: Although used with the top hat mount on the L115A2 the KN203D is half a kilogram heavier than its predecessor which may have caused problems that resulted with a much more robust mount and two locking levers. Also note the desiccation warning window on top of the battery housing.

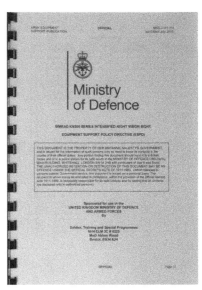

ABOVE: The KN203D fitted to the L115A3 during a night shoot on the range. The device's Operating Information booklet is also illustrated which covers the KN200 series of devices. *(FIG Left © MoDCrown copyright)*

Sniper Thermal Image Capability Sight

Qioptiq SVIPIR-2, or Sniper Viper sight Mk2, was purchased and designated STIC (Sniper Thermal Image Capability) by the MoD, being allocated NSN 5855-99-361-2969. The thermal imaging sight was introduced to the field army as the final part of the SSIP to improve the night fighting ability of the L115A3 rifle. Since its introduction it has been used in conjunction with the L118A1, A2, L115A1 and A2 sniper rifles all sharing the same offset picatinny rail attachment that accommodated the 3-12x50mm Schmidt & Bender telescope which of course was in the end mounted on all of the aforementioned weapons, all of which used the same fore-end block that accepted the Parker-Hale style bipod. However the device was first introduced to British forces under the classification of Urgent Operational Supply just prior to the SSIP when Special Forces units as well as their supporting elements such as SFSG

(Special Forces Support Group) were the first to deploy it, and were not slow to capitalise on the new device, making it compatible to the L96 through a new revised design of fore-end block. This block was never issued to the sniper units of the field army so it is unclear if its creation was SF led or if Qioptiq themselves created the fore-end block at the request of the MoD, but either way it was manufactured by Accuracy International and included as part of the weapon integration kit which comes with the STIC device, which in turn was only ever issued to Special Forces units. They were after all the only organisations who had the full complement of sniper rifles to which the integration kit fitted, however it was produced in relatively small numbers to seemingly satisfy the requirements of SF only.

The device is currently in service with the L115A3 sniper rifle which

is mounted in the same fashion but with a picatinny rail attachment that has altered dimensions so as to seat the device accurately in front of the much larger objective lens of the L24A1 PM MkII telescope.

Thermal imaging capability gives the sniper an alternative method of seeing in the dark and is particularly useful when the starlight and moonlight that image intensifiers like SIMRAD and CWS rely on is insufficient for those devices to work efficiently. It is also capable of finding a well camouflaged and concealed enemy in daylight as it simply reads the heat signature. Sniper pairs are equipped with two devices, one handheld, NSN 5855-99-614-4596, for the spotter which has a mildot reticle and one which mounts on the weapon so the pair can operate with the same thermal view of the world. The device was used extensively during the Afghan conflict and attaches to the picatinny rail attachment on the right hand side of the weapon which is at an angled offset position to the day scope. The picatinny allows for the device's exact fitment marrying the STIC sight to the objective lens of the day scope via a light cancelling sheath. The picatinny also allows the fitting of the device to take into account the position of the day scope on the rifle in terms of how the sniper has the scope set for eye relief. Once attached the sniper uses his day scope in the same fashion, utilising the scope's own reticle and adjustments for correction of the bullet's path.

The STIC system has had a mixed reception with criticism of the device's resolution and being thermal provides only a thermal signature of the target, enabling the sniper to engage targets at realistic distances of 300 to 400 metres although the

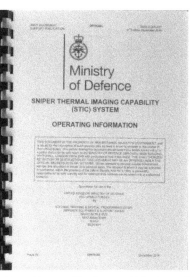

The STIC integration kit is pictured in its hard transit case. The fore-end blocks and rails contained within fit all of the Accuracy International sniper rifles, including the L96. The STIC Operating Information booklet is also pictured.

ABOVE & LEFT: The L115A3 is illustrated with the Sniper Thermal Imaging Capability Scope fitted via the offset picatinny rail. The close-up shows the device connects with the L24A1 telescope via the rubber light cancelling sleeve.

manufacturer advises the device is capable of detecting a man at over 1,000 metres, which it is perfectly capable of. However as targets appear over 400 metres and out to the manufacturer prescribed 1,000 metres, PID (Positive Identification) of the target becomes a major issue with the device being blamed for several "blue on blue" engagements on friendly forces during the Afghanistan conflict. Additionally, the device's performance suffers when the barrel begins to heat up.

The heat signature emitted from the barrel creates a mirage effect, distorting the target image in the viewfinder which gets worse as more rounds are fired. Previously, and particularly with the L118 rifle, a mirage band was issued for use

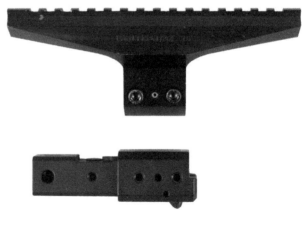

LEFT & ABOVE: The picatinny rail used for the attachment of STIC is illustrated with its fore-end block. The light alloy block allows the rail attachment to be removed if desired. The accompanying image shows the block from a forward angle that also reveals the block is capable of accepting the Parker-Hale style bipod.

ABOVE: The thermal imaging capability provided by STIC is undoubtedly significant; however this device has brought about an unnerving amount of uncertainty on the battlefield due to it being used in a number of friendly fire incidents.

with STIC which sat flat horizontal to the barrel and ran its full length from muzzle brake to picatinny rail, however this item appears to have been omitted from the L115A3 CES.

For live fire training purposes the thermal imaging device requires a target which it can see; therefore an impressive range of TI targets which offer varying levels of detail are available, however for the purposes of the sniper a Figure 11 and 12 target is commonly used for range work. The targets when presented appear through the device much like a standard daytime target and can be presented "White Hot" or "Black Hot" as can the features within the target, allowing definition of certain features such as weapons which can be made to stand out, or alternatively a target can be made to look unarmed – a useful aspect depending on the type of training being carried out.

ABOVE: The spotter's handheld version of STIC is the same device as the weapon mounted sight with an eyepiece opposed to a light cancelling sleeve as found on the weapon mountable version. The spotter's device also has a mildot reticle enabling both spotter and sniper to view the target in the same way. The accompanying image shows how the sniper dressed in conventional ghillie camouflage appears through the device with "White Hot" viewing mode selected.

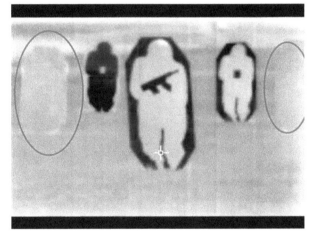

ABOVE: A sniper using STIC during a night shoot on a gallery range. The targets used for this application are specialist thermal imaging targets. The accompanying images illustrate three thermal imaging targets flanked by two standard Figure 11 type daytime targets. The targets are also shown as they appear through a TI device; the two standard Figure 11s are still present with their positions circled in red. Note the thermal targets appear in both "White Hot" and "Black Hot". *(FIG Top © MoDCrown copyright) (FIGS Above Courtesy MJ Services (GB) Ltd)*

The Sniper's Garments

The army is entering an age whereby civilian companies are offering excellent kit across the board and which soldiers take good advantage of. The practice of soldiers personalising their equipment with privately purchased items is nothing new; it's been happening for centuries but the growing trend of specialist companies offering personalised assault vests to cold weather kit and everything in between that rivals and even betters the issued kit is a growing one. Sniper kit is no exception; one piece of commercially produced kit offered to snipers was the concealment vest which first appeared in the early 2000s. The hooded mesh overcoat is worn over the normal combat clothing and is secured at the front with two quick release clips on the chest as well as one further clip at the waist. The arms are full length and baggy and the whole garment is covered with fabric loops so hessian and natural foliage can be attached. The versatile garment, which can be stowed in the Bergen and used as and when required, has become hugely popular and has almost eliminated the need for a handmade ghillie suit.

Clothing evolved so much through the nineties that it took a technological leap forward around 1998 with the introduction of the TICS (Thermal Individual Camouflage System) which was adopted by the MoD in 2000 and NSN coded 8415-99-925-2407. The Mk1 TICS suit is a five piece system consisting of head shroud, smock, trousers, gloves and glasses. The suit is manufactured in a perforated fabric which is formed in pleated layers and is designed to be multi-spectral and able to defeat ultra-violet, visual, near infra-red and far infra-red sensors as well as thermal imaging devices.

But with all the advances to this day the trusty sniper smock is still officially issued to badged snipers and unchanged in its build specification since the late seventies, however the camouflage pattern

ABOVE: The hooded concealment vest on the left is a commercially manufactured product, and the vest on the right was privately made for a sniper deploying to Afghanistan. The vest is largely responsible for ending the practice of handmaking a ghillie suit.

ABOVE: The Thermal Individual Camouflage Suit is heavily technology led. The suit is supplied in DPM as well as in a U.S. desert camouflage pattern.

ABOVE: The snipers seen here are from the resident battalion in Warminster and are demonstrating the TICS next to a conventional ghillie suit. *(© MoDCrown copyright)*

LEFT: This thermal image shows the effectiveness of the TICS. In the image there are three figures equally spaced. The figure clearly visible on the right is wearing standard combat clothing, the figure to his right is wearing a traditional ghillie suit and spaced at an equal distance to his right is a soldier wearing full TICS.

is currently the MTP (Multi Terrain Pattern) adopted in 2011 under the PECOC (Personal Equipment and Common Operational Clothing) programme.

The large square knee pads traditionally issued to snipers seem now to have been dropped, having given way to the padded cupped knee and elbow protection that have elasticated straps for attaching as well as many other types which typically have padded protection behind a rigid knee plate. The head and shoulder net which has been a standard issue item to snipers since the end of WW2 has also disappeared from the sniper's array of garments; the design unchanged for decades is however currently under review with a new take on this old idea being planned.

British snipers were not slow to test the L115A3 and its long range capability that had been shouted about so loudly by the MoD during its 2008 launch. Its sole purpose was

ABOVE: The trusty sniper smock is still in service forty years after its creation. Now produced in the relatively new MTP camouflage pattern and to the same build specification generations of snipers have previously used.

after all to give snipers a long reach on the enemy in an environment that often offered vast arcs over far stretching Afghan plains. After years of being armed with the L96 which delivered harassing fire out to 1,100 metres and then to suddenly have the harassing distance turned into your deadly fire distance must have been a groundbreaking moment for every sniper who experienced the transition. From 2008 the distances out to which deadly fire was being delivered were constantly being tested and it was only a matter of time before someone would pull off something astonishing.

2009 saw the Blues and Royals, one of the Household Cavalry regiments, deploy to Afghanistan on a tour which would bridge 2009 and 2010. In November 2009 Corporal of Horse Craig Harrison was with his spotter operating south of Musa Qala providing sniper overwatch for a dawn patrol that would move up a vast open valley floor. The sniper pair selected a position on high ground that provided a commanding view of the entire valley which was loosely urbanised in that it had a manmade retaining wall which was holding back earth at the same height as it, enabling the pair to stand against it. Craig sat the rifle on the wall which was around waist height and utilised the earth behind it to rest his bipod. It was a good well supported fire position.

The pair observed the valley and watched the patrol slowly advance when at some distance they spotted a "Dicker", an individual on the corner of a compound building watching the patrol and reporting what he was seeing into a radio. Clearly spotting for the Taliban, the individual's activity was with hostile intention which made him a legitimate target under the NATO 429 rules of engagement. Craig engaged the "Dicker", however he

was so far away that to reach his position his spotter had to walk his rounds in towards the target. It took nine rounds before he was within range of the target who by this time realised he had been compromised and wisely disappeared into hard cover. To deliver his rounds on the Taliban spotter's position Craig had maxed out the adjustments in his scope's elevation drum and was holding the lowest stadia line in his reticle above the spotter's head.

The patrol remained in the valley active for most of the day when in the afternoon they came under heavy automatic machine gun fire. A vicious fire fight ensued between the patrol and the Taliban, who to the amazement of the sniper pair had set up a crew served weapon in the exact same place the "Dicker" earlier in the day had been sat. Craig recalled his hold over on the Taliban spotter and engaged the two Taliban fighters manning the Russian made 7.62mm calibre RPD machine gun. His first shot fell slightly short, of which he saw the dusty impact, corrected and then immediately sent his second round which hit the gunner in the chest. He took aim over the gunner's number two and sent his third round. The distance was so great the flight time of his rounds was roughly six seconds in which a lot can happen. The number two sprang to his feet in an effort to exit the situation and as he did so Craig's third round missed, passing between the dead gunner and the number two but seriously damaging the insurgent's machine gun, however, Craig had immediately cycled the action and a fourth round was already on its way and as the second man stood vertical and about to flee the fourth .338 Lapua round passed through his side.

After the engagement an Apache helicopter flew over the area and

measured the distance between the sniper pair's position and that of the Taliban gunner's which was a staggering 2,475 metres. The shots performed by Craig with his Accuracy International built L115A3 rifle set a new world record for a sniper confirmed kill which stood for eight years before a Canadian sniper took the title in May 2017. Such successes were seized upon by the MoD to justify to our public the use of snipers, which in this day and age is incredibly still a necessary part of the winning of hearts and minds as it still carries something of a stigma. In the case of Craig Harrison his world record shot made him something of a poster boy for the army who in turn actually named him. From that point his life was turned upside down by death threats from his own countrymen, culminating in the police uncovering a plot to kidnap and murder him.

The huge expense involved with the delivery of the SSIP had to be justified to the taxpayer as well as the continued use of snipers and therefore regular press releases by Defence Media Operations regularly reported on the activity of British snipers, stamping a positive spin on anything they did. The following passage is an original DMO press release featuring a sniper operation carried out by 1st Battalion Royal Welsh and highlights strongly the surgical precision with which their targets were selected, quite rightly suggesting only snipers could have made such an operation successful without many civilian casualties. I would suggest it also imparts a further suggestion that the British Government is also acting on its responsibilities, doing all it can to limit the risk of civilian casualties, which further strengthens their case for the use of such combatants.

WELSH SNIPERS SHOW COURAGE AND CONSTRAINT

Members of Fire Support Company, 1st Battalion the Royal Welsh have been showing courage and constraint whilst clearing insurgents from positions near Shahzad in South West Helmand. Tasked with providing flanking protection for army bomb disposal teams, army marksmen held insurgents back from positions in a towered compound as their colleagues moved through the area. The action was part of building on the progress of Op Moshtarak.

The team had been tasked to secure a compound, but on patrolling towards the location came under heavy fire from Taliban fighters.

Sniper two, "We left our patrol base just before first light towards the compound we wanted to go to and came under contact. We carried out our drills and observed, but couldn't see anyone so pushed on and that's when all hell broke loose. We were attacked by different weapons and people, so we moved under fire towards the compound."

The commander in charge of the team, continues, "Straight inside, after the complete adrenaline outside, we were expecting them (the insurgents) to be in the compound, but we were confronted by four children, an elderly man and his wife. The lads switched on straight away, cleared the compound of the locals and the interpreter dealt with them.

From there, I co-ordinated the two snipers up onto the roof.... As soon as they started observing, we took fire from small arms....with shots hitting the compound wall to our front."

The snipers had to use their observation skills to clearly identify the insurgents from the locals. Using the British Army .338 L115A3 Long Range Rifle, which has state-of-the-art telescopic day and night all-weather sights, the soldiers were able to win the fire fight without injuring civilians.

Sniper one comments, "Once we got up into the tower, we identified the enemy with a weapon, and distinguished between them and civilians, who they were using as human shields at the time. We had sniper rifles, the .338, which is a precision weapon, so we were able to take clean shots without injuring any civilians."

Sniper two, "When I was observing, first of all I saw women and children. I was trying to find the firing points, because they had been using 'murder holes', holes in walls which they've knocked out so they can stick their rifle through. I was checking the walls for that. At the end of the wall, I saw an insurgent take a knee, raise his weapon up to his shoulder and fire a burst at our compound, so I took my aim, took my time with the shot and engaged him."

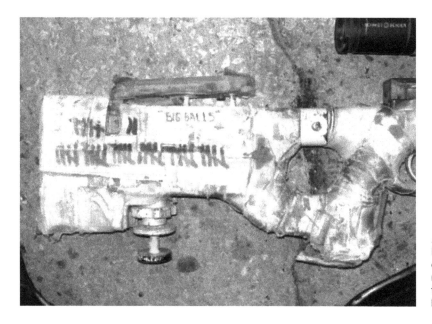

LEFT: During a deployment to Operation Herrick, Afghanistan, the sniper who carried this L115A3 rifle kept a macabre running tally of his kills on the butt. The tally in the image is at 37. By the end of his tour it was 61.

ABOVE: The weight of the L115A3 rifle was unfortunately the trade-off for the accuracy and reach it provided. This sniper has improvised and has rigged up a makeshift harness from a tree branch allowing him to maintain his aim over difficult ground. *(© MoDCrown copyright)*

The L115A3 delivered an exceptional long range capability which snipers were quick to capitalise on but it is a heavy weapon to lug around and was during the conflict viewed as a specialist weapon by many who used it. Complaints within the ranks began to gather pace, with a call for something lighter to enter service alongside the L115A3 that could hit out to around 1,000 metres as accurately but more importantly be wielded with ease when engaging at much shorter distances, as it was common for snipers to have their L24A1 telescopes pre-set at 300 metres; this was the distance many targets would most commonly present themselves.

Many called for the L96 to remain for this role as for those who had used it the rifle was ticking many of the boxes. The calls grew louder and for a short period it looked as though the L96A1 rifle would return, albeit in a new guise. In 2011 Accuracy International responded to feedback from snipers identifying

a solution to the problem the troops had which lay in the L96A1. This led Dave Walls back to the drawing board where he prepared a combat-ready upgrade of the rifle, a design specifically for close to mid-range

range engagements. The rifle's new design incorporated a complete overhaul of the chassis and receiver and was made to be compatible with many of the Arctic Warfare rifle's components. Dave designed

ABOVE: The remodelled L96A1 sniper rifle. First impressions would suggest this is an AW rifle but under it all lies an L96. The image is a sad reminder of what the rifle could have become had the decision not been made to destroy it.

a hybrid weapon which received a twenty inch barrel with the .338 tactical muzzle brake allowing the rifle to use the L115A3 short suppressor. The top of the receiver was converted to a continuous picatinny rail and the bolt was upgraded to incorporate the AW three stage safety catch. Incredibly the butt was converted to the AW folding butt and was finished with AW stock sides and the L96 type bipod fitted with the Parker-Hale style spigot as used on the L115A2 rifle. Accuracy International made these modifications to only one rifle for MoD assessment which history now tells us was rejected quite early in the process. This unique one-off rifle now resides in Accuracy International's own reference collection.

The government answered the call but not with the L96; its days were over. The weapon the troops received was the L129A1 Sharpshooter Rifle, NSN 1005-99-226-6708, which is a 7.62mm/.308 calibre weapon ordered under the Urgent Operational Requirement banner and it joined the ranks not with snipers but as its name suggests with an appointed sharpshooter. Designed to fire standard Radway Green L2A2 155 grain (10.04 grams) ammunition, the weapon was designated L129A1 LMT 7.62mm MWS (Modular Weapon System) fitted with a six power Trijicon ACOG (Advanced Combat Optical Gunsight) sight with a forty-eight millimetre objective lens, hand grip under the fore-end and Harris bipod.

The rifle is an Armalite rifle platform built by the U.S. Lewis Machine and Tool Company and was ordered with a specific brief. It had to be ideal for close combat engagements and be capable of consistent hits on a man out to 800 metres. The AR receiver is fitted with a quick change sixteen inch stainless steel barrel and brought to the fight a semi-automatic rate of fire and being modular in its design enabled the user to fit an array of accessories including an inline MUNS (Magnum Universal Night Sight) sight which mounts on the continuous picatinny rail directly in front of the ACOG and adds three pounds to the combat weight of the Sharpshooter Rifle.

The L129A1 was well received and much liked by those who use it, so much so that within a year the L129A1 was formally adopted by snipers as the SSW (Sniper Support Weapon) carried by the spotter and is modified for this role with the addition of a Surefire suppressor and replacement of the ACOG with a L17A1 Schmidt & Bender 3-12 x 50 sniper scope. Interestingly since its introduction the RAF Regiment have tried, so far unsuccessfully, to replace all of their SA80 L85A2 assault rifles with the L129A1.

Rifle 7.62mm L129A1 LMT Sharpshooter/Trijicon ACOG
NSN 1005-99-226-6708

Technical Specification	
Calibre	7.62mm
Magazine Capacity	20 round double stack
Overall Rifle Length	990mm max
Barrel	Stainless Steel Match Grade 16 inch
Twist Rate	1 in 11
Combat Weight	6.2kg
Iron Sights	Yes
Approval Date	December 2009
Manufactured By	Lewis Machine and Tool Co.
Scope Mounted	Overbore
Contract Qty	400

ABOVE & NEXT PAGE (BOTTOM): The accurate and hard hitting L129A1 rifle pictured with the ACOG sight. The Sharpshooter rifle was quickly adopted by snipers as the SSW. *(© MoDCrown copyright)*

ABOVE: A sniper taking part in a gallery range night shoot with the L129A1 rifle. He is using MUNS which is an inline night sight being used in this case with the ACOG. *(© MoDCrown copyright*

The L129A1 Employment. A Sniper's Overview.

In past conflicts there has always been an element of marksmen on the battlefield, but it has only recently been a skill that has been brought into the spotlight of the armed forces. Sharpshooters as they are known are a necessary part of any ground combat force, but should not be confused with sniping. These special marksmen require and deserve weapons, scope and ammunition specially manufactured for their needs and requirements.

Currently the weapon that has been brought into service is the 7.62mm L129A1. Since starting pre-deployment training (PDT) this rifle, I believe, has been deployed in the incorrect manner. Currently the L129A1 has either been given to second in command (2IC) or to individuals that have limited training. It has been found that sufficient expert riflemen within Rifle Companies exist but it still needs to be deployed correctly to fill the gap of accuracy employment. We must not forget that in most cases accuracy rather than volume will win.

We have found that you cannot just conduct limited training whether in the United Kingdom or on a makeshift range in theatre. These potential Sharpshooters are required to attend a course which will enable them to best bring the weapon to bear against the enemy to our advantage. Not only do these marksmen have to learn how to fire, but they also need to learn how to judge distance, become skilled observers, and most importantly be able to estimate the speed of the wind so as to be able to aim off at the correct distance.

Having deployed on Operation Herrick 13 myself with a L129A1 it has been proven to be a competent weapon, but does not exceed its expectations. There are minor

ABOVE: A sniper from the Rifles with a L129A1 rifle fitted with a L17A1 telescope. After the L96 was withdrawn there was a surplus of these scopes which were utilised on the SSW.

issues which have been brought into light over this period of time. These issues which have been brought up are the following: ammunition, optics, rifle butt, and suppressor.

Ammunition

The current ammunition being used is the 7.62mm sniper Green Spot round. Individuals have been using de-linked ammunition for the General Purpose Machine Gun (GPMG). It does state in the PAM that you are able to do this, but must be adopted as a last resort. With current climate, and working environment of winter season, the weapon has at times been subjected to wet muddy conditions. With this the round and the working parts have difficulty sliding forward fully which in turn leaves a gap between bolt face, and the base of the round. On most similar weapons such as the Diemaco C8 there is a forward assist unlike the L129A1. Further to

this firers have found that if the top round in the magazine is subjected to constant chambering and extraction without being fired it will eventually detach, leaving the bullet inside the barrel whilst ejecting the case. More than often when this case, whether being subjected to constant use or not, gets extracted the bolt face can rip the outer rim of the percussion cap off causing further stoppages.

Rifle Butt

The butt which comes with the L129A1 is standard issue throughout the armed forces. Having done research and fired various sniper rifles, we have found that with a butt spike and cheek piece that can be raised to aid the firer, this increases the stability of the shot, thus creating excellent results and diminishing the need to waste ammunition.

Optics

The rifle (L129A1) has been issued with an Advanced Combat Optical Gun sight X6 (ACOG). This sight has been proved to be robust as well as accurate. If soldiers were to attend an advanced marksman course using scopes there is no reason why it should not have a Schmidt and Bender optic sight attached to aid with precision firing.

Suppressor

Having a suppressor fitted to the L129A1 reduces not only the noise of the shot being fired, but can hide the signature of the location of the firer, day and especially at night where the flash from the muzzle is extremely bright; doing this will create fear and confusion in the enemy.

ABOVE: This sniper also has a L129A1 rifle fitted with an L17 scope and GPS device. Note the map, aerial photographs and PLRF-15c next to him. Interestingly he is using a GPMG sling on the weapon.

"A Sniper's Overview" was provided by a Parachute Regiment sniper serving as a sniper instructor at the Household Division Parachute Regiment Combined Course, Pirbright.

With the successes of the L115A3 over the last decade and cumulative successes of the AW series of rifles as a whole the AWSM will eventually pass the baton of British Army sniper system to the next series of rifles, the AX series, which has already entered service designated L115A4, NSN, 1005-99-269-0095 with Special Forces units. The field army can expect to receive the new system around 2030 which is when the L115A3 service life is expected to expire and is when Accuracy International are set to continue as the primary supplier of the British Army sniper system with the L115A3 upgrade to L115A4 specification. It will provide much improved ergonomics and usability as well as safeguarding the system's employment by UK armed forces

long into the future, enabling British snipers to enter future conflicts armed with cutting edge equipment which will enable them to maintain their fearsome reputation on any battlefield.

We have travelled through a century and seen how the British military sniper rifle, scope, observation optics, ancillaries and clothing has evolved. The equipment has certainly changed and conflicts have come and gone and have been as varied as our enemies. We have read the accounts from the men who used it all and amongst it all runs a common thread which is how the basic principles and core skills which were first established in the trenches over 100 years ago when the British Army was on a back foot have barely changed. Through excellent leadership and forward thinking officers and men the highest standards were set, so high in fact they still form the main body of sniper training and best practice today.

The British Army has for the last forty-five years been fully engaged with sniping, probably the longest unbroken period since 1915, and the future of sniping within the British Army looks to be secure. The worth of the humble sniper was proven many times during the conflicts of more recent times. With the Islamist terrorist threat that still looms and an increasingly threatening and aggressive Russia flexing its military might wherever it can in the world, the MoD's commitment has been underlined with its planned adoption of the L115A4 rifle and continued improvement of associated equipment.

The challenge of bringing the capability of weapons and optics in line with that of the capabilities of the men that use them seemingly having been long met now puts us in a position whereby ever advancing technology and improved engineering has made huge leaps in sniper rifle performance with every new mark of rifle. The performance of each new sniper rifle and optic is quickly going beyond the ability of those selected to use them. We are indeed moving in a direction which is increasingly exposing the vulnerability of the human interaction in the process. I truly believe only computerised technology will be able to maximise the performance of future sniper rifles and indeed electronic devices are already taking over the calculations of distance, wind strength, angle of shot and humidity, however the corrections still need to be physically dialled into the telescope and the physical skill of the individual behind the rifle is still a major factor as to whether or not the bullet will be delivered on its target.

With the ever increasing advances in the materials being selected to build a sniper rifle, and the tough anti-wear and corrosion finishes applied to them coupled with the precision engineering involved to bring the components together, the evolution of the sniper rifle seems limitless. An incalculable amount of effort is being expended in the drive to perfect this weapon of which the accuracy can only be likened to that of a technologically advanced missile which costs tens of thousands of pounds; the sniper rifle costs considerably less and is reusable. Of course I am not suggesting the sniper rifle is the answer to all the problems troops may encounter on the battlefield, but its accuracy and reach along with calibres and types of ammunition available is rapidly making it the weapon of choice for the surgical destruction of enemy combatants and equipment which in years gone by would have involved some sort of expensive ordnance.

The one thing that simply does not keep pace with this technological evolution is the human mind. The equipment is tougher than ever before, capable of operating twenty-four hours a day regardless of conditions, killing indiscriminately. It is therefore ironic that the human mind, which can create this equipment which many individuals have stepped up and used in anger for the purpose it was created, now as a result have a personal fight in the form of PTSD (Post-Traumatic Stress Disorder). One of the biggest differences between a rifleman in an infantry section and a sniper is the personal aspect of the sniper's role. Although the rifleman will find himself in combat and often in a sustained fire fight with the enemy he fires in the direction of the enemy to kill and suppress in an effort to overwhelm him and end his will to fight, forcing a withdrawal or surrender. The sniper chooses his target with a powerful telescope through which he can see the man in detail and he is often not a dark silhouetted figure running around the battlefield; he can clearly see the face of the man whose life he has selected to end and indeed when the trigger is pulled both the sniper and spotter have a front row seat at the violent death of another human being.

A great many snipers who served on Operation Telic and Herrick have lived this scenario many times and today suffer the ongoing effects of PTSD which to many men is a crippling disorder. Being haunted by sights and sounds as well as reliving some experiences make it difficult to lead a normal life, particularly later, after their military career has ended and one has to adjust back to a civilian life.

One hundred years ago the disorder was only just being recognised and its effects, which could crush a man's ability to function, were largely unknown. Sadly this was often misinterpreted as a refusal to fight, resulting in many men being court marshalled and forced to pay the ultimate price of execution, an utterly brutal method of enforcing discipline when in fact many who paid this enormous price needed care and understanding. Subsequently many men who have returned from Britain's wars and skirmishes have carried with them the mental scars, never having gone in search of treatment for fear of being labelled crazy, or weak.

My own father, Harry Houghton, who in WW2 was a Chindit and fought the Japanese in Burma, suffered PTSD until the day he passed away in 1986. He never sought help or tackled the disorder head on but tried to bury it, which of course he could not, and he was still haunted by nightmares of being back in the Burmese jungle surrounded by Japanese voices. I to this day know very little about the detail of his trauma; he never spoke of it and what little I do know was told by my mother. Thankfully the disorder is today recognised which has opened a new battle which is to make those who suffer the disorder realise there is help; they don't have to suffer in silence and there is no weakness in your character by openly admitting you have PTSD. Unfortunately snipers for the foreseeable future will have to endure but the intervention of technology will hopefully go some way to resolving this burden and perhaps the telescope will be at the centre of a solution.

The closing statement is from a former senior sniping instructor of the Household Division Parachute Regiment Combined Course, Pirbright.

A Sniper's Perspective

We can be under no illusion that Dave Walls, Dave Caig, Malcolm Coopers and later on Tom Irwin's Accuracy International's sniper rifles have changed the face of warfare, not only through the design of superior and extremely accurate rifles, but by producing exactly the right tool for the job. With their weapons playing a major part in virtually every conflict since the end of the Falklands War, these rifles have significantly increased the effective range of our snipers. In doing so, they have not only allowed us to reach the enemy from a safe distance but have also saved countless British lives by driving the enemy back beyond their effective sniping range. In an often misunderstood profession, sniping is not just about killing important enemy targets on the battlefield, it is also about keeping your own guys alive by defeating these individuals before they can inflict loss and damage to one's own troops. In sniper speak this is referred to as the "Sniper Umbrella". In the capacity as a Counter Terrorist tool, these rifles have proven highly effective and to this day create fear amongst determined terrorists and insurgents globally.

I have personally witnessed the enormous leap in capability when the L96A1 rifle came into service, replacing the trusty L42A1 a few years after the Falklands War. Literally overnight, we snipers discovered that we could shoot with precision out to and beyond the given 600m lethality range of the time and in a few years, our prowess leapt with the introduction of more powerful optics and training, from 900m to 1,100m, no mean feat using the 7.62mm calibre.

Later, we snipers armed with the .338 calibre rifles were outshooting the Taliban by twice the distance that they could shoot back. Only years later was this publicly announced that a significant number of effective shots were made beyond 2000 metres, something that was never dreamed off back in the early 1980s. Some of the earliest engagements were made in Sierra Leone where the 252 grain .338 Swiss P ball round proved so effective against problematic drug fuelled rebels. These insurgents could absorb a number of 5.56mm shots, but the .338 knocked them down like playing cards.

In 2013 the L96 rifle was eventually withdrawn from service by the MoD and we snipers watched it go with great reluctance, quite remarkable for a weapon that was 25 years old. This rifle when carried with just a 9mm pistol as a side arm and nothing else, gave you the ability to rely on your pure sniper stalking skills, crawling across the ground, unseen in search of your targets. You had every confidence in this set up and although you were carrying only a bolt action with 10 rounds to hand in the magazine, when the chance encounter happened the firepower was deliberate, slow, but deadly accurate. Bettered probably only by carrying a GPMG!

Today, the L96 lives on in the guise of the L115A3, the rifle credited with the longest ever recorded sniper shot for a .338 in November 2009. During the war fighting period in Afghanistan from 2006 – 2014 we witnessed the combat effectiveness of the .338 round and saw the long range engagement capability leap forward almost another 1000 metres of range from 1500 – 2474 metres. This feat was in part due to the introduction of the A3 version of the L115 rifle coupled with the improved 5-25x56 rifle scope, entering service in 2008 and coupled with actual combat operations pushing the boundaries of tactical effectiveness of the weapon systems as combat often does. The A3 is a good tool for the job, although larger and heavier than the L96 it is less manoeuvrable when stalking although once stable the shooting platform allows long distance engagements at almost double the 7.62mm 155 grain NATO round. By increasing the ability of the sniper pair by issuing the spotter with the L129A1 the combat effectiveness of the sniper team could be, and has been proven, greatly increased even more.

As man's ability to wage war continues, snipers are required more than ever before. The trust and confidence in such excellent rifles is important. Designs that give you the edge against your opponents greatly help in the fight, which today is not all that dissimilar to 100 years ago, whereupon regardless of the technology leaps you still have the old "cat and mouse" sniper versus sniper warfare taking place on some corner of the modern battlefield.

Appendix
Principal Rifles

SMLE MkIII & MkIII*, Periscopic Prism Co (PPCo) Conversion/PPCo Telescope

SMLE MkIII & MkIII*, J. Purdey & Sons Conversion/Aldis Bros Telescope

SMLE MkIII & MkIII*, Holland & Holland Conversion/Aldis Bros Telescope

SMLE MkIII, Whitehead Brothers Conversion/Winchester A5 Telescope

Pattern 1914 Mk1* W (T), Periscopic Prism Company Conversion/PPCo Model 1918 Telescope

Rifle No. 3 Mk1* (T) A, Alexander Martin Conversion/Aldis Bros Telescope

Rifle No. 4 Mk1 (T) ex Trials Rifle RSAF Enfield Conversion/No. 32 Mk1 Telescope

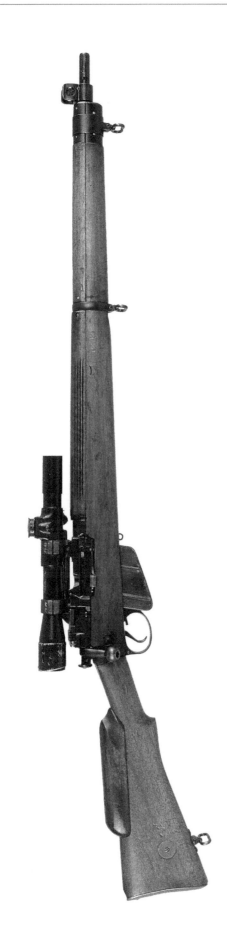
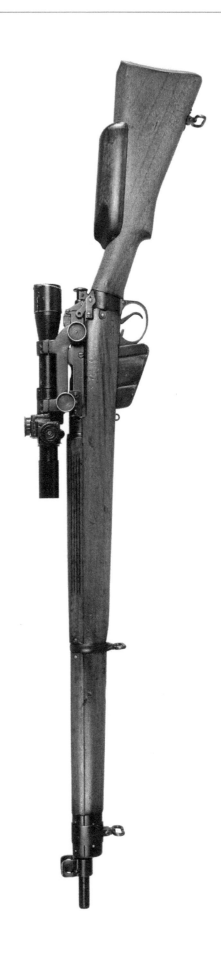

Rifle No. 4 Mk1 (T) Holland & Holland Conversion/No. 32 Telescope

Rifle 7.62mm L42A1/L1A1 Telescope, NSN number B1/1005-99-963-3786

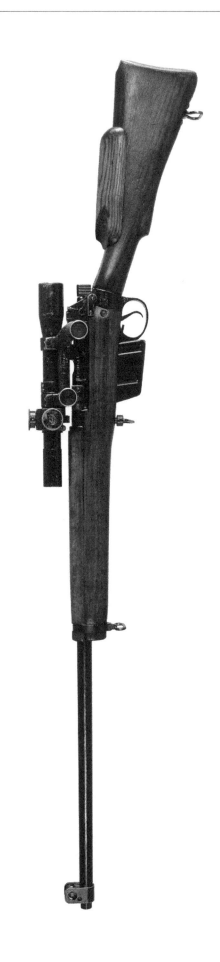

Rifle 7.62mm L96A1/L13A1 Telescope, NSN, B1/1005-99-967-3405

Rifle 7.62mm L118A1/A2/L17A1 Telescope, NSN 1005-99-535-4279

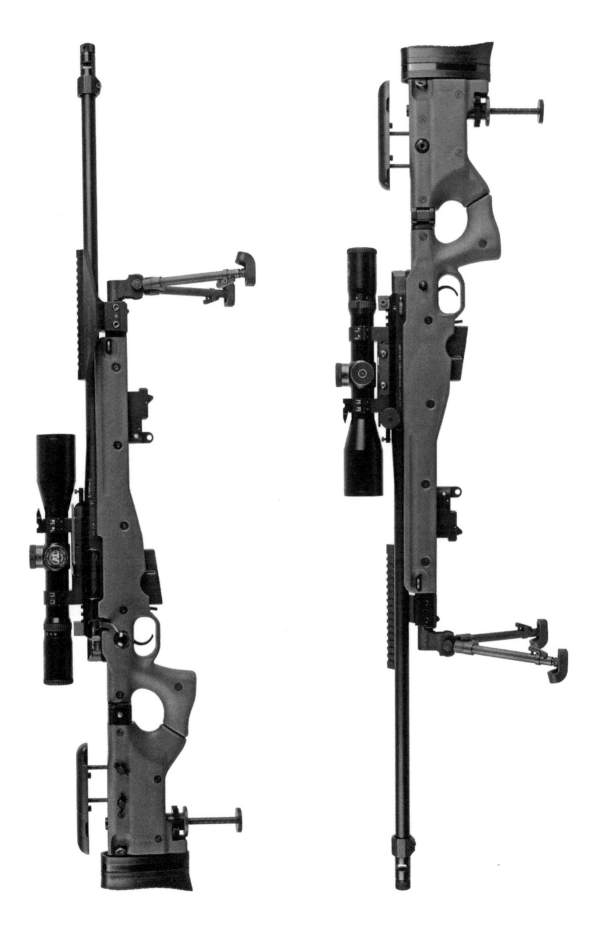

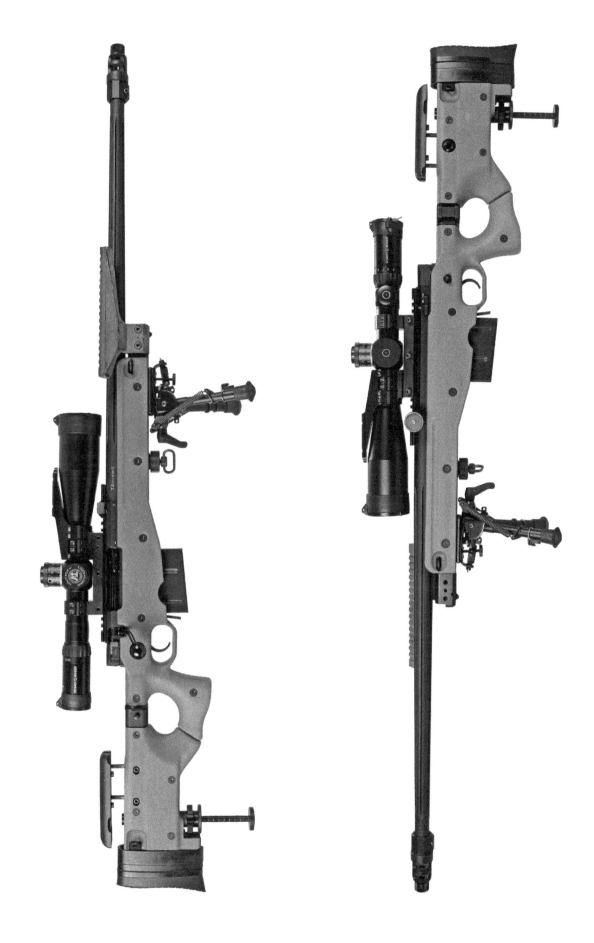

Rifle .338 Lapua AWSM L115A3/L24A1 Telescope, NSN 1005-99-372-3045

CPSIA information can be obtained
at www.ICGtesting.com
Printed in the USA
BVHW022222281122
653009BV00010B/62

9 781399 93783